To Jim,

I hope when you look at this book, it brings back happy memories of your stay in Budapest.

With all good wishes,
Love
Tina
10/6/98

AN ILLUSTRATED HISTORY
OF HUNGARY

ISTVÁN LÁZÁR

An Illustrated History of
HUNGARY

C · O · R · V · I · N · A

Published by Corvina Books, Budapest
(Vörösmarty tér 1, Hungary 1051)
Fifth edition, 1998

Translated by
ALBERT TEZLA

Translated from *Kis magyar történelem,* Gondolat, Budapest, 1989
First English language edition, without illustrations, was published
by Corvina 1990.
Illustration selected by Géza Buzinkay
Maps by Ágoston Dákány
Design by Miklós Beniczky

On the cover:
Recapture of Buda Castle in 1686
by Gyula Benczúr (1844–1920. Detail)
Hungarian National Gallery, Budapest

ISBN 963 13 4542 4

Printed in Hungary, 1998
Offset Printing House, Budapest

CONTENTS

INTRODUCTION

Horsemen. On short-legged, shaggy, brawny horses sweating mud, they climb upward among the mountains, following a path edged with dense pine forests. They stop on the height of the pass, in the dividing ridge. They look ahead intently and cock their ears to the rear. Are they the advanced guard or the main force?

Are they only soldiers or everyone together: the elderly, children, women, and wagons loaded with belongings?

(Are they forging ahead, bent on conquest? Are they fleeing in defeat?) Let's not begin with questions or inquire about details, circumstances, or causes, whether we know the answers or not.

Horsemen. On their shoulders, reflex bows composed of layers of sheets of horn cemented together with glue rendered from fish, hide, and bone, strengthened with coils of stag's sinew, and their tips and grasps made of antlers. On their left side, bundles of iron-tipped arrows in quivers; on their right, oriental sabres with curved, single-edged blades. Their saddles are high and rise sharply in front and back. This saddle and the Avar-type stirrup make it possible for both hands to be free in battle with reins flying to tear along hurling a shower of arrows in an attack on their enemy or, half-turned on their horses, to do so backwards fleeing from a superior force or feigning flight deceptively. They have become one with their horses, like centaurs; their horses, on pressure from their knees or on command, wheel, stop dead, and start off.

Horsemen. Their hair braided into pigtails held together on two sides by brass disks, those of the chiefs by gold ones. At their waists, the many studs on their leather belts as well as the embossed, stamped and paunchy U-shaped plates on leather satchels containing their smaller belongings flash in the sunlight. They are hardy, like the wolves on the plains. They are fond of splendor, like the potentates of the East.

They are forging ahead from the east toward the west, meanwhile having to cross the mountain range from north to south. They are the ones about whom the chant of supplication fearfully concluded at this time in the monasteries and churches of Christian Europe with two lines: "From the arrows of the Hungarians...", the precentor shouted to Heaven, and "... spare us, Oh Lord!" the choir boomed thereupon.

Árpád's Hungarians.

They stand high on the ridge of the Carpathians in the Verecke Pass. On the border of an unfamiliar world? Definitely not. They have roamed there before. Perhaps, as their legends claim, this is the land of their forefathers, and thus a reclamation of a lawful ancient inheritance.

Or did the flattering authors of chronicles only later think or contend that this was what they thought? We do not know. Did early bands precede them by generations perhaps? We do not know. But we know for certain that they had been in this area during the preceding year and the years before. The scene spreading out below is familiar to them. Down below await water they have tasted, grazing meadows for the cattle they have tested, and land for their plows and vegetable seed-beds they have found to be rich and fertile.

They have come to settle down.

That part of the Hungarian armies led by Árpád—as we know and believe today—crossed the Verecke Pass and parallel passes in AD 895 and descended to the fields of the Carpathian Basin which seemed to be defendable.

895?

At this same time, around the decade of the 890s, France was emerging from the ruins of Charlemagne's empire. Giving the Normans, who were long believed to be invincible, a lesson in defeat, the Capetian dynasty was establishing its power. In the west, the German Carolingians were also struggling with the Normans; in the east, they were seeking an ally against the Moravian-Slavic state of Svatopluk. (We shall see

A Hungarian horseman from the age of the Hungarian Conquest—A pastel by Árpád Feszty (1856–1914). *According to a romantic view, Avar and Hungarian warriors were buried on "horseback." This is not quite true. Nor is the belief that the equestrian way of life of the ancient Hungarians evolved only a couple of centuries before the Conquest under Turkic influence. The keeping of large livestock and the use of horses for riding and battle were an inheritance of several thousand years for Árpád's Hungarians. And, befitting its everyday and wartime role, the horse found a significant place in their cults. The close bond between the warrior and his horse is indisputable. Though only a relatively small number of the graves are of this kind, the interments of horsemen from the time of the Hungarian Conquest reveal that it was not the horse of the warrior or that of a man of rank that was buried with him; instead, at the funeral feast celebrated at the deceased man's grave the mourners consumed the flesh of a horse, whose parts, its head and legs left in its hide, were buried immediately or later on beside the deceased.*

Feszty prepared this sketch for his monumental panorama entitled The Entry of the Hungarians, *in which he attempted to depict the momentous event of the Age of Árpád, the Hungarian Conquest itself, in accordance with the knowledge and sentiments prevailing at the time of the Millennium. The colossal picture, actually painted by a team of artists, was badly damaged during World War II. After its restoration, it was again put on display at Ópusztaszer, in the southern Alföld: at that historical spot where—at the time only in personal tribute—Árpád's fellow chiefs, raising him on a shield, chose him as ruling prince, the founder of a dynasty which was to reign for 400 years.*

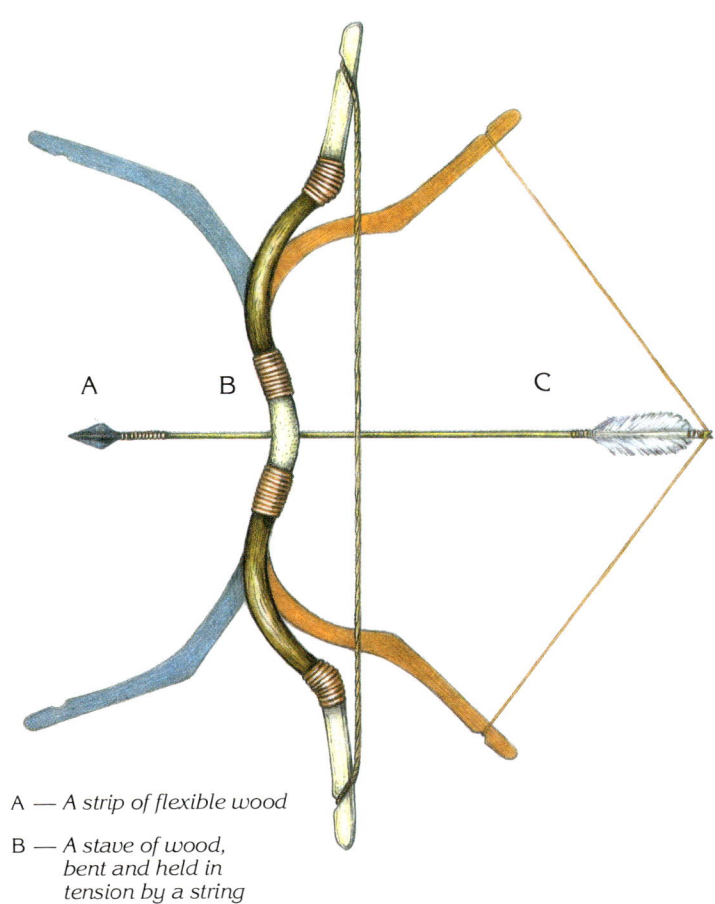

A reflex bow from the age of the Hungarian Conquest—A drawing by Gyula László, based on Károly Cs. Sebestyén's reconstruction. *The making of a bow like this could take as many as five to ten years because of the need to rest the materials, the repeated gluing of the layered sheets, and the slow-drying character of the organic matter used as the adhesive. And, as with ancient weapons generally, this one was both a prized piece of property and a decorative work of art. At the same time, because of its range and the effectiveness of the mobile tactics of warfare based upon it, its role was much more important than that of other weapons in the victories of the Hungarian light cavalry—or in their defeats. For a sudden downpour, in effect, "disarmed" the Hungarian forces by slackening the bowstring; at such times, they either avoided the battle or lost it.*

A — *A strip of flexible wood*

B — *A stave of wood, bent and held in tension by a string*

C — *Bow drawn back*

whom they found.) Not long ago, the other branch of the Carolingians had driven the Arab conquerors from the south with the help of Byzantium, and they were now dividing the Italian Peninsula between themselves and the pope. About that time, no small part of the Iberian Peninsula had long been in the hands of the Moors (Arabs); at this time, a certain Abdullah ruled the Umayyad Caliphate of Córdoba. Already apparent was that intellectual effervescence through which the center of European learning was to blossom in this Islamic world. In Scandinavia, first one and then another Viking (Norman) king had become a Christian, although paganism struck back for a long time in the divided and restless population of the Danish–Norwegian–Swedish trinity. A Norwegian king happened to be ruling across the Channel on Irish soil. Alfred I, the English king, had to conclude a humiliating peace with the incursive Danes, abandoning East Anglia to them, in order to gain time to build a fleet, organize a standing army, and strike back. On the Adriatic-Dalmatian seacoast, Ragusa (Dubrovnik), Zara (Zadar), Spalato (Split), Trau (Trogir), Cattaro (Kotor), and Bar were already veritable city-states. On Russian soil, the challenge of the Varangians (Vikings) promoted the concentration of power among the princes with the participation of the Varangians, who, assimilating, became Slavs. In Byzantium, Leo (the Wise) VI's tripartitum of laws was being diligently prepared, while the border marshes of the kingdom were everywhere in flames.

8

THE PREHISTORY
OF THE REGION

Where were Árpád's Hungarians preparing to settle? Could it have been an uninhabited land? Unpopulated for hundreds of thousands of years, where only plants ran wild and animals roamed freely, unmolested by man? A heated debate about this question raged barely a century ago. It was mainly geologists who insisted that an ice-age, diluvial man never lived in the region of the Carpathian Basin. However, evidence from accidental finds could not long be denied; diggings that commenced crammed the prehistoric archaeological map of the region with symbols, whether we consider the ancient historical homeland or the territory of present-day Hungary shrunk to a fragment by the Versailles peace treaty (Trianon) in 1920. From among these symbols on the map we shall select only a few, without any connections among them.

At Vértesszőlős, barely a stone's throw from the M-1 highway running between Vienna and Budapest, is sheltered one of the oldest sites in Europe, with scattered tools, petrified footprints, and an exact copy of the nape of a prehistoric man. He gained the pet name "Samuel" from his excavators. He made crude tools from pebbles, he already used fire and had fed it with fatty pieces of bone. He came here about 350 to 400 thousand years ago for several hundred generations, taking pleasure in the thermal springs of that time, the mild microclimate of the spring basins; he belonged in the domain of "upright man", or *homo erectus*. His delineator named him *homo sapiens palaeo-hungaricus* on the basis of the estimated volume of his brain and his tools. Is he, perhaps, the very first who properly fits into the classification of *sapiens*?

Over and above its age, the great value of the site is its completeness: it indicates an often interrupted but very lengthy residence. The spring-water limestone preserved the camp and hearth, heaps of tools, the bones of captured animals, and the imprints of plants, indicating the climate. Careful analysis of the legacy layer-by-layer clearly shows how the stockpile of tools became more advanced and better designed and formed. Here the rapidity of man's evolution seems mathematically measurable. All this is enormously interesting even if today much uncertainty still surrounds Samuel, who was unearthed in 1965. Uncertainty surrounds even the identity of the "owner" of the nape: is he the one who ate in the camp or the one who was actually devoured there?

About 35 to 40 thousand years ago, the Carpathian Basin was populated by the Neanderthal man of prehistory, with his "specialized" hunting tribes, who cannot be included among our presumably extinct direct ancestors of a later time. At Érd, near Budapest, his hunting specialists pursued the cave bear (thus in name only, not in his habit), at Tata the young mammoth, likewise settling down beside hot springs, and in the Bükk mountains, around the Subalyuk cave the ibex and the chamois.

After the hardly comprehensible distance of 400 thousand and 40 thousand years, we place the time of our

The Vértesszőlős prehistoric man—As reconstructed by anthropologist László Kordos and graphic artist Miklós Kolozsvári Grandpierre. *His scientific name is* homo (erectus seu sapiens) palaeohungaricus. *As the anthropologist states: "... Samuel precipitated many disputes. He amalgamates in a peculiar way the brain capacity characteristic of modern man and the marks of a more primitive wide and thick occipital bone. Samuel was given his odd name because he stands close to either* homo erectus *or* homo sapiens"; *in other words, to "upright" or "intelligent" man. Formerly, he was thought to be "the oldest European," though incorrectly so. Unfortunately, since the death of his discoverer, palaeoarchaeologist László Vértes, research on Samuel has slowed down, even though the site where he was found has not been uncovered in its entirety.*

next segment at 4000 years before the Christian era, or 6000 years from today. For several reasons. On the basis of anthropological investigations, it can be stated about a small fragment of the original inhabitants in the Carpathian Basin assimilated by Árpád's conquerors that by that time they had been living in this very region for four to five thousand years, something rare in the history of a Europe diversified by many mass migrations. A very special historical occurrence also accounts for the choice of our third segment of time: the sudden and prolonged halt of neolithic development in our region. It was only recently that the knowledge of the raising of food, of animal husbandry and agriculture, coming from the Zagros mountain range and Mesopotamia, or more directly from Asia Minor and the region of the eastern Mediterranean, had reached the Carpathian Basin, taking hold in its soft underbelly, the southern part of the Alföld, or great Hungarian plain. However, for a while it came to a stop here and in a section of Transylvania.

An amazing phenomenon prevailed at this time, one that had never occurred before and would never happen again: the civilization *east* of the Danube was superior to the one to its west. A part of the Alföld was the border area of the most developed center of civilization at the time, a place where the mother culture still emanated directly from the Mediterranean. We can say, "it was carried in by hand": in all probability, it can be linked to a migrating population. To the west and the north, however, only an indirect influence could be demonstrated later as well; indeed, even a counterforce appeared in these regions.

No doubt, this line of demarcation marked by the advanced development and lasting for many generations was due to nature and the climate. The well-watered and immensely rich soil of the Alföld made permanent settlement and agriculture possible. Proof of this is provided by a spectacular form of settlement, whose name also points to the Near East: the artificial mound of settlement or *tell*. This is the outermost instance of this type of settlement in Europe. When, however, the knowledge of agriculture finally spread farther west, the clearing of forests for agricultural purposes began in Transdanubia, the later Pannonia, i.e. the western part of modern Hungary, with the appearance of different kinds of dwellings and villages and with frequent onward migration, because the soil was quickly exhausted there.

Of course, the size and richness of the settlement mounds in the southern Alföld did not equal those of the ancestral *tells* in the Near East. Nevertheless, it is worth mentioning not only the numerous cultic and other material finds related to the centers of Mesopotamia and the Mediterranean but also the ruins of a two-story house from the Neolithic Age that recent excavations in Hungary have uncovered. This was already a neolithic "city" and not a "village."

Finally, I mention that special feature which influenced the prehistory of our region from the Mesolithic Age to the Bronze Age with varying intensity. In addition to the Aegean and the Caucasus, that remarkably chippable volcanic glass, *obsidian,* turned up in Europe only in the Carpathian Basin, or more precisely in the region of the Eperjes-Tokaj mountain range which today partly falls in Slovakia and in Hungary. This rare, valuable mineral substance was, from time to time, the reason for sudden migrations or slow infiltrations and also for powerful conflicts; in its raw form or shaped into tools, it was the object of continual commercial exchange and brought into existence early and advanced modes of the division

The late Neolithic in the Tisza region. *In the exploration of the ancient past of the Carpathian Basin, research in the Roman period occupied the forefront for a long time because of the numerous spectacular finds. However, at the turn of the century, the Age of the Migrations and the Hungarian Conquest came to the fore on the strength of the interest in the nation's thousand-year-old past celebrated in 1896. Meanwhile, the answers to many problems attending the establishment of the Hungarian kingdom probably still lay hidden beneath the earth. In recent decades, however, the results of widespread archaeological studies of the Neolithic in the Carpathian Basin have aroused the most striking and far-reaching international attention, particularly those that surfaced in the systematic diggings of the late Neolithic period in the Tisza region. The general public is hardly aware of the fact that in the disputes about the single or multicentered character of the Neolithic revolution, its development and spread how frequently references are made to finds excavated in the southern and southeastern Carpathian Basin, in addition to those of the Mediterranean Basin and the Balkan Peninsula.*

Part of a villa in Pannonia—A reconstruction in the permanent exhibition of the National Museum. *At first, the Pannonian culture developing and stabilizing at the beginning of the first millennium of the Christian era displayed the strong influence of the earlier local barbarian, or Celtic, tradition. Later on, though it retained its provincial character to the very last, this culture was increasingly integrated. The durability of the Roman domination and the military importance of Pannonia elevated the region's economic and cultural level, despite the fact that it was a frontier zone. Though frequently disrupted by barbarian attacks, exports from Italy, Africa, and other areas flowed into the region, and this commercial activity was, through the deployment of the legions, accompanied by the mingling of cults, religions, and customs.*

Aquincum, the civilian town. *The existence of Pannonia's sometime capital during the Roman period in Óbuda, now a Budapest suburb, is attested to by several fields of well-preserved ruins and by several known but reburied and many uncovered but unsuccessfully preserved remains of buildings as well as a number still undiscovered but believed to exist. In this picture we see the largest contiguous remains of Aquincum's civilian town, on Szentendrei út running parallel with the Danube. A short section of the Aquincum aqueduct has also been partially reconstructed in the middle of the six-lane highway. In the lower left corner of the picture a mere segment of a circle recalls the ruins of an amphitheater which had formed part of the civilian town. The military town, with its garrisons and its own amphitheater, stretched to the south of the civilian town, also along the bank of the Danube, while the sumptuous palace of the proconsul, built by Hadrian, who later became emperor, was situated on today's Hajógyár (Shipyard) Island and is now partially destroyed and partly hidden under land occupied by the now defunct Ganz-Danubius Shipyard.*

4

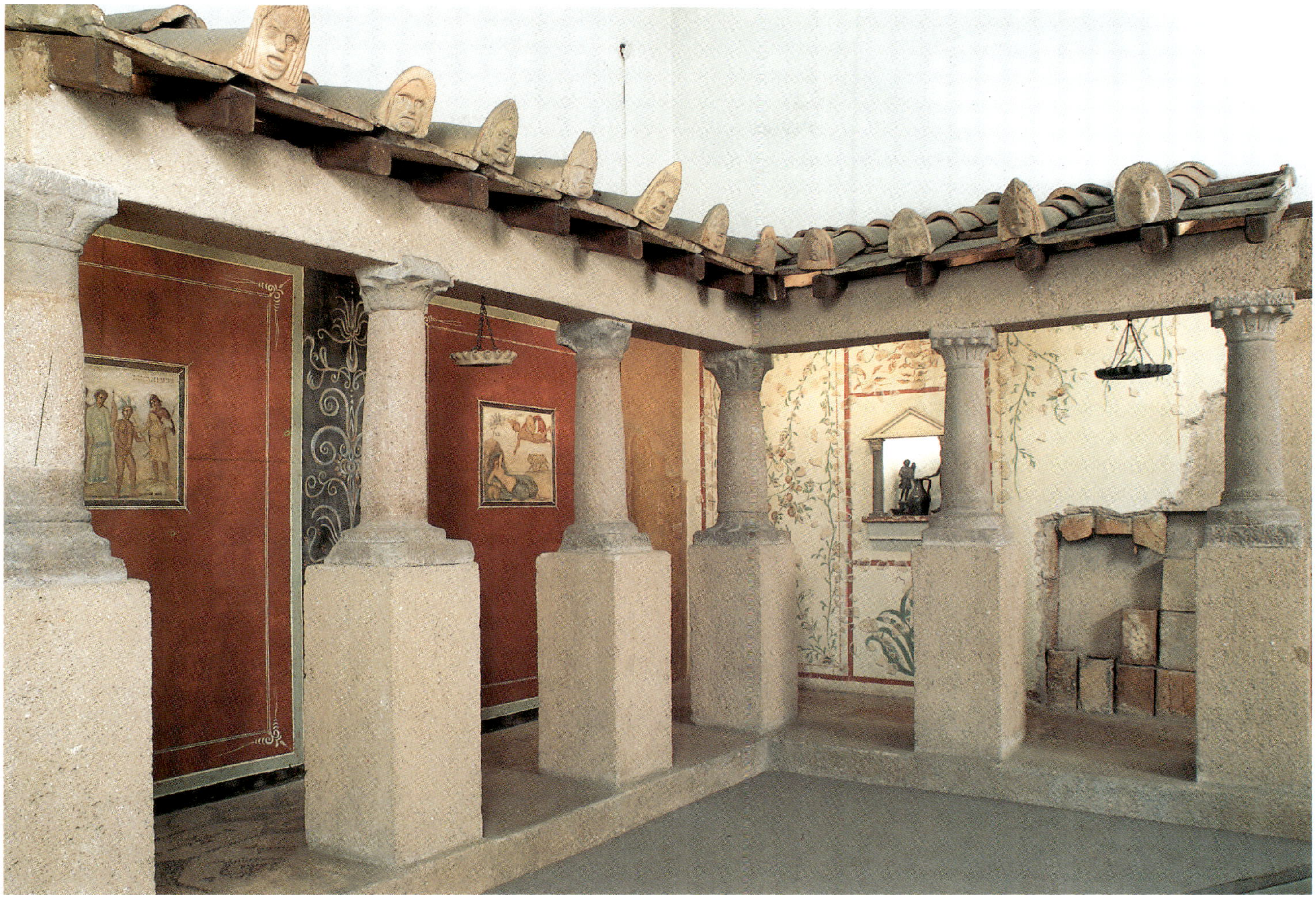
5

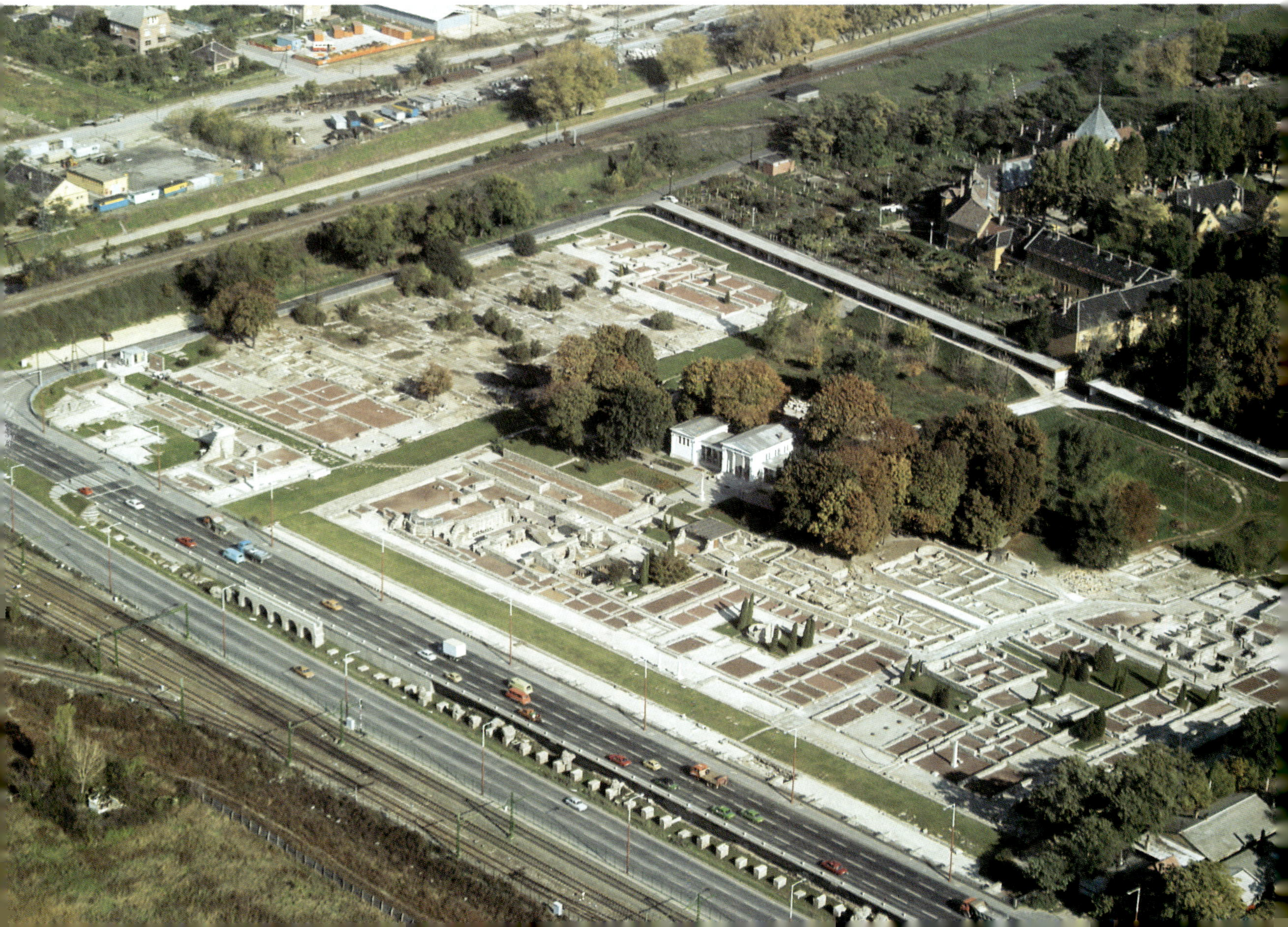
6

of labor. Since through their trace elements the Aegean, Caucasian, and Tokaj obsidian are today clearly separable, we can determine the connection of the Carpathian area and Tokaj with many distant archaeological sites in Central Europe. As is the case with amber, because of the presence of certain shells or, later, different kinds of money, the basic trade routes for obsidian can be traced, which were simultaneously paths for cultural expansion and exchange.

The history of the Copper, Bronze, and Iron Ages in the Carpathian Basin does not lack for points of interest in finds whose significance extends beyond Hungary's own borders. As a consequence of a slightly drier climate, tribes of herdsmen replaced, or rather absorbed, the early agriculturists and keepers of animals. Long-time migration mainly from the southeast was time and again interrupted and replaced by the more southerly movement of peoples from the northeast and the Steppes, among them those of Iranian origin, but migrations from the west also took place and later on actually became determinative. During the Bronze and Iron Ages, a row of mountain centers, secured by powerful fortifications, developed in the western reaches, and their warlike lords of various ethnic origins brought the agriculturist in the neighboring, lower-lying areas under their control. Meanwhile, a fraction of a mysterious people who originated in Iberia and who made bell-shaped utensils arrived in the Carpathian Basin, bogged down in the Danube Bend, and were assimilated by the people living there. To the despair of anthropologists, the close tracking of the migrations and amalgamations was made difficult by the fact that beginning with the early Bronze Age, burial by cremation became more common. The Bronze Age also brought to the settlement hills agricultural *tell*-dwellers, who further increased the height of the abandoned, long uninhabited neolithic mounds, although they set up new ones as well. The Copper, Bronze, and Iron Ages were crammed with armed clashes, which sometimes disturbed the surface only slightly, sometimes produced a slow but far-reaching wave but sometimes brought about sudden, blood-soaked transformations that set back civilization for centuries.

The prehistory of what we today call Europe closed with the Iron Age, not so much in a geographical as in a historical and cultural sense. This half continent first entered real history on fleet Greek legs and then with the supple strides of diverse, sandal-shod, moccasined peoples.

So let us now take a good step into the future, all the way to the time when the location in the Neolithic Age of "civilized" and "barbarian" became reversed. From the dividing waters of the Danube to the east and on the mountain ridges to the north, the watch-fires of advanced guards burned: barbarian tribes looked covetously at rich Pannonia. During a pause in a grueling military campaign conducted against the barbarians, "on the land of the Quadi, on the bank of the [River] Garam," somewhere across from today's Esztergom, Marcus Aurelius, the philosophical Caesar, the last Stoic, who did not like to govern and even less to wage war, wrote his *Meditations* in the flickering lamplight in his camp.

Those who gave their name to the province of Pannonia were other Pannonian tribes which lived more to the south and were of different origin; the Roman legions penetrating into the Carpathian Basin from the south and southwest had to subjugate mainly Celtic tribes and make peace with them. It is surprising that the tribes of this very dynamic ethnic group, long settled in the region and a branch

of which had recently ravaged Rome, hardly resisted the Romans. They integrated much more peacefully than the Dacians who had moved up from the Balkans and whom the Roman legions tried to pacify in what is now Transylvania and on the eastern slopes of the Carpathian Mountains. Thus the history and fate of the two parts of the Carpathian Basin which became a part of the Roman Empire temporarily, today's Transdanubia and Transylvania, which now belongs to Rumania, diverged. Between them lay the Alföld—a wedged-in, barbarian strip where Sarmatian tribes of Iranian origin, the Iazyges and the Roxolani, faced the Romans sometimes in open hostility, sometimes in shaky alliance.

Roman occupation of Pannonia lasted for four whole centuries, from the years after the birth of Christ to the beginning of the fifth century, during which, though disturbed by barbarian incursions and smaller turbulences, the development of the Danubian *limes,* the line of military defense, made excellent economic expansion possible. However, in Dacia, to which Transylvania belonged, Rome's supremacy was much shorter, lasting from AD 106 to 268–271, barely more than a century and a half, and severe uprisings also frequently disturbed this period. As a matter of fact, the occupation was never total, because individual Dacian tribes remained independent throughout in their earthen fortifications on high mountain tops. This view runs contrary to theories that proclaim the strong Romanization of the Dacians, the fusion of Dacian and Roman inhabitants, and then the unbroken survival of this alleged ethnic group; and henceforth, in the future history of Transylvania and Moldavia as well as the Wallachian plain, these theories see nothing more than the continual battle for independence of the pre-Rumanian and Rumanian population respectively. Actually, the evolution of the Rumanian ethnic group—its history and locality—as well as the history of the peopling of this region, of the successive appearance of the ethnic groups living intermingled here today, is much more complicated than that: the first Rumanian inhabitants settled down later and at various times in individual parts of the region over an extended period.

It is very tempting to plunge deeper into this theme at this point. The sources available are numberless. In Hungarian archaeology, the Roman Age has always, and perhaps excessively, stood in the foreground. Pannonia is one of the provinces about which we know the most. And it is not merely pictures of local life that present themselves—their colors like those of a most resplendent mosaic—but also the piquant historical circumstance that during the later period of the caesars, Pannonia was the cradle of the caesars. After all, because of the *limes,* the concentration of military might was very great in the region. Stationed comparatively close to Rome, Pannonia's legions were swiftly deployable against the capital to overthrow and elevate rulers. So much so that—was "the tail wagging the dog" perhaps?—in the third century the expression "Pannonia's world domination" was coined. Yet it was precisely the numerous "putsches," garrison revolts, and changing "juntas" of the legions that formed one of the reasons why, in the end, the barbarian Germanic peoples soon did not look longingly at Pannonia and the Sarmatian Alföld and pounded directly on the gates of Rome, instead.

The destruction that quickly followed Pannonia's period of false glory was severe but not devastating. Although it is shocking to see the archaeologist dig up wretched huts in the nooks of villas, palaces, and bath halls—the occasional abodes of vagrant shepherds and agriculturists clinging, like swallows' nests, to the broadstone walls—certain signs manifest the continuity of life. In some towns and encampments we can find the traces of Pannonian inhabitants who did not leave their localities during the period of the great migrations. Nor did urban life cease completely. On the edge of Budapest, the thick encrustation deposited on the aqueduct of former Aquincum proves such long utilization that we must conclude it was used for a long time even after Roman domination ended. Moreover, we know about Christian bishoprics that were active in Pannonia as late as AD. 670–580. One of them was Sabaria (today's Szombathely), where Martin was born in 316 or 317 as a pagan but into a milieu becoming Christian. This is that Martin who, following his father's example, was first a soldier, a cavalry officer of the Guards in Italy, but later became the Bishop of Tours and then the patron saint of the whole of Gaul (his name day is November 11).

In the footsteps of the progressively withdrawn Roman legion, the Huns of savage reputation swarmed all over the region. What is more, their center was also located here at the peak of this nomadic empire's power—very warlike but disintegrating because it was based on a loose mixture of peoples—at the time of Attila, who was honored as the Scourge of God. This center was either in the southern Alföld near Szeged, in the border area between Hungary and Serbia today, or, perhaps—collaterally as a winter and a summer encampment?—in modern Óbuda, which is identical with the Roman Aquincum mentioned above. This is that Sicambria which the Hun-Magyar cycle of legends describes as Attila's city. And—again a "French Connection"—some ancient legends of Gaul record it as the place where, in flight from a destroyed Troy and after centuries of wandering, the ancestors of the Gauls lived for a long time and where they moved on from to Western Europe.

What more shall we say about the tumultuous times of the great migrations?

We know the route of one of the Germanic peoples frequently turning up in Pannonia with an accuracy unusual for this period. The Langobards, cast out of the valley of the Elbe, arrived in fairly large numbers in 546, densely populating the northern and eastern perimeters

7

St. Martin and the beggar—An altarpiece in the Dunántúl (Transdanubia, Western Hungary), c. 1490. *According to the legend,* Martin, *the bishop of Tours, impetuous as a youth and later all the more ascetic, who was born in Pannonian Savaria (Szombathely) or possibly in Sabaria (Pannonhalma), encountered a beggar at the gate to Amiens while he was still a soldier. Because he had lost all his money playing dice, he tossed his cloak to the naked mendicant as alms. This episode illustrates nicely how the typically bohemian behavior of a rowdy soldier becomes, in the end, part of a canonized saint's repertory of virtue. The original legend mentioned a snowy day; this picture from about 1490 knows nothing about it.*

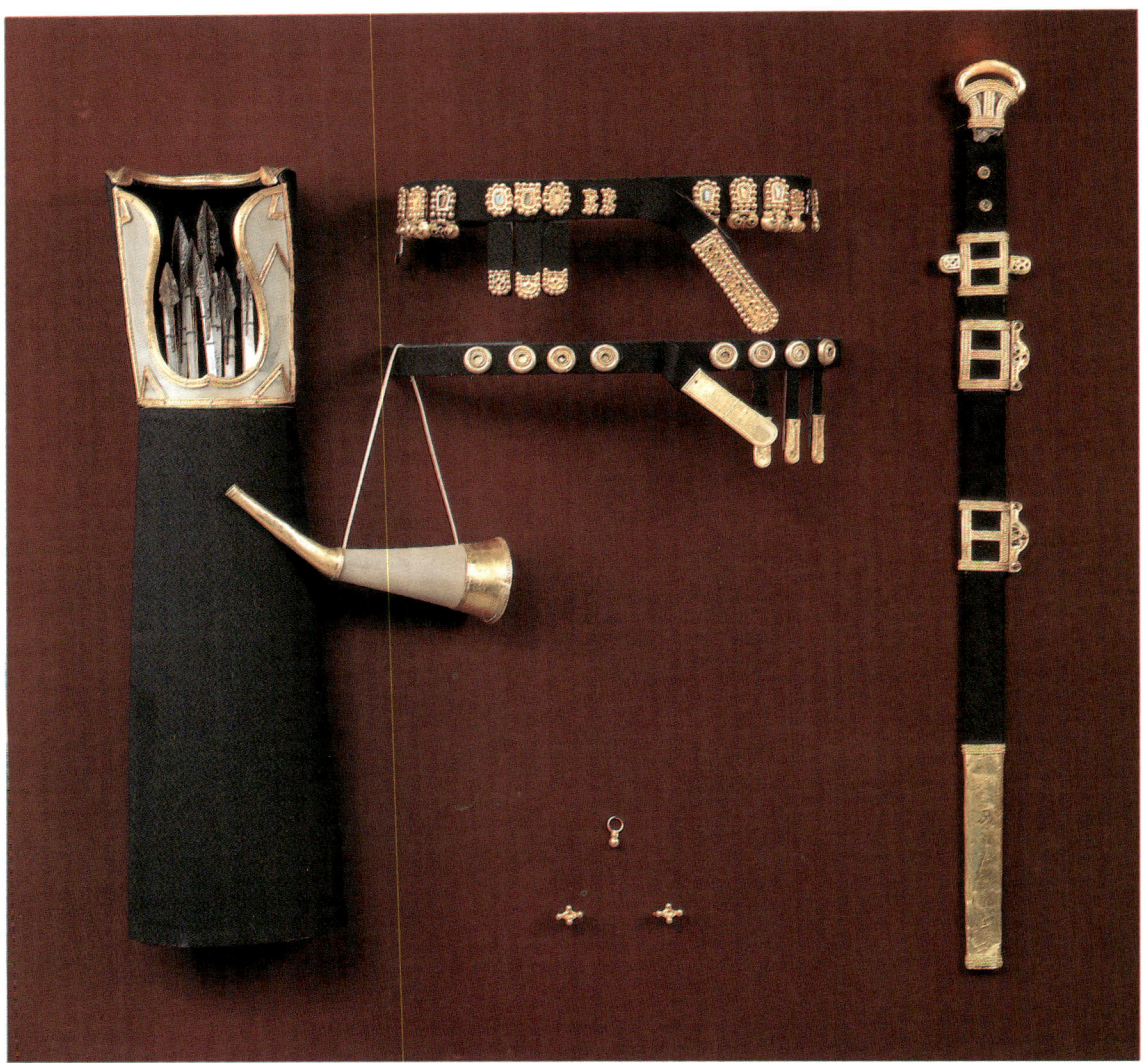

Dignitaries' insignia found in the grave of an Avar prince at Bócs
—Sword, quiver, and goblet. *The Avar question is one of the dilemmas
of Hungarian prehistory. Our archaeologists divide this eastern people
of Turkish origin from the Steppes, to whom Byzantium was also forced
at times to pay tribute, into two groups: earlier and later Avars.
Professor Gyula László's hypothesis maintains that the later Avars were
in fact an earlier migratory wave of "Hungarian" people, whom Árpád
and his clans joined and mingled with later. But only this much is
certain that the conquering Hungarians had found a diminishing group
of Avars in the Carpathian Basin whom they quickly assimilated
without a trace. However, numerous finds in their graves give evidence
of the Avars' former greatness.*

of Pannonia along the Danube, areas not uninhabited
of course. However, in 568, they moved on
to the southwest beyond the Alps almost to the last person,

something tremendously rare in this period. They founded
Lombardy in Italy.

The Avars advanced into their place from the east,
a people warlike and of Turkish blood, who had grown
stronger in the Eurasian steppes. A portion of them can
still be found in the Caucasus, although some deny
the continuity to the Avars living there today.

Our Avar dilemma is entirely different. According
to material finds and anthropological data, the bloody and
uneven "Avar" domination of the Carpathian Basin for three
centuries falls into two periods. The question has arisen
as to whether, in contrast to hardly any relationship with
the people of the early Avars, we are not or were not
ourselves, the Hungarians, really identical to those whom
anthropology calls the late Avars. Of course, for this
we have to clarify what the Hungarian is.

ONE MUST DESCEND
FROM SOME PLACE

The wondrous stag prances at the opening of the chapter with a magical and shiny-haloed crown of antlers on its head. Two princes, burning with hunting fever, gallop on two chargers in its steps. The wondrous stag leads them, lures them on for days ever deeper into the marshy area. Suddenly it vanishes. Without any trace whatsoever. But at this moment, the two disappointed young hunters, called Hunor and Magor, hear merry laughing and singing. Dismounting, they stalk stealthily until they come across a lake in which two beautiful maidens are splashing. Screaming, the daughters of King Dul flee. The two youths, again astride their horses, take after them. They meet. Passionate love immediately flares up. Hunor takes one as his wife, and Magor the other. The Huns are Hunor's descendants, the Magyars are Magor's... This is the way I remember the legend of our origin. These two rhyming names instilled an awareness of the Hun–Magyar kinship in me long before I learned to read.

In Simon Kézai's chronicle, entitled *Gesta Hungarorum* and written about 1283, the same mythical tale is slightly more somber and, irrespective of the factual truth of its essence, much more realistic. Hunor and Magor are Chief Ménrót's grown-up sons who had reached maturity and had moved into a separate tent.

"One day it happened that, as they were going out to hunt, a hind suddenly appeared in front of them on the plains, and as they undertook to pursue her, she fled from them into the Maeotian marshes. Since she completely disappeared there from their eyes, they searched for her a long time but could not chance upon her traces. After having traversed the said marshes, they decided the marshes were suitable for raising livestock. They returned to their father, and securing his consent, they moved into the Maeotian marshes with all their animals to settle down there. The region of Maeotis is a neighbor of Persia. Apart from a very narrow wading place, it is enclosed by the sea everywhere. It has absolutely no streams, but it teems with grass, trees, fish, fowl, and game. Access to and exit from it is difficult. Thus settling in the Maeotian marshes, Hunor and Magor did not move from there for five years. In the sixth year they wandered out, and by chance they came upon the wives and children of Belár's sons, who stayed at home without their menfolk. Quickly galloping off with them and their belongings, they carried them off into the Maeotian marshes. It so happened that among the children they also seized the two daughters of Dula, the Prince of the Alans. Hunor married one and Magor the other. All the Huns descend from these women."

How did the stag turn into hind? The theft of women and possessions into a romantic love story? Why are there no separate Hungarians in this version, why only Huns? It is not worth spending any time on these questions now. Instead, let us mention that, according to another myth about the origin of the Hungarians, which also provides a year (819), Chief Álmos, the ancestor of the House of Árpád, was born under wondrous signs: "... in his pregnant mother's dream a divine apparition appeared in the shape of a *turul* and, so to say, got her with child." According to some, the *turul* is an eagle or a hawk; however, it is most probably a falcon—the totem animal of the Árpád clan.

What interests us in the first tale of our origin is the place—the vicinity of Persia—and the mention of the warring lifestyle of the nomads. The chief's two sons search for good grazing lands, and without hindrance they wrest away the wives, children, and cattle from the men of another people who are apparently away at war. In the other tale, the mythical animal ancestor emerges directly. But whereas, for example, in Italy the female wolf only nurses Romulus and Remus, our *turul* himself impregnates the ancestral mother (similar to the way Leda falls in love with the swan, or rather Zeus in the shape of a swan in Greek mythology).

Let us point out that both tales of our origin take us to the East. Following their mythical references, we come across Iranian and Turkish kinship. In Kézai's chronicle, the stag occupies a prominent place in the frequently repeated eponyms of Scythia, in Scythian mythology; in the world of the Turkish peoples, the most common totem animals are the winged masters of the hunt, the birds of prey. (In Mongolia and among the peoples of the Steppes generally, these birds are all, to this very day, inviolable and taboo.)

Later on, a lasting and unyielding ideology was founded on this legacy of eastern mythology. Among Hungarian leading circles, an awareness of some kind of "Scythian origin" lived on vividly, and those who proclaimed themselves the descendants of ancients bearing bows and sabres and mounted on horses seemed to hold hunting, in addition to fighting, to be the sole pastime of a gentleman. Rooting their class privileges in the mythical past, they cited ancient rights paid in advance in war by shedding their ancient blood to the point of extinction. This attitude experienced a renascence in the nineteenth century; it peaked in the millennium of the Conquest (1896), in the fever of national celebration occurring at that time. It flared up once again between the two world wars, littering the country with the totem animal, with throngs of smaller and larger statues of the *turul*. (The largest of them rises above Tatabánya, barely a couple of kilometers from the site of the "Samuel" of ancient Europe. From the distance it is an awe-inspiring spectacle, up close it is a frightening monstrosity.)

Today, it is quite difficult to picture the indignation two astronomers studying linguistics as a hobby created in their time. In 1768, Miksa Hell and János Sajnovics, Hungarian Jesuit priests, traveled to the island of Vardö, in Norway, to observe the passage of Venus across the Sun. Since the observation of the planet left them with ample time on their hands, Sajnovics, prompted by Hell, began to study the language of the Lapps, many elements of which sounded suspiciously familiar to his Hungarian ear. On his return home, Sajnovics wrote a treatise on the similarities between the Lapp and Hungarian languages. With this, the Hungarian people entered a section of the extensive northern Finno-Ugrian (Uralic) family of mankind on the basis of its language in a single stroke.

The public outcry was tremendous. Those proud of their connections with eastern lineage bitterly denied that we could possibly have anything in common with some poor northern relatives. The company of the Finns and Estonians could not compensate for the Lapps and for those still hardly known at the time, the little Finno-Ugrian peoples, who seemed to live at the level of the Neolithic Age, somewhere in the massive prison for human beings, in czarist Russia.

Meanwhile, however, the large bronze *turuls* perched in rows on the tops of monuments, the pillars of bridges, and the façades of public buildings in Hungary. In the aftermath of Sajnovics and his followers, linguistics indisputably ascertained, within a century and a half, where, given its determinant percentage of Finno-Ugrian vocabulary and grammatical forms, the Hungarian language with its basically Finno-Ugrian character is to be placed exactly in this family of languages, designating the Ostyak (Khanti) and the Vogul (Manshi) languages of the Ugrian group as its closest relatives.

This group of smaller Ugrian peoples is also called the "people of the water fowl." The reason for this is that in their myths swimming and wading birds filled a role

similar to that of birds of prey among the Turks. Indeed, in their world of marshes, fishing and gleaning were the important activities; animal husbandry or agriculture could expand only slightly for natural geographical reasons.

Which won out in the end? The warring falcon, the *turul*, or the gentle wild duck? Actually, neither did. The question is open, its threads are so snarled that, unable to unite it in a proper way, we must deal with it like the Gordian knot: we must cut it with a sword.

As for the language, this much is certain, that during the "living Hungarian" population's extended and long migration in historical time and geographical space, which produced connections and minglings with ever different peoples, Iranian, Turkish and then Slavic layers were abundantly deposited on its Finno-Ugrian (Uralic) foundations; but it is difficult to measure their weight precisely and to reconcile clearly the circumstances of language with the facts of history, way of life, migration, and other elements. In the end, however, the strength of the Finno-Ugrian link is hardly disputable with linguistic arguments. So much so, that in the middle of the century there was hardly anyone who did not seek the distant trails of Hungarian prehistory in maps determining the ancient settlements and migrations of the Finno-Ugrian peoples and tracing them back to the Neolithic Age, without denying that later, on paths leading into the Carpathian Basin, the early Hungarians came into frequent contact with Iranian and Turkish peoples, which influenced not only the language and style of life but also the ethnic group.

Recently, however, a new counterattack was launched. There are those who base their arguments on the gests and ancient chronicles and on either the obscure mythical tales

Route followed by the Hungarian conquerors to the Carpathian Basin

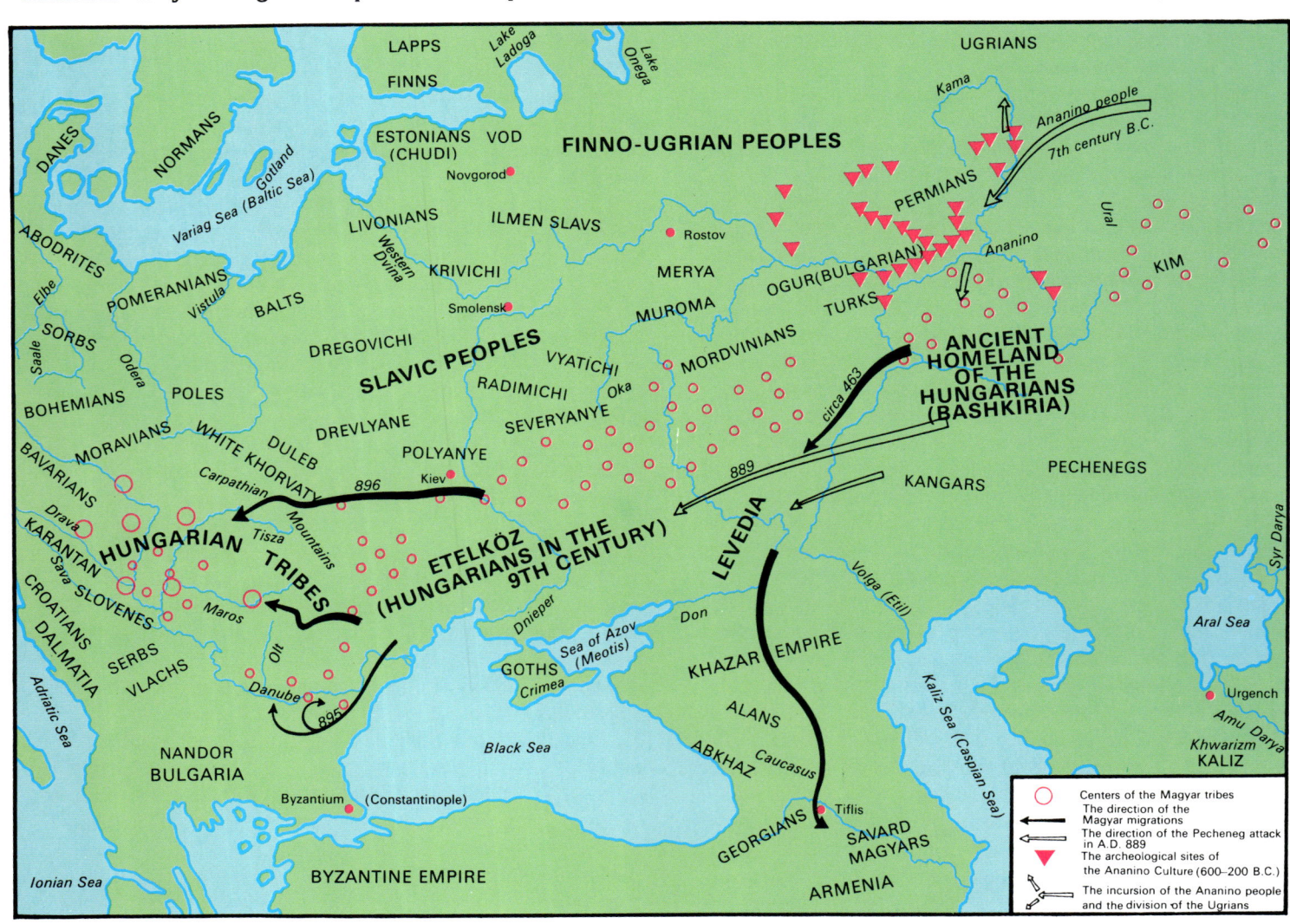

The pursuit of the wondrous stag—From the series entitled "The Myth of Origin," 1921, by Mariska Undi (1877–1959). *In this author's childhood recollections, the wondrous stag being pursued was undoubtedly a male, a stag. And in some of the illustrations showing the stag, he bore an apostolic cross between his antlers. The reason for this is that the myth of origin describing the pursuit gradually changed in such a way as to intertwine its prehistoric elements with the adoption of Christianity, thus indicating that the Hungarians became Christians already on the shore of the Maeotis, or the Sea of Azov. The early acquaintance with Christianity is, of course, a historical fact, and largely in the same way the ancient Hungarians also became acquainted with the principles of the Mohammedan and Jewish religions before they came to the Carpathians. The actual choice, however, was made in the new homeland.*

of origin or the eastern motifs in the art of the conquering Hungarians, their resemblance to those found in the steppes. Others call bones as witnesses from the burial grounds of the conquerors to those of people living today. There is no doubt that the anthropological standard establishes remarkably few Finno-Ugrian traits and many more of the Turks and others. And this is cause for reflection even when we know that the Finno-Ugrian component was minimal in the population that was found and then assimilated in the new land by Árpád's people and that, in addition to the Slavs, many of the people who had already settled there earlier were of Iranian and Turkish origin; moreover, during the centuries following the Conquest, the eastern component, genetic stock, and anthropological character became stronger with the admission of the Pechenegs, Cumans, and Iazyges.

Thus, the conclusions of linguistic history and anthropology are today so greatly contradictory that this

writer not only does not dare to suggest a solution; he does not even see a satisfactory middle road. Perhaps, we have an inadequate knowledge of the evolution of language usage, the paths of language exchange, and the interaction of ethnic and language factors.

A proposal has been made for cutting the Gordian knot; it maintains that we cannot speak of Hungarians as a people who have come from outside the Carpathian Basin, because they have evolved here. Namely, the people who came here under the leadership of Árpád comprised only a small fraction of the ancestors of today's total population; those they found here, those who made their way after them in the later stages of the great migrations, and those who later entered the Carpathian Basin and were settled here formed a very large proportion of the population...

This is a striking proposition. Still, I do not accept it. We shall see that the age of marauding raids following the Conquest and then the establishment of the kingdom presume that a sturdy core of people, full-fledged and prepared, existed outside this region by the time of the Conquest, a conclusion which demands and completely justifies our speaking of this people as Árpád's Hungarians. Nevertheless, the above proposal is useful in shortening the section of the road we must necessarily travel to trace the migration of this people, our ancestors, so extended in time and space, outside the Carpathian Basin. We shall not immerse ourselves in distinguishing between what we know and what we infer about the formation of the Hungarians living in parts of the Eurasian steppes.

Instead, let us take the hand of Julianus. Let us go as far as he penetrated. In 1235, Julianus, a Dominican friar, set out with three brethren to find Magna Hungaria. At that time, it was certainly common knowledge that the Hungarians had split in two before the Conquest, and that only the smaller group came west and the large remained in the east, in the Great Ancestral Land.

The bold Julianus eventually reached on his own the people he was searching for. He actually came across Hungarians beyond the Volga, in the area of today's

beyond the Volga, who then, keeping ahead of the Avars, reached the Carpathian Basin and placed the region under their rule permanently. This much can be taken for granted, that the group of Hungarians that Árpád's people sprang from had spent a long period of time around the middle of the first millennium A.D. some distance on this side of the Volga along the middle reaches of the Don, above the Sea of Azov. Here they stumbled upon an entirely new

The turul or falcon—Decorative disk for braids found at Rakamaz. *A large number of the most beautiful finds from the Age of the Conquest come from Hungary's northeastern parts, the region of the Upper Tisza and the Bodrog rivers. On the one hand, this fact helps to verify the traditional historical view that during the conquest, the major route—or at least one—led across the Verecke Pass into the Carpathian Basin; on the other, it indicates that many members of the first generation of the conquerors immediately settled in the upper border regions of the recently found homeland, so abundant with fish, wild game, and fertile grazing land. Though the Hungarian*

Gesta *by Anonymus is a later compilation and not completely reliable, it is, nevertheless, worth mentioning that its author, "King Béla's nameless scribe," relates the occupation and settlement of this specific area in the greatest detail and most graphically, almost as if he had been a witness. This disk, decorated with the totem animal of Árpád's tribe, seems to confirm that Chief Árpád and his people passed through this region. The hypothesis that a branch of this ever more powerful dynastic tribe actually settled on the banks of the Bodrog river is verified by the frequent occurrence of characteristic place names in clusters.*

Bashkiria, whom he could clearly understand. From them he obtained knowledge about the approach of the Tatar (Mongolian) forces, and he immediately returned home with the news. In 1237, he took to the road again to "summon home" this very small, yet significant number of people in Magna Hungaria, to persuade them to relocate in the Carpathian Basin. But by the time he reached Suzdal he had learned that the Mongolians had already swept away these remaining relatives in the Volga region. His attempt to unify the separate groups failed.

Well, this is what we know about our direct ancestors. However, even today we can only guess as to when they split up at the Volga's bend in today's Kuibyshev area. Certainly not close to the time before the Conquest; we can put the date at any time between the fourth and the eighth century.

In this period the domino principle prevailed for centuries from one end of the vast Eurasian plains to the other. The leading ranks of various nomadic peoples acquired ever greater power; they crushed the neighboring and then the more distant, mostly related peoples. Because nomadism was not sufficiently conducive to agriculture, expansion, pillage, and occasional exacting of ransom or permanent taxation formed the basis for the existence of every powerful group. And wherever the military forces of such a "realm" extended, there—never without loss of blood or material—other peoples either allowed the flood to pass over their heads and tried, if possible, to hang on somehow or become allies or auxiliaries and split the spoils of war, or leaving their place, they avoided the armies' main routes to areas more protected and removed from the swiftly moving horsemen, or rather into the vicinity of groups more capable of opposition.

It may have been the Avars who dislodged the Hungarians from their original home in Bashkiria

environment. They already knew how to till land with a plow in Magna Hungaria, but in the new place, named Levedia after one of the Hungarian chiefs, the Hungarians, who were still largely nomadic breeders of animals, encountered agriculturists using a more advanced, heavier plow with iron fittings, a rich horticulture and livestock, buildings and fortified towns indicating permanent residence among the Sarmatian Alans and the Onogurs and Volga Bulgarians belonging to the Turkish ethnic group living here. The Hungarians themselves acquired much from their agriculture and way of life.

Constantine VII Porphyrogenitus, Emperor of Byzantium from 912 to 959, who was also a painstaking historian, put the stay of the Hungarians in Levedia at three years. But apparently he was mistaken. Linguistic, agricultural, and cultural interpenetrations allow us to conclude that the Alans, Bulgarians, and Hungarians lived together about three hundred years. (Let us remember Hunor and Magor, the double marriage with the kidnapped daughters of the Alan chief.) However, what was Levedia to us was, at the same time, the border area of the Turkish Khazars' state structure, the Khazar Kaganate, which varied in size and power but remained permanently important. Thus, with respect to power, the Hungarians were sometimes subjects of the Khazars, sometimes supporters of their adversaries. The elements of Finno-Ugrian animism and shamanism and the veneration of totem animals by the peoples from the Steppes blended into the Hungarians' still completely pagan beliefs. However, in Levedia, they encountered three types of monotheism. Mohammedanism was widespread in the Khazar Kaganate, Eastern Christianity had a bishopric there, and its leading social class converted to the Jewish faith with great suddenness. (History hardly knows of another instance when non-Jewish ethnic groups converted to the Jewish faith not individually, as through

Hungarians at Kiev—A painting by Pál Vágó (1853–1928). *Though many attempts, based in part on archaeological finds and in part on old accounts, were made to depict Hungarian prehistory and the Conquest at the time of the Millennium and the turn of the twentieth century, much uncertainty still attends the prehistory of Hungarians, the period before they arrived in the Carpathian Basin. At present, it is extremely difficult to maintain, on the basis of archaeological relics more or less datable to the proper time that have turned up in territories now forming part of the Ukraine and Russia, that these objects are unmistakably the relics of the ancient Hungarians. It is probable, though, that as a result of the extensive and multibranched archaeological research that has been going on for a long time, many such finds today lie hidden in the area of the former Soviet Union, mainly in smaller regional museums, which more thorough scientific investigation will identify as being of ancient Hungarian origin.*

marriage, but in such large numbers. The explanation of this exceptional case is that, in the absence of a Jewish core with powerful aspirations in the region, and both the Mohammedans and Christians having such a core, the Khazar nobles, by converting, counted on avoiding a situation in which the choice of belief would also call for a political and power alignment.)

Like every contemporaneous concentration of power—it is not accidental that we can hardly speak as yet of nations or states, particularly of nation states—the structure of the Khazar state too was unstable. At the close of the Hungarians' Levedian period, external and internal challenges rocked the Kaganate. The main problem was posed by a new Turkish people attacking from the east, the Pechenegs. Our own ancestors also began to move farther west, while a larger group of people, a small portion of them from the Khazar Empire, joined them and moved on with them half as allies and half as subject auxiliaries. Though perhaps, they themselves formed and separated into three tribes, they would, under the name of Kabars, make up the eighth tribe of the Conquest, in addition

to Árpád's seven Hungarian tribes; they were the "black" Hungarians beside the "white" Hungarians. Among them there were certainly Mohammedans and also Jews in all probability; and possibly a very small part of the Hungarians and Kabars may have been Christians.

We hardly know the exact time, but before the mid-ninth century, while Hungarian advance guards were already appearing at the Lower Danube—where they came across a familiar people, the Onogur Bulgars who had moved to that point—the future conquerors could be found in the Etelköz (*köz* = area between two rivers) directly in the foreground of the Carpathians, along the Dnieper, the Dniester, the Bug, and the Siret. Here they whiled away one and a half or two generations. Then perhaps another Pecheneg attack moved them onward again.

The migration of peoples continued; the unruly peoples of the Steppes, craving better land, rushed headlong with renewed strength from the east to the west. Facing them in the foreground of the Carpathians, unprotected from the east, made it impossible to withstand their onslaught. And the Etelköz Hungarians were very familiar with the shores of the Black Sea down to Byzantium, the Balkan Peninsula, the Carpathian Basin itself, and, indeed, all of Central Europe to the west. In alliance with Byzantium and in other alliances or on their own hook, they had already dashed along on journeys of many days. Only a part of them were staid farmers, the rest were an unruly nomadic military breed; they had a real need for the prizes they acquired through military plunder—slaves, gold, and silver—and the freer, warring life of wandering also became a passion with them. They were fond of home in the winter, of the splendidly decorated yurt and the women they were accustomed to, the ones who raised their heirs faithfully, but, at the same time, they enjoyed the embraces of the new slave women they gained in battle.

"FROM THE ARROWS OF THE HUNGARIANS"...

The *Gesta Hungarorum* was not passed on to us in its original form, but this ancient chronicle about the Hungarians can be reconstructed fairly well from various transcriptions. One of its episodes tells about how Árpád dispatched an ambassador spy by the name of Kusid, the son of Künd, to the interior of the Carpathian Basin.

"When Kusid reached the middle of Hungary and descended to the Danube region, he found the place delightful, the land all around good and fertile, and its streams and meadows splendid. He had a liking for it. Then he went to the prince of the domain, named Svatopluk, who governed after Attila. He hailed him in the name of his people and stated the reason why he came. Hearing this, Svatopluk rejoiced greatly because he thought they were settlers come to cultivate the land. For this reason he joyfully sent the ambassador back. Filling his flask with water from the Danube, loading his goatskin with meadow grass, and taking a sample of the black sandy soil, Kusid returned to his people. As he recounted everything he had heard and seen to them, they rejoiced greatly. He showed them the flask of water, the soil, and the grass. Tasting them with their tongues, they saw that the soil was very good, the water sweet, and that such grasses grew in the pastures as the ambassador had told them. Surrounded by his people, Árpád filled his drinking horn with the water from the Danube, and, in front of all the Hungarians, he asked for the grace of Almighty God on the horn, that the Lord grant them that land forever... Then they sent the same ambassador back to the forenamed prince by general agreement and sent the price in payment for his land, a large white horse with an Arabian saddle gilded with gold and a gold halter. Seeing these, the prince rejoiced even more, for he believed they had sent them for the land as prospective settlers. But the ambassador asked the prince to provide land, grass, and water. Smiling at this, the prince said, 'Take as much as you want for this gift!' And so the ambassador returned to his people. At this, Árpád and the seven chiefs invaded Pannonia, not as immigrants but as the lawful owners of the land in perpetuity. Then they dispatched another ambassador to the prince, sending him off with this message: 'Árpád and his men tell you not to remain any longer in any way on the land with a horse, your grass with a halter, and your water with a saddle, and because of your penury and greediness you have yielded your land, grass, and water over to them.' When the message was delivered to the prince, he spoke as follows: 'Beat that horse to death with a club, throw the halter into the meadow, and cast the saddle into the waters of the Danube!' At this, the ambassador said: 'What loss would this bring to our lord? If you beat the horse to death, you provide food for his dogs; if you throw the golden halter into the grass, his men will come upon it at harvest time; if you cast the golden saddle into the Danube, his fishermen will pull it to the bank and take it home! Whoever owns the land, the grass, and the water, he owns everything!' Hearing this and fearing the Hungarians, the prince quickly assembled an army and called upon his friends for help, and gathering these together, he started off to do battle with them. In the meantime, the Hungarians arrived beside the Danube, and at the break of day they arose on a lovely field to do battle. But the Lord's support was with the Hungarians, at the sight of whom the forenamed prince took flight. But the Hungarians pursued him to the Danube, and there in his fright he cast himself into the Danube and he drowned in its swift waters."

This historical tale about how Árpád outwitted Svatopluk, the Slavic prince, with a deceitful give-and-take agreement eerily resembles the one about how a couple of centuries later, the whites swarming over America duped the poor redskinned Indians. But can there be any kind of historical basis for the tale about the white horse?

Thus did the Hungarians reach the place where they have lived to this very day. Now let us rephrase in a declarative mode what we had posed as a question in the introduction—at least to the extent that it is possible.

In 895, the main forces of the Etelköz Hungarians, as allies of Byzantium or as mercenaries—which amounts to the same thing—were waging war on their former Levedian comrades, the Bulgarians, west of the Black Sea. Meanwhile, a Pecheneg attack—instigated, perhaps, by the Bulgarians—was launched against the Khazar Kaganate, and hearing news of the assault, those remaining in their Etelköz quarters suddenly headed off and moved across the northern passes of the Carpathians into the basin protected by the ring of mountains. The main forces did not return to the Etelköz but also headed for the Carpathian Basin, almost from the opposite direction. These two troop movements indicated the existence of a well-established communication link and forced but planned military operations.

This idea also refutes the romantic notion that the Hungarians were purely a battered, fleeing army of males who, their wives and children having perished, had to generate their own bloodlines in the new homeland with women they took as slaves. It is not only our sources that contradict this idea, but also the fact that the conquerors of the Carpathian Basin have immediately devoted themselves to bold new adventures, indicating a secure home front. At the same time the Hungarians dislodged by the great migrations and having reached the Carpathian Basin, in a manner unique among the traditionally nomadic peoples (the Scythians, the Sarmatians, the Huns, the Avars, the Pechenegs, the Cumans, and the Tatars), did not assimilate, disperse, or lose their language; instead, they were able to found a national state which has endured to this very day.

About 895, various Slavic peoples on the perimeter of the Carpathian Basin and the Avar population in its

Attila's banquet—A painting by Mór Than (1822–1899), 1863–1866. *With the Millennium, that ecstatic celebration of the thousandth anniversary of the Hungarian Conquest, still distant, this picture anticipated the mood of that event. When the artist presented Attila amid the theatrical scene at his court, whom myth-making Hungarian history attempted with great effort to register as one of our ancestors, he could rely on a dependable historical source for support. Priscus Rhetor, a contemporary historian who in 448 was present at Attila's court (then certainly situated in the Alföld) as a member of a Byzantine delegation, provided a vivid description of the wooden palace of the great prince of the Huns, "the Scourge of God," and was his guest at a banquet.*

lowlands were the decisive elements, while the power of the Moravians from the northwest, of the Franks (Bavarians) formerly in Pannonia from the west, and of the Bulgarians from the south exerted—what? At this time "dominion" in this region was not very efficacious. Sometimes it signified little more than the fact that the leaders of agricultural village communities living permanently in a place and bound to the soil by their mode of life reinforced their positions through some tribute paid in kind for first one and then for another of the chiefs of more mobile and warlike peoples. The burial grounds of the age, mingling bones and artifacts, clearly reveal the continuity or changeability of power and might, ethnicity and culture, and the diverse variety of the motifs of permanent coexistence and assimilation.

Árpád the Conqueror's entire army consisted of about 20 thousand horsemen. Since we can assume that there were four or five peasants, as well as artisans, serving as support personnel behind each warrior horseman, the total number of Hungarians can be estimated at 100 thousand families, or about half a million persons. On the other hand, researchers put the local population of the Carpathian Basin at not more than 100 to 200 thousand inhabitants. Though these estimates are based on reliable archaeological, settlement geographical and demographic data, the writer of these lines, nevertheless, thinks of more balanced proportions. Perhaps it was more their own dynamics than their superior numbers that gave the Hungarians their strength. Also the conquerors' cautious behavior suggests that at first they were not as confident of their own abilities as they were entitled to be. The hypothesis that the late Avars living in the region before 895 were also Hungarian ethnics (or users of the language) and thus formed, so to say, the advance guard of the Hungarian conquerors is not provable. Still less believable is the romantic postulate, based on a close Hun–Hungarian kinship constructed at a later time, according to which the Székely guarding the frontiers of Transylvania and of southwest Transdanubia (Göcsej) were descendants of kinfolk who had lived there since the time of the Huns, the people of the Hun Prince Csaba, one of Attila's sons. On the other hand, we cannot preclude the possibility that during the earlier marauding raids small fragments of the Hungarians remained in the Carpathian Basin who then helped Árpád's Hungarians.

The Hungarian Conquest—A color sketch of the painting by Mihály Munkácsy (1844–1900). *This picture shows the fifth color sketch made in 1892 for the gigantic panel painting being created with the utmost care at the beginning of the 1890s for Parliament in the way of preparing for the Millennium. Although the artists of the time tried to make use of the historical and archaeological knowledge existing then, the painting reflects, instead, the romantic notions invented about Árpád and his people rather than authentic historical reality. And this is true even if in this sketch Munkácsy portrays on the basis of Anonymus's Gesta the surrender of "Chief Salán's" people—in other words, the local Slavic inhabitants—when at Árpád's request they brought earth, water, and grass to "taste" in "exchange" for Árpád's twelve white horses and other gifts he sent to their chief. According to Anonymus, the Hungarians really viewed this "exchange" as a purchase, as compensation for Salán's domain, which, in today's view, would be as large a ruse as the one the Greeks perpetrated with the wooden horse at Troy.*

No matter how small a kernel of truth is concealed in the tale of the white horse, in the legend of the subjugation of the Slavs through trickery, one thing is certain: the movement of the Hungarians inside the Carpathian Basin slackened for a couple of years. First they only reached the Danube; it was only after five years, near the end of the century, that they took possession of earlier Pannonia to the west of the former Roman *limes*—the chronicles at times extend this name mistakenly to all of the Carpathian Basin. At this time, however, their mobility returned. Hardly a year passed without their swift, ransoming armies appearing in ever more distant regions. Their horses waded in the waters of the Baltic Sea in the north and in the Channel in the west; they reached the middle of the Iberian Peninsula in the southwest; they cast a glance at Sicily from the Italian Peninsula in the south; on Greek soil they left only the Peloponnesus untouched; and the Bosporus barred their way in the east. They cut their way through peoples, countries, and borders "like a knife through butter."

The pagan *legendarium* of these Hungarians is full of deeds about their own glory: about Botond the Champion, who smashed the iron gate of Byzantium with his own mace; about Chief Lél, or Lehel, who, having fallen prisoner and awaiting execution, slew the German prince Conrad, saying: "You will precede me and be my slave in the hereafter," in accord with the pagan belief that those whom warriors kill become their slaves "on the other side." Monastic annals of aggrieved individuals are also filled with their unholy atrocities. They are themselves from

Hell, the breed of Satan, a scourge of God. A friar of St. Gallen, though not as a witness but years after the event, presented an account of the Hungarians' encampment in his monastery in 926 with such vivid liveliness that, whether he writes something bad or not so bad about them, we must accept it. What makes his history particularly believable is that while the friars of St. Gallen fled in panic, one of them stayed there—because he had not received leather for his sandals. Ekkehard, the chronicler, called this fellow member, named Heribald, a half-wit. He is our witness. Let us not smile: the simple-minded speak the truth.

"At last they burst in, with their quivers and loaded with menacing javelins and arrows. They hunt through every room carefully, and it is certain they show no mercy to sex or age. They find him alone, just standing unperturbed in the middle of the room. They marvel at him: what can he want? why does he not flee? Meanwhile, the officers order their forces, ready to kill, not to use their weapons, and they interrogate him with the help of interpreters. When they become aware that they are dealing with a half-witted freak of nature, they all laugh and spare his life.

"They do not even touch St. Gallen's altar, for they had suffered disappointment in such things previously, never finding anything more than bones and ashes...

"Two of them climb up the belfry in the belief that the rooster on its peak is made of gold, that it could not be the local god with this name unless it was made of precious metal. (*Gallus* = rooster.) One of them leans out more sharply to force it off with his lance, falls to the courtyard from the height, and is killed outright. Meanwhile, the other climbed to the top of the eastern façade to desecrate the god's shrine, and while he prepared himself to empty his bowels there, he tumbled backwards and crushed himself to death....

"The officers take over the courtyard and carouse copiously. Heribald also gorges himself so much that, as he himself kept saying afterwards, he never lived better. And since, according to their custom, they sat down on the grass without chairs to eat, Heribald brought chairs for himself and a cleric taken prisoner. After having gnawed and torn the sacrificial cattle's shoulders and other half-raw parts solely with their teeth, without knives, the others kept tossing the gnawed bones at each other in sport. Everyone, without exception, drank as much wine as he wanted, which was placed in full buckets in the middle. After they became heated with wine, they began shouting frightfully to their gods, and they forced the cleric and the half-wit to do the same. And the cleric, since he knew their language well, which was why they let him live, shouted with them as hard as he could. But when he had behaved madly enough in their language, he began the antiphony on the Holy Cross tearfully, beginning with 'Bless us'—which Heribald also sang with him, though his voice was very hoarse. (The feast of the Holy Cross was to be the next day.) At the prisoners' strange song, all who were there crowded together, and releasing their jollity, they danced and wrestled in front of the leaders. Some clashed with weapons to demonstrate how skilled they were in military science."

With this sentence, let us leave our brave Friar Heribald to himself, who, perhaps, was not so simple-minded after all. Skill in military science—this was one of the key maxims of the Hungarian marauding raids. Now, we have to unravel what sent this newly arrived people time and time again on fearless attacks from their recently occupied homeland immediately after they settled on the boundary of the western world of that time, in between the Christians of the east and the west, in the vicinity of the parturition zone where the formation of the European nation states was just going on, having abandoned the region of the easily developing and disintegrating eastern "empires".

As for their warlike traditions, they are, in part, simply the routines of the eastern nomads. Without them they could not have survived during the long and bloody wanderings of the earlier centuries. In a curious way, they were enjoying the benefits of their late arrival in their new environment.

Economic and social developments achieved a new level from the Leitha to the west; they created new values and a new order. The city and the monastery, the handicraft industry and commerce, increasingly subsisting on money, demanded security and more effective protection of the achievements that existed under Rome before it collapsed under the attacks of the Germanic barbarians.

Now, however, the political framework and the power essential to it were missing.

Byzantium was the frightening example of ossification, of centuries' long decline caused by ruinous dogmatism. In the west, technical development, Christian thought, and feudal society—the feudal subordination and superordination—transformed mental attitudes just as it did the way of life, and weaponry or the methods of waging war. Yet all this was endangered by a series of challenges by greedy Arabs (Saracens and Moors) from the south, by Normans (Vikings) attacking with their swift boats from the north, and first by Avars and later by Hungarian light cavalrymen from the east. Europe reacted slowly. Fragmented and quarreling over the spoils of the collapsed parts of the former Roman Empire, it not only offered itself unwittingly to its extortioners but even summoned them as allies in their anarchic struggles against one another.

At this time, the half-nomadic Hungarians could no longer content themselves with rich meadows, well-stocked streams, and fertile plowlands. Their agriculturists, we know, did not participate in raiding parties; most of these campaigns commenced in the spring, the time of the greatest agricultural activity, and rarely ended before the harvest. Thus the marauders constituted the remaining one-fifth of the population. Did they, perhaps, have to abandon the nomadic life in their new smaller homeland? No. The sharp division of society had already taken place outside the Carpathians, with the elevation of a leading class that was so much the master of the tillers of the soil that its power was based on strong military retinues, in addition to material wealth.

These military retinues knew virtually no time of peace. It was not solely bravado and hot blood—the maintenance of warlike knowledge—that impelled the retinues and their leaders. With respect to sheer existence, the hoeing and plowing agriculture, horticulture, and still rather nomadic animal husbandry of this period were more than adequate to meet the needs of the entire population. But the leading

14

Male and female apparel from the Age of the Hungarian Conquest —A reconstruction sketch by Gyula László. *Since the climatic and soil conditions of Hungary seldom allowed organic material to survive in the graves of the Conquest period, Professor of Archaeology László's reconstruction sketched out the clothing of the Hungarian military leaders' class that settled in the Carpathian Basin*

mainly on the basis of the durable finds, those of metal and bone, which might have been pieces of costume jewelry. To this end, he studied the archaeological relics of other nomadic peoples from the Steppes and also their apparel, aspects of which apparently survive to the present. The possibilities of our learning how the agricultural classes were clothed in the Age of the Conquest are more modest.

classes' aspirations for power and fondness for pomp required riches and money, nor did the large military retinues content themselves only with the small portion that was tossed like a bone to them from the surplus yields of the new homeland.

The most dependable source of income for Árpád and his fellow officers, and for their descendants, was the regular annual tax exacted from neighboring peoples who were more peacefully inclined and settled, or who, for whatever reason, were seeking military allies. Yet for this, they had to display military strength, in order to cause fear among the neighbors in case they lagged in paying their taxes. And if this display of military power was insufficient, they had to strike hard and bloodily. The leading classes preferred first the certain and enormous peace taxes collected in a lump sum and second the military pay handed directly to them. On the other hand, the common soldiers in the military retinues were, with reason, more pleased with ransom and punitive campaigns when robbery was permitted; after all, on such occasions, most of the plunder wound up in their own knapsacks; but they also valued mercenary military expeditions, during which they had to spare the land of the employer's people but could pillage elsewhere at will.

For two generations, hardly a year passed without larger or smaller Hungarian armies being engaged in military ventures, sometimes strictly on their own but mostly on call. And in today's Czech, German, French, and Italian territories or in the Balkans there was scarcely a province, principality, kingdom, or other national structure whose leaders did not call for their occasional military assistance at one time or other and endure their attacks in service to their adversaries at another time. They seemed to appear on schedule on numerous military routes in many distant regions. Their guides came from the party that hired them, and they crossed most rivers peacefully—until they reached the lands of the next enemy. The great distances covered, the many battles they fought successfully, the ample ransom, the large number of prisoners—whom they did not often take home but released immediately for a ransom or sold as slaves, not really needing the manpower of prisoners of war (slaves) at home—all this proves that from the end of the ninth century to the middle of the tenth, the military retinues of the Hungarian leading classes obtained, in addition to some systematic taxation, substantial additional income by regularly hiring out their battle prowess.

Now then, what advantages derived from the lateness of their arrival? The Hungarians' mode of Asian nomadic warfare—the division of the army into several parts, its lightning fast movement, the deceptive retreat, its very powerful bows, and its far-soaring arrows—surprised foot soldiers accustomed to the more cumbersome, closed battle formations, to moving on large horses, and to heavier weapons, and it muddled the inhabitants of cities and castles who often sought protection singly. On the other hand, their enemies were only slightly able to exploit their weaknesses—the fact that they were less able to wage war in the winter, that rain slackened their bowstrings, that they dispersed to pillage, that they had to lug their booty with them. Perhaps the Hungarians faced their greatest danger when their friends and foes suddenly regrouped themselves and, amid the disturbed power relations, the road back to the homeland became more difficult for armies roving so far away.

A Hungarian horseman shooting an arrow—A tenth or eleventh-century fresco in the crypt of the cathedral at Aquileia. *This fresco, apparently painted by an eyewitness, is of no small assistance in our efforts to reconstruct Hungarian weaponry, war tactics, and apparel at the time of the Conquest and the marauding raids. The reflex bow and the quiver appear in the picture as well; and it is an extremely graphic image of the warrior securely seated in the saddle on a galloping horse and,* turned around, *shooting an arrow at the enemy while fleeing—either as a ruse or in actuality. Armor-clad cavalry would have been unable to execute a similar movement.*

From the middle of the tenth century on, the dynamics of the incursions could no longer be supported. The employers—the rulers and aspiring rulers of Europe—gradually realized their own stupidity. Politically, they recognized that by constantly weakening each other's people and economy through destruction by the roaming Hungarians, they were all ruining themselves. Militarily, they recognized that the warfare of Hungarian light cavalrymen was easy to see through and vulnerable, that this voracious people wedged in Central Europe could be tamed by answering trick with trick, by attacking the dispersed forces separately, not isolated in towns but with united forces.

Contrary to the contentions of western chronicles, it was not one and not two battles lost, not primarily the defeat inflicted by the German Otto I at Augsburg in 955 that staggered the marauding Hungarians. The victors exaggerated this news because of their intoxication with the triumph and the defeated because they wanted to calm the war fever back home. Did the ideals of gentle Christianity begin to exert influence on pagan traditions? Cause and effect were reversed. The wiser leaders of the Hungarian tribes and tribal confederations themselves awoke to what those they had blithely taxed until then or had served with blood for pay had suddenly realized to their dismay. The realization was mutual and affected both sides. The restless, full-blooded Hungarians must be settled among the ranks of the more prosperous peoples within the more secure borders of Christian Europe. Or they must be destroyed. And we must become a part of a Europe with a strange religion. Or the enemy will destroy us.

SAINTS OUT OF WOLVES

The remnants of the army headed homeward from Augsburg. Although the loss of human life was not disastrous, internal relations in the homeland were undergoing realignment. Change was occurring in part, perhaps, because the Kabars and other ethnic groups that had joined the Hungarians also participated in the marauding raids, and thus also in the defeat at Augsburg, in significant numbers, while the leading ethnic group, the Hungarians, had remained more entire. (True, the men lost in the war hardly left an irreplaceable void. Polygamy was still common, and the custom of levirate whereby the oldest brother of the decased warrior was obliged to marry his widow, to raise his children, and to beget additional offspring, still existed. Thus the capacity of women to bear children and the rate of infant mortality determined almost exclusively the increase in population.)

The remnants of the army headed homeward from Augsburg. What was their final destination? We know this much, that the leading circles of Hungarians still kept dual lodgings, changing dwelling-places in winter and summer, leading a nomadic life. In keeping with the custom of the peoples from the Steppes, they also maintained marshes in the Carpathian Basin, that is, uninhabited zones of land all around, with marsh gates and with auxiliary forces stationed there to guard the borders. The process of laying out these marshes was easy in a region broken up by mountains, and also in the south where rivers and swamps protected them. This was also the case in the west, at the feet of the Alps. At this time, the upper marshes along the Danube stretched somewhere into the Vienna Basin.

While we know all this, our information is, in certain respects, less than that about earlier times. The traces of the frequent raids survived, often in the form of chief warriors' names, in the chronicles of the affected regions which at first were filled with lamentation but later with exultation. News about the Hungarians withdrawing to their borders was more rare, the facts fewer.

What was the situation in Europe in the second half of the tenth century? Across the Channel, King Edgar was the first to rule all of England. On French soil, the Capet dynasty was supplanting the Carolingians; it had strong dukedoms, and a weak royal house. The German (Saxon) Otto I, the victor at Augsburg, was more than a match for his own princes; waging war in all directions, he became so powerful that in 962 he had himself crowned emperor of the Holy Roman Empire in Rome. His son, Otto II, married the daughter of the emperor of Byzantium —it raised a dream of reviving the Roman Empire. On the Iberian Peninsula, the ousting of the Moors was invariably the aim. In Scandinavia, in addition to the growing separation of the Danes, Norwegians, and Swedes, the counteractions of the pagan opposition hindered Christianization; with the age of Norman (Viking) marauding raids in Europe coming to an end, the nimble ships turned northward: Erik the Red reached Greenland, his son America at Labrador. Byzantium temporarily gained ground, while leaders distinguishing themselves against the Arabs seized the imperial throne with hands stained with each other's blood. On Bohemian (Moravian) soil, a complicated German–Slavic mudwrestling match went on in the disintegrating kingdom of Greater Moravia, which actually never existed; Prague developed into an important European city and was a bishopric from 972 on. On Polish soil, too, Christianization gained momentum, and a monarchy formed over the small principalities. On Russian soil, the endless metamorphosis of power factions could barely be followed; here the slow expansion of Christianity came from Byzantium, and its effect can be felt to the present day in the development of the region.

What is the most striking feature of this fleeting panorama? It is the raising of the cross in the sky throughout Europe, and the subjugation of lesser power centers, although setbacks mark both processes. Meanwhile, conversions, Christianization—particularly its western course—served to unify: it strengthened what is termed "supranational" in peoples. In the centralization of power and in the organization of worldly dominion, the integrating role of ethnic groups grew rather secretly, one can say, unconsciously. To the Hungarians' good fortune, it was precisely those among Árpád's descendants holding the greatest power who recognized both the direction and importance of these processes.

At the same time, our facts about this more peaceful time are, as we mentioned, more limited. This much is certain, however, that during the generation following Augsburg, Gyula, the leader of Transylvania, the eastern part of the country enjoying considerable independence, cast an eye upon Byzantium; he welcomed missionaries from there, became a Christian himself, and founded a bishopric. Looking westward instead, Taksony, the chief prince and man of armed peace, sought political tranquility with the Germans but did not commit himself with respect to religion. Meanwhile, "old-fashioned" military campaigns were occasionally launched both east and west, but the age of marauding raids was irretrievably over. And those Hungarians with the most restless blood had no opportunity to set sail for new continents, as the Vikings had; nor could they return to the former homeland, as the Moors had to Africa. If not expressed as clearly as the nineteenth-century poet, Mihály Vörösmarty, will in his hymn entitled *Szózat*, the same conviction was already rooted among the most foresighted Hungarians:

> *No place exists for you*
> *In the whole world but this;*
> *Fate's hand may bless or damn you:*
> *Here must you live or die.*

Taksony's son, Géza, who was chief prince from 970 to 997—perhaps he also wore the title of king at the end of his life—was willing to become a Christian, but he

25

continued to participate in pagan rites, and, according to one story, when his attention was called to this fact, he replied haughtily: he was such a wealthy lord that he had enough treasure to sacrifice abundantly to two gods.

Géza's son, Vajk, who received the name Stephen on becoming a Christian—the same as his father's, though thereafter he used his new and not his old name—was prince from 997 to 1000 and king from 1000 to 1038. His coronation could have taken place on December 25, 1000 or on January 1, 1001, with a crown sent by Pope Sylvester II, or by Otto III, the emperor of the Holy Roman Empire, according to another opinion.

Stephen defeated Koppány, and had his body quartered for his rebellion and had the parts nailed on the gates of the country's four cities. This episode occurred later, however. First, let us see how the date of the coronation may have been chosen, which was, in certain respects, only a formal but still indispensable ceremony for Stephen. Was the day accommodated to the pagan holiday of the winter solstice occurring a couple of days earlier, though at this time it was not accurately determined, so that the pagan part of the population—the majority—would understand once and for all who their ruler is? Or exactly the opposite, to December 26, to the Christian name day of Deacon Stephen? After all, Taksony's son, Géza, and then Géza's son, Vajk, hardly received the name of the early missionary and martyr in Jerusalem accidentally. Or, instead, was the commencement of the new, the second millennium according to the Christian calendar to which the papacy attributed unparalleled importance at this time taken into account? Whichever one of these or all three together was the case, Stephen's coronation was carefully planned not only as a binding political and religious act but also as a pure ceremony.

With what date can we begin this historical epic poem broken into prose that Stephen I, the Hungarian king, undoubtedly deserves? With 997 or 1000, or the year

of the final event when King Ladislas I, who was also raised to the ranks of Rome's saints not much later, had sainthood conferred on Stephen, his son, Prince Emeric, and Emeric's tutor, Bishop Gerard (Gellért), simultaneously on August 20, 1083?

We shall not begin with any of these. The prose epic poem is not our genre. And anyway, not wanting to diminish Stephen's greatness, we must not stress date or narrower time periods. Passage from Taksony to well after Stephen was constant, despite every breach and regression. The Hungarian nation was not founded by a single act nor by a single ruler, though Stephen's reign was very long, extending over more than four decades. What commenced in the middle of the tenth century bestowed enough tasks upon a whole line of rulers, even to the extinction of the kings of the House of Árpád, to the beginning of the fourteenth century.

Still Stephen's lifework is so significant that he cannot be described simply as one of the figures in a long historical process.

Taksony and then his son, Géza, already saw the triumph of the cross in Europe; they themselves, however, were leading a people, a conglomeration of peoples, who to a great part remained pagan in their beliefs. Taksony and his son perceived that some other, stronger sword would carve out ever more power, territory, and population everywhere in Europe for itself; that mass

Vajk's baptism—A painting by Gyula Benczúr (1844–1920), 1875. *Vajk was the pagan name of Géza's son, Stephen, during his youth; in addition to the contemporary chronicle of Thietmar, the Bishop of Merseburg, the name is preserved by several place names in Hungary. Could St. Stephen actually have been baptized only after he became an adult? This is not impossible even if we now believe that Prince Géza, his father, had already become a Christian, if only ostensibly so. (The notion that he too had ruled with the name of Stephen also crops up. If this were true, then historiography would have to commemorate St. Stephen as Stephen II, not Stephen I.)*

migration would abate; that security would no longer be provided by mobile manpower but by walls and the producers and valuable goods they protected. They themselves, however, were leaders of a social class—their own military retinue—that was so restless and accustomed to constant changes of place that they remained subject to their will. Walls could hardly be found in the new homeland in the Carpathian Basin, unless they were odd, foreign Roman ruins. Craftsmen lived in exactly the same fragile villages as the plowing and planting peasants did, and a goodly number of valuable objects wound up in pagan sacrificial places as gifts to the gods or were buried, in keeping with pagan rite, in graves.

How could one hang on and create security here? When necessary, Taksony even gave up some of his newly gained territory; for example, the Vienna Basin, where the border marshes ran farther in and more to the east. However, we can, it seems, only guess at his political thinking and plans for action: he was maneuvering, gaining time—for his descendants.

The wife of Taksony's son, Géza, was a Christian; she was Sarolt from Transylvania, Gyula's daughter. Géza gave his own daughters in marriage to Boleslaw (the Brave) I, the ruler of Poland, to Samuel Aba, the leader of the

The Holy Right Hand—The largest relic of St. Stephen, the right hand of the nation's founder. *The right hand of Stephen I, who was buried, possibly embalmed, at Székesfehérvár, survived relatively intact in his tomb, precisely because, placed on his chest, it remained dry and mummified. The Holy Right Hand is highly esteemed in Hungary to this very day through the Roman Catholic Church in which the fanatic veneration of relics ever since the Middle Ages still remains, even if to a less fervent degree.*

Kabars, and to Otto Orseolo, the Doge of Venice. For his son, Stephen, he chose Gisela, a princess of Bavaria, as bride. This unheard-of deliberateness elevates Géza so high in our esteem because we do know that he still had not changed as much in his heart as in his politics. He became a Christian, but only half-heartedly: he made his offerings in two directions. But, we think, we suspect, this was hardly a tactic on his part: he did not want to deceive the gods or the people by appearing to be a Christian externally and a pagan internally. It was simply that that was what he was like. His feelings still pulled him back; listening to his intellect, he looked ahead.

Recently, a belief entered the realm of probability, to the effect that the foundations of many structures reputed to be from Stephen's time had already been laid down by Géza. And this can be extended symbolically. In the founding of the state, no matter how long this process took, the roles of the two rulers, Prince Géza and Géza's son, King Stephen, were unquestionably enormous. Géza handed down the decision. The burden of execution was bequeathed to Stephen.

The son and grandson of half-pagan Géza were both canonized by the Catholic Church. With cause? Definitely. But probably not entirely for what was ascribed to them in the writings of the legendmakers in the monasteries. Some sources described Stephen and especially Prince Emeric as pious souls. Actually, there was hardly a Hungarian king who was more iron-handed than Stephen, and Emeric, as far as we know, died while hunting wild boar.

The reign of Stephen I began with Chief Koppány, the lord of the southwestern part of the country, putting his

18

Gyula's capture—Illustration from the Illuminated Chronicle. *The war or rather the military expedition against and the subjugation of Gyula and Ajtony who had their landed estates in Transylvania and along the banks of the Maros river did not serve St. Stephen's desire for general centralization only. Direct control and use of the Transylvanian salt mines and the roads to transport the salt were indispensable to the early kings of Hungary. Later, the fact that Stephen had to take up arms against his relatives, Gyula and Ajtony, gave cause also for mistaken conclusions about Transylvania's independence in times past. It was limited and varied in degree, and other border regions of the country sometimes experienced something comparable.*

rule in jeopardy while Stephen was still prince. By right of levirate, Koppány demanded that Stephen's mother, Géza's widow, Sarolt, become his wife. And, of course, he laid claim to the throne. Since we know that Koppány was not Géza's brother, he could have been his cousin. Perhaps he was the son of Taksony's other son, whose name is not known. But he could also have been the descendant of another Árpád branch. (Here history is obscure because the chronicles were written mostly by the lettered slaves of the victors, who, crudely correcting the facts at times, were capable of falsifying genealogy, of amending points of legality, and of altering disasters and victories to their opposites; they redrew maps, made documents disappear; they distorted the tales in accordance with changing interests.)

Later, with the Géza branch dying out without progeny, the male line of the Árpáds continued through the descendants of Taksony's other son. However, Stephen defeated Koppány and his clan with his own military retinues and the German knights taken into service at his court before his coronation. The chronicles described this conflict mainly as the struggle between the still pagan and the already Christianized parts of Hungary. Although this motive played a role—and will frequently return in the wars for the Hungarian throne—the real opposition was more related to power than to faith. (In all probability Koppány himself did not follow the pagan rites any more.) Two lines of succession had collided: who should succeed to the throne, the oldest male within the ruling house or the son of the deceased ruler?

In 1002, Stephen had to wage war against Gyula of Transylvania. One can hardly speak of a pagan rebellion here: Gyula, we remember, had been a Christian for a long time. Later—the year is not known—Stephen defeated the chief of the southern region of the country, Ajtony, who was also an Eastern Christian. However, when Vászoly attacked him—who was probably Koppány's brother, but at the time of his clan's rebellion still so young that he evaded the bloody reprisal—it again seemed that pagan–Christian hostility was flaring up. Moreover, it also appeared—especially if Vászoly's campaign can indisputably be put immediately before Stephen's death—that he was preparing for nothing more than the sacral murder of the king in compliance with pagan customs, when he made his attempt on Stephen's life precisely in the fortieth year of his reign. (According to another, more romantic hypothesis, every nineteenth year, power crises, rebellions, and emerging pretenders to the throne disturbed the reign of the House of Árpád with such consistency that this seemed to prove the survival among the pagans of the lunar year used by many ancient peoples and equivalent to nineteen solar years [Metonic cycle]; in this case, Vászoly rose against his royal nephew after the passage of two lunar years.)

St. Stephen commends Hungary to the patronage of the Virgin Mary—A painting by a disciple of A. Maulbertsch, the second half of the eighteenth century. *The cult of the Virgin Mary, which developed quickly in the Roman Catholic Church and is emphasized to this very day, can be discerned in Hungary as early as Stephen's time. The wide response that this cult received from a people not exactly overly devout may, perhaps, be partly due to the fact that the Christianization of the Hungarians came about shortly after the disintegration of a matriarchal society and its transformation into a patriarchal one.*

The church at Karcsa. *The little round church in the village of Karcsa, in the Bodrogköz region, is undoubtedly from the time of the Árpáds, in all probability from the time of Stephen. It is a relic resulting from Stephen's decree that every ten villages were obliged to build a house of God. But if not one village but ten settlements, though each was small, founded a church, the people of ten congregations driven under the Cross could not fit into the early round churches, which barely covered a few square meters of ground. Did these ancient churches at first provide shelter only for the priest and his assistants or some dignitaries, while those flocking to the Mass stood under the open sky? (Or perhaps, were the latter not even present? Was the divine service conducted "in their name"? in their absence?) Later, by opening a side of the early round church at Karcsa, a Romanesque nave was built, which, however, remained unfinished because of the Mongol invasion or some other reason. Thus the church at Karcsa, which today belongs to the Reformed or Calvinist Church, is a beautiful relic of ancient church architecture and, at the same time, a symbol of the first stormy centuries of Christianity in Hungary.*

Pannonhalma. *Curiously, the present-day name of this community originated with poet Ferenc Kazinczy (1759–1831), who was a leading light of what is known as the Reform Age in Hungary. Yet, the Frankish ruler Charlemagne had built a church in this place to commemorate his extraordinary victory over the Avars. Prince Géza laid the foundation of the Benedictine Abbey still standing today, and the consecration of the church and the monastery occurred at the very beginning of Stephen I's reign, in 1001. The monastery's history almost epitomizes Hungary's entire history, whether it is in the form of the important peace conference that took place here in 1091 following the war once again being waged between the Holy Roman Empire and the papacy, or that of the several hundred people who fled to the monastery in 1945 during the last weeks of World War II, many of them the victims of Nazi persecution (it was the only place in Hungary that both sides in the war agreed to declare "open"). Despite all this, let us this time emphasize, instead, what can be substantiated by the examples of Tihany Abbey, the Romanesque church at Zsámbék, and many other buildings of the church: the builders of these early representative church institutions were endowed with the genius to create a harmony between edifice and landscape with the structures positioned on some height as if they were lifting into the sky to God the abodes of the communities devoted to serving Him.*

Stephen had Vászoly's eyes gouged out and hot lead poured into his ears. His three sons, Andrew, Béla and Levente, escaped to Poland. They were to return home from there some day.

Amid the terrible domestic and foreign wars, which, however, never reached a tragic scale, Stephen had the means and strength to organize and build the state. His most important act in the secular sphere was the elimination of the earlier tribal and clan structure. He appropriated two-thirds of the lands belonging to the clans, made them the estates of the royal crown and their people the servants of castles, and divided the country into some fifty counties. The mobilizable people of the counties, under the leadership of *ispán*s (bailiffs), served territorial defense. The land and people ruled by the chief prince's tribe, supplemented by the new crown lands and their inhabitants, were independent of the counties, and, at the same time, supplied the economic support and manpower for the king's standing army.

An extremely strong central power was necessary for this enormous appropriation. Obviously, the land was then sparsely inhabited, and only a small portion was under cultivation; furthermore the abandonment of dual quarters

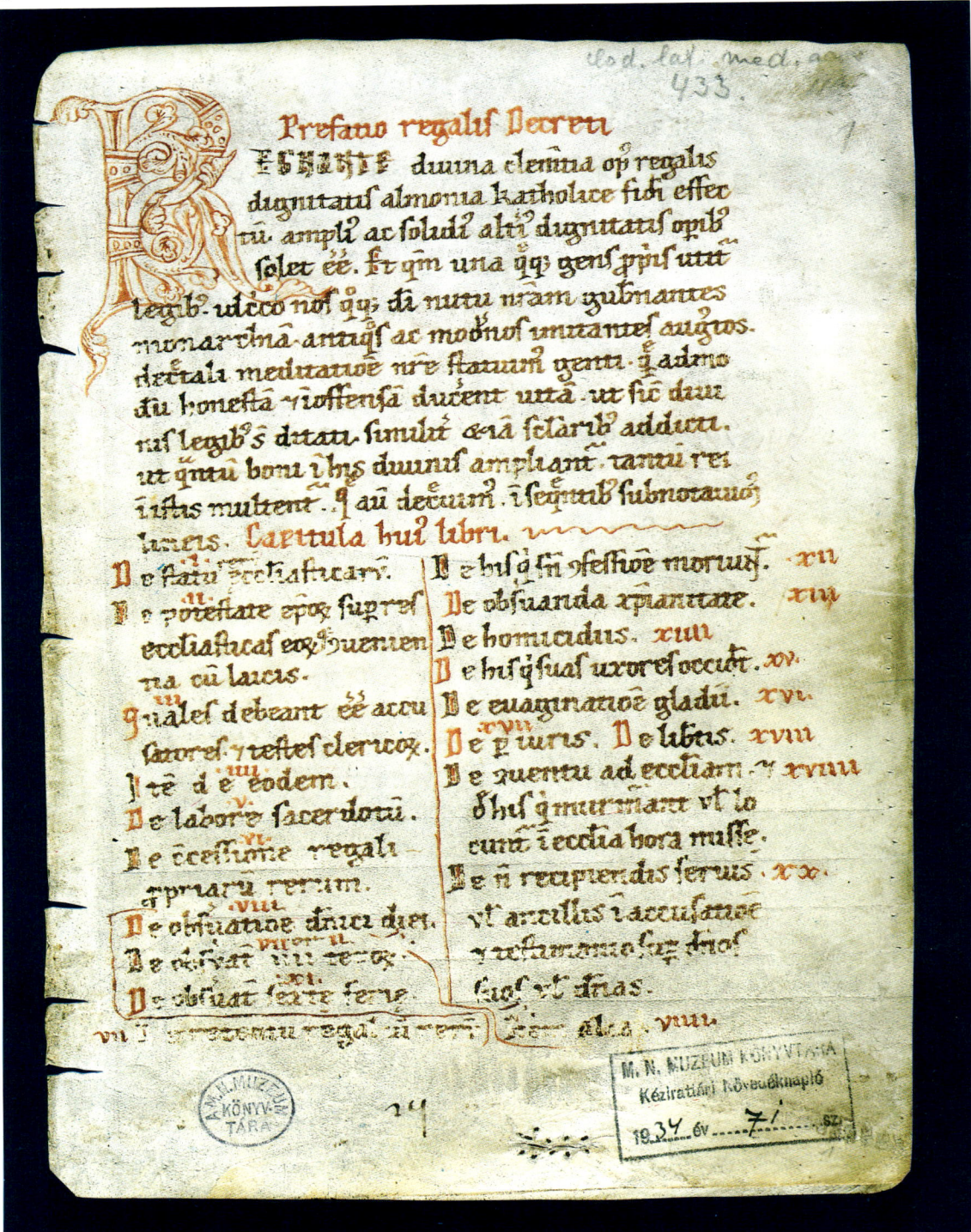

St. Stephen's laws on the first page of the Admont Codex. *We know the provisions of St. Stephen's first code of laws, dating to the beginning of his reign, only from a later copy, the pages of the twelfth-century Admont Codex. In part, these laws followed Western examples almost word for word; in part, however, they were shaped by specific local conditions and demands, and reflected the new requirements for the stabilization of Hungarian society, which found itself in a transitional state, its becoming a part of Europe, the organization of Church and State, and the security of life and property. Moreover, the Latin language in its written form was certainly in use at Géza's court and expanded at Stephen's. This is all the more so because the tradition of written communication was already familiar to the nomadic societies of the Steppes. The élite classes of the conquerors definitely did not know how to write—nor did most rulers of the House of Árpád—since this task was for a long time still the duty of a separate "caste" of scribes and priests. However, in Stephen's time, the written word, communications, the exchange of messages, and the administration of justice were no longer considered to be an absolute novelty.*

(winter along the rivers and summer amid good pastures) and the cessation of what remained of the nomadic way of life opened up large territories. In choosing *ispáns,* the king placed his trust in foreigners dependent only on him and in a few leaders of the ancient clans—this way, the two checked and balanced each other.

Laying the foundation of the church structure paralleled that of the secular reorganization. The new decanal districts and the counties were more or less identical; ten bishoprics came into being, and the one in Esztergom immediately and the one in Kalocsa shortly became archiepiscopal sees. Stephen was generous in granting privileges and estates to the Church. While earlier the Greek Orthodox rite spread predominantly east from the Danube and in some places actually crossed into former Pannonia, Géza and then Stephen steadfastly assisted the conversion and organizational activities of the Roman Church. The fact that

Stephen founded a Greek monastery for nuns in Veszprém Valley for the Greek princess chosen as wife for Emeric was not inconsistent with this policy.

We know about Stephen's correspondence with the famous French Benedictine center, with Abbot Odilo at Cluny: he asked for relics of saints for Hungarian churches. But one of the chief centers of domestic religious life, the Abbey of Pannonhalma, molded its life and rules after the example of the also Benedictine Monte Cassino, in Italy.

In the course of his major measures in religious matters, Stephen transformed the custom relating to the markets. He decreed that markets be held every seventh day sanctified in compliance with the commands of the Church. Thus the name of this day was first *vásárnap* (market day) and then *vasárnap* (Sunday) in Hungarian. Every group of ten villages had to build a church, and two households, or families, were obligated to perform socage

St. Stephen's herm—The work of Giovanni Lorenzo Bernini (1598–1680). *Through time, each age had its own portrait of Stephen. Though his likeness on the coronation robe can be considered authentic, later delineations, whether originating in Hungary or abroad, can hardly have a real basis. However, it is the depictions of his spirit and temperament that truly matter. Shortly after his death and mainly at the time of his canonization—when Ladislas was king—his benevolence, piety, and sanctity were emphasized. When he became the symbol of royal legitimacy, the traits of an iron-handed ruler and strong-willed state organizer and leader were discerned in him. The fact that Hungary became "Regnum Marianum" (the land of Mary) is linked with his name on the basis of his vow. But this is uncertain to a degree since according to Pope Gregory VII, Stephen commended his country to Peter, the founder of the Church—i.e. to the papacy—when he requested a crown from Rome. He is hardly the author of his* Exhortations, *though its text probably reflects his guidance. And what is said in this work about "The Reception and Support of Guests" served in later years as the basis of "St. Stephen's conception of the state's role" which cannot be considered authentic in its entirety, and is, in part, an anachronistic interpretation. In spite of all this, it is beyond question that though the views about St. Stephen have altered during the nearly one thousand years since his reign, his reputation has not dimmed.*

service in its support, with a stallion and a mare, six oxen, two cows, and thirty small animals.

It is worth visiting a church from the time of Stephen or one not much later but still constructed at his command. The nave of the Romanesque church at Karcsa erected of ashlar and built in the thirteenth century, is surprisingly small. A closer look reveals that today's chancel, built of bricks and having a three-quarter arch, was a much earlier, eleventh-century village church that was attached to the new nave as a chancel during its expansion in the thirteenth century. It is impossible, we should think, that this tiny round church met the needs of ten villages for two hundred years. Could the pagan tradition have remained this strong, attendance at Mass so small? They were, perhaps, content to have the roof only above the priest and the altar and people stand about in the open during the contemporary Mass.

The tragedy of Stephen—and of the entire House of Árpád and of the nation as well—was that among the children of the king who ruled for forty-one years only a single son reached adulthood, who himself died as a young successor to the throne. According to written sources of the Church, Emeric led such a saintly life that he vowed chastity with his Greek (Byzantine) wife, and they never consummated their marriage. Was this so? Who knows? In the light of what we know about the temperament of the members of the House of Árpád or the political prudence with which they wove their dynastic marriage bonds, we are inclined to doubt it. Would the only adult son of Stephen have behaved this way whom Géza so carefully prepared to rule and who himself so carefully groomed Emeric for his future independent life and his reign with fatherly and kingly advice? (We can consider Stephen's Book of Exhortations *[Intelmek könyve]* to his

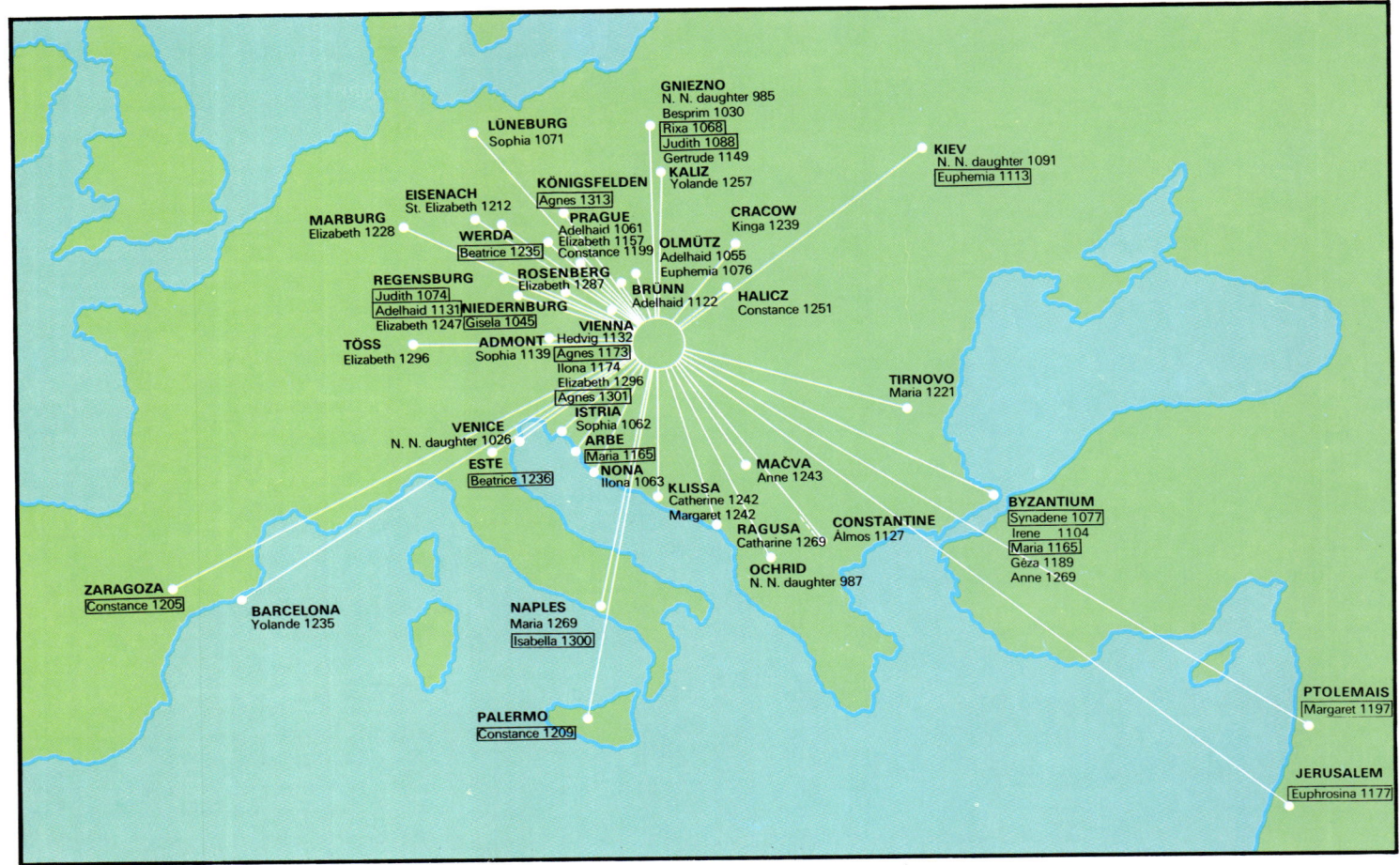

The House of Árpád and Europe—I.

*Queens, princesses and princes who returned to their original
homelands or left Hungary or were buried abroad during the reign of the
Árpád dynasty. The names of queens crowned are given in frames.*
(After Alán Kralovánszky)

son as the first known Hungarian literary work.) A son
whom his father had already entrusted with the leadership
of the army while he was quite young in order to strengthen
his stature as successor to the throne? Collateral
succession to the throne always, and in this age
particularly, concealed great perils, and not solely
for the "defeated" family.

It is, however, a fact that Emeric remained childless, and
became, in 1031, the victim of a hunting accident (perhaps
a murderous attack?). We even know the date of his death:
September 2. But we do not know his age at the time.

After Emeric's death, Stephen designated his sister's
son, Peter Orseolo, as his successor; he summoned him
to his court and prepared him to rule. His other sister's
husband, the Kabar Samuel Aba, wore the honorific
of palatine (in case of need, the palatine replaced the king).

In 1038, Peter ascended the throne. However, internal
opposition ejected Peter, who had to depend heavily on
foreign lords, and in 1041, the opposition made Samuel
Aba king. By 1044 he also had to fight internal rebellion,
over which he could triumph only by murdering fifty lords
mercilessly. Emboldened by this, Peter returned with
the help of the troops of Henry III, the Holy Roman
Emperor. Samuel Aba fell during one of the battles for
the throne—or a treacherous assassin killed him.
The crown again belonged to Peter for two years, but he
was forced to flee in the fall of 1046. Then his successor,
Andrew I, one of Vazul's sons, had him apprehended and
blinded. Hereafter, the descendants of Vazul of the House
of Árpád sat on the royal throne of Hungary for a quarter
of a millennium. However, fortune reversed itself. In the age
of marauding raids, those who wanted to increase their
power in the neighboring regions called on Hungarian
auxiliary forces for assistance; then a balance of power
largely prevailed for a period of time in East European
territories surrounding the Carpathian Basin; in the middle
of the eleventh century efforts to make vassals
of the Christianized and settled Hungarians occurred ever
more frequently.

CURSED AND BLESSED KINGS

If Shakespeare had, perchance, been born on Hungarian soil—if we may play with this completely absurd notion—he could have written every one of his historical plays and tragedies about the age of Árpád and his descendants who sat on the throne. What a portrait gallery they would have also formed! Brooding Prince Hamlets, meek Ophelias retiring into nunneries, high officials of gray eminence, loyal captains and unfaithful sweethearts, Richards offering kingdoms for a horse, knights errant from foreign courts, Rosenkrantzes and Guildensterns, Iagos, noblemen of the white and red roses, kings dogged by fate and triumphing over it—spectacular and cathartic chivalry and villainy and thus the very stuff of drama and acting.

But would that magnificent Anglo-Saxon have had the audacity to place on stage such an unreal occurrence as befell King Béla I in 1063 in Hungary? On whom, after three years of rule, the throne toppled, killing him in his summer palace at Dömös? The spectacle of the throne tottering and falling on the king is, of course, inevitably comical, even though bones break and blood flows. Only the consequences make the occurrence tragic. But again, how dramatic—indeed theatrical, if not "corny"—are the scenes that preceded Béla's reign.

Thus Vászoly, made blind and deaf, had three sons who fled to Polish soil and returned from there later. Of them, Andrew wound up on the throne. However, he entrusted one third of the country to his younger brother, Prince Béla, who operated so independently in his territory that he minted his own money, which was the right of a legitimate sovereign. Andrew, though he did not hand his rule over, crowned his son Salomon king in 1057, and betrothed him to a princess of the Holy Roman Empire in 1058. Yet, as if the question were still open, Andrew I placed the crown and the sword before Prince Béla at Várkony along the River Tisza: choose between the throne and the sword. The machination was obvious. But the astounded Béla reached for the sword only at an emphatic sign from one of his councillors. His fate would have been sealed if he had chosen otherwise... Even so, after having placed his stake on the right card at the ordeal called the "Várkony scene" in Hungarian historiography, the prince again fled to Polish soil. Returning with an army, he defeated his enthroned elder brother, who died soon after. Béla I began his reign, which was constantly disturbed by Salomon and his supporters and which ended under the wreckage of the Dömös throne after three years. However, after the childless Salomon, the unfortunate Béla's two sons sat on the throne, and of them, the magnificent Ladislas I became the second but not the last saint in the House of Árpád.

Seeing all the fratricidal wars, insurrections, and disputes that dominated his homeland after Stephen I, the dejected patriot is overcome by a yearning to reach for a surmise even more futile than the literary one: what would have happened if Emeric, like his father, had been granted four decades on the throne, if the enormous central power created by Stephen had not dissipated during the ten-year struggle for the throne waged by Peter and Samuel Aba?

In the meantime, however, the marauding raids had ended for the Hungarians a century ago, although in the vicinity of the Carpathian Basin, there still remained a group of those restless Pechenegs who had driven the Hungarians from Levedia and then from the Etelköz region. Continual internal instability increased the danger of Pecheneg invasions, and so the Hungarians, though, in relation to the incursions, they had changed "from thieves into gendarmes", were forced to defend themselves at the cost of heavy casualties. On the other hand, when Géza I finally reconciled the parties by accepting the Pecheneg group into the country, he did so to boost his military power against the ousted but still unsubdued former King Salomon.

The eighteen-year reign of (Saint) Ladislas I began in 1077 under a lucky star. Salomon fled to a group of Pechenegs—or a newer nomadic people on horses who had already taken their place, the Cumans—and he later perished during one of their incursionary military campaigns. There was no other claimant to the throne "on duty" on the scene. The pope and the emperor of the Holy Roman Empire were tied down by the war of investiture being waged over the right to name church leaders. To Ladislas, the Germans were a more immediate danger than Rome; for this reason, he sided with the pope, though he did not submit to the feudal authority of the papacy in place of the Germans. Actually, he supported Rome in a way that seemed to reject the cause of the conflict between Pope Gregory VII and Emperor Henry IV: the precedence of the Church's power over the secular in earthly matters. (Incidentally, Henry IV was the brother-in-law of Salomon, the former king of Hungary; he was the one who was forced to do penance: during one of the darkest times in his struggles with the pope, he made amends by crawling on his knees before Gregory VII at Canossa.)

The laws of Ladislas I, compared with the first recorded laws of Hungary, those of Stephen I, attest simultaneously to continuity and change in Hungarian society. That legal system slowly solidified which was so unfamiliar to the conquerors, who held entirely different views of private ownership or the value of life and who probably were more steadfast in their morality in the ninth and tenth centuries than their eleventh-century descendants, though they based it on the completely different norms and customs they had brought with them from the Sian steppes. Meanwhile, it is difficult to evaluate every factor correctly. For example, the relationship between slaves and freemen—also changing in time—implies the presence of some form of slavery in Hungarian society in the Middle Ages. With much cause. Namely, this word can conceal several meanings. No doubt, slavery was totally different in ancient African societies from that of modern America;

The west gate of St. Adalbert cathedral in Esztergom, the "porta speciosa," 1196—An oil painting, the middle of the eighteenth century. *This is not the only instance in which we can today show only an old illustration of one of the best relics from our past. Roman ruins—aqueducts traceable for long among them—vanished, of which precise engravings could be prepared as recently as the last century. Not to mention engravings showing scores of medieval castles that were blown up at the time of Rákóczi's War of Independence (1704–1711) at the Habsburg emperor's orders. In 1010, Stephen I began to build on the site of today's Esztergom Cathedral the basilica dedicated to St. Adalbert, which was extensively damaged by frequent sieges and the Turkish rule but whose western gate this unidentified artist was able to depict in the mid-1700s, though possibly with a measure of his own additions on the canvas. Today, its few remaining fragments are on display with other stone finds in the Castle Museum.*

it was different in ancient Rome from that of the nomadic and half-nomadic peoples of the Steppes; and it was different when its remnants still persisted in a Europe becoming feudal. Similarly, when the elements of the feudal system appeared and gained strength in Hungary—among other things, through the laws

of Ladislas and his successors—the kind of feudalism that came into being was not the same as the kind found in Western Europe nor like the kind that was institutionalized farther to the east. At times, even specialists are not capable of adequately discerning or rendering discernible the regional hues or their fine or rough differences; and more than one dispute of historians stems from the fact that they cannot even agree among themselves on the meanings of words.

In 1083, Ladislas began a "campaign" of canonization. First, he had two hermits of Polish descent, Andrew and Benedict, elevated to sainthood, then Emeric's tutor, Bishop Gerard (Gellért), who died a martyr's death during one of the pagan uprisings, next Stephen I, and finally Emeric. By this means he also certified his nation's and his family's integral presence in Christian Europe, meanwhile issuing a warning to the remaining followers of pagan rite. And though his character, like Stephen's, hardly met every requirement of sainthood in the mirror of undistorted sources, legends were quickly woven around him as well. Ladislas, the creator of saints, was not the only one who

The figure of St. Ladislas in the church at Székelyderzs—*A fresco, 1419, the legend of King Ladislas, who was buried at Nagyvárad and as especially popular in Transylvania, is perpetuated in many of our medieval churches, in the form of frescoes serving as a kind of picture book, which tell of his freeing a Hungarian maiden from the captivity of a marauding Cuman. Interpretations of the episode branch out in many directions, partly a long way from the traditional legendry of saints, all the way back to pagan times. The fight between the king and the Cuman can be taken also as the mythological struggle between the powers of light and darkness. However, certain scenes of the St. Ladislas frescoes are extraordinarily profane and not exactly appropriate to a saint. For example, one picture shows the liberated maiden "looking at the head" of Ladislas or delousing him, an act that a woman performed only for her lover.*

The crypt of Tihany Abbey with the tomb of Andrew I. *Andrew I was the first member of the Vazul branch of the House of Árpád to gain supreme power. The year of his birth is not known, but he ruled from 1046 to 1060. In 1055, he founded the Benedictine monastery at Tihany; after his death at Zirc, he was buried there in an already completed church. This was a very fast pace of construction for the times. Now only his tombstone remains; later, the former monastery served military purposes for a long time. The abbey, built on a splendidly defendable point at the tip of Tihany Peninsula, blends spectacularly into the setting. Its deed of foundation, which has uncommonly survived, is one of our priceless language monuments. Several Hungarian place names and passages appear in the Latin text.*

later gained for himself the glory he obtained for others. His daughter, who became empress of Byzantium—Piroska was her Hungarian and Irene her Greek name—was to become a saint of the Eastern Church.

Were there any remnants of paganism among the Hungarians? Yes, now and for some time to come. We have little direct and all the more indirect evidence that a clandestine paganism lasted for centuries after Stephen. In vain did the Church decree—to the great regret of today's archaeologists—burial without "furniture"; coins and amulets crop up in graves. Sacrificial ceremonies went on in secret groves under pikes bearing the skulls of horses; the sorcerer (táltos in Hungarian), the shaman, lived on as magician, as medicine man, not for centuries but for a thousand years, almost to our own day. Fragments of unmistakably pagan texts were handed down in children's ditties, in the incantations of old women casting spells in secret healing, and even in Christian prayers. Zsuzsanna Erdélyi, an ethnographic researcher, not long ago collected hundreds of apocryphal prayers containing structurally intertwined Christian and pagan elements. This tenacity of the pagan tradition is quite understandable. After all, accommodating the several waves of Pechenegs and then portions of the Cuman and Iazygian (Alan) peoples, this pagan population underwent baptism, but it did not become truly Christian overnight; instead, the remaining paganism of the Hungarians was reinforced.

Ladislas I, who frequently engaged in combat in person—he himself killed a Cuman chief on the battlefield—successfully defended himself diplomatically and militarily against German expansion from the west and Cuman incursions from the east, while in the south he acquired Dalmatia, whose small city-states considered vassalage to the "distant" Hungarians more favorable than to the "nearby" Venetians. The thought of heading for the Holy Land also occurred to him, but fortunately, news about the eruption of a struggle for the Bohemian throne kept him at home. Thus the enormous capital he had amassed was not squandered away in some dubious adventure in the Near East, which vitiated the potency of so many ambitious European rulers. (The record of the Crusades, launched to liberate the Holy Land, hardly changes if we believe their motive was faith, religious zeal—or the desire to control the commerce of the Mediterranean Sea.)

Ladislas I's successor was his nephew, Koloman—who acquired "Bookish" as his sobriquet (Coloman Beauclerc)—whose first wife was Buzilla, a Sicilian Norman princess, and his second Euphemia, the daughter of Vladimir Monomakh, the Suzdal prince; he managed the wealth he inherited with varying success. After the athletic and chivalrous (Saint) Ladislas I, who was also called elegantissimus rex, this physically stunted man, who according to one source, was "dishevelled, hirsute, half-blind, hunchbacked and lame, and stammered"—if only half of this is true, it is too much—at the same time, buried himself in codices like a bookworm, and he was, not entirely incidentally, a consecrated bishop who could not be crowned until he received dispensation from the Church—this man had to march constantly at the head of his armies.

In the very first year of Koloman's reign, in 1096, the challenges of the Crusaders' armies heading east on their European routes reached Hungary one after the other. His relations were good with the forces led by the French knight Walter the Penniless (Sansavoir), or Godfrey of Bouillon, the prince of Lorraine—it is true that, enlightened by his bad experiences, Koloman and his troops accompanied the latter until he left Hungarian territory; however, he could not prevent the army of Peter the Hermit of Amiens from assaulting and occupying the castle at Zimony (Zemun); he had to defeat the armies of the French Folkmar and the German priest Gottschalk, and he did not permit the armies of William the Carpenter or Guillaume Charpentier, viscount of Melun, and Count Emich of Leiningen to cross the Hungarian border.

In addition, Koloman had a substantial number of domestic difficulties. His younger brother, Prince Álmos, rose against him. At the first opportunity, their armies met where the "Várkony scene" had taken place. At this time not a single one of the chief lords was willing to enter the war on either side; so the two brothers made peace with each other. Later, however, Álmos invaded Hungary time and again with foreign supporters.

When Koloman felt his death approaching and the enthronement of his teen-aged son was at stake, he hunted down and blinded Álmos, and Álmos's son, Béla. To complicate the story further in the manner of Shakespeare, Álmos escaped to Byzantium under the reign of Stephen II (1116–1131), while his son hid in the monastery at Pécsvárad. However, when the chief lords, noting the illness of the childless Stephen II, had already chosen three kings from among themselves, the king swept down bloodily on the insurgents. Meanwhile, he found out where the blind Prince Béla was hiding—Álmos had died in the meantime—and had him brought out of hiding, gave him his daughter in marriage, and named him heir to the throne. He was to become King Béla (Blind) II, his fate showing that gouging out someone's eyes would no longer make him unfit to wear the crown.

The ten-year reign of Béla (Blind) II (1131–1141) was threatened from Poland by the pretender to the throne, Boris, so extensively that at a national meeting held in Arad in 1132, sixty-eight barons suspected of siding with Boris were slaughtered as a preventive measure at the instigation of the queen. Who was this Boris? Well, the life of King Koloman was already on the wane when his second wife, Euphemia, became pregnant; at the time, her husband also caught her in adultery. We cannot be sure whether this occurred in flagranti or whether the king simply knew that the child could not really be of his loins. Be that as it may, he sent the fallen woman home to her father in Suzdal, where she gave birth to a son, who bore the name Boris.

But are we writing the kings'—sometimes scandalous—chronicles or the life history of a people? We should like to do the latter, though it can hardly be superfluous to provide a sense of the circumstances under which one of Europe's youngest nations came into being and survived under Árpád's descendants. Meanwhile, a sweeping economic and social tranformation took place

St. Ladislas's herm—A reliquary from the early 1400s. *What is so interesting about this reliquary, originally from Nagyvárad and now preserved in Győr, is that when the sculptor Károly Árpás recently prepared a reconstruction of the faces of Béla III and his wife, Anne of Antioch, on the basis of skulls which had survived in an exceptionally well-preserved condition, the king's facial features showed an astonishing similarity to those which this herm had immortalized, though according to our present supposition, it was probably made at least a hundred years after the reign of Béla III.*

in Hungary resulting in part from the conscious intervention of the rulers and their councillors and in part from the automatism of accommodation in Europe. Amid the new circumstances of ownership and rank and the new differentiation of social strata following the disintegration of the system based on joint families and clans, the new leading classes, the *ispán*s and other officials, were soon dissatisfied with the privileges attending their commissions; instead, because the separate and private possession of one's land was so important to royal supremacy, they themselves also aimed at acquiring landed estates that would be under their free and perpetual control. At the same time, the Hungarian serfs were still a privileged group compared to servants, they inherited much from

stronger—commerce in salt and horses, mining, the ownership of customs stations, and income from fish ponds. Two cities, Esztergom and Székesfehérvár, developed, though the royal court still traveled from place to place for a long time, to consume produce gathered in at some subcenters in various parts of the country. The export of horses was the sole state monopoly as regards agricultural products—the horse was an important implement of war at this time, too—but the subject of cattle export already turned up in the laws.

By this time, the development of one basis for the envied wealth of medieval Hungary had begun in Transylvania and Upper Hungary: the extensive and highly profitable mining of copper, gold, and silver (and

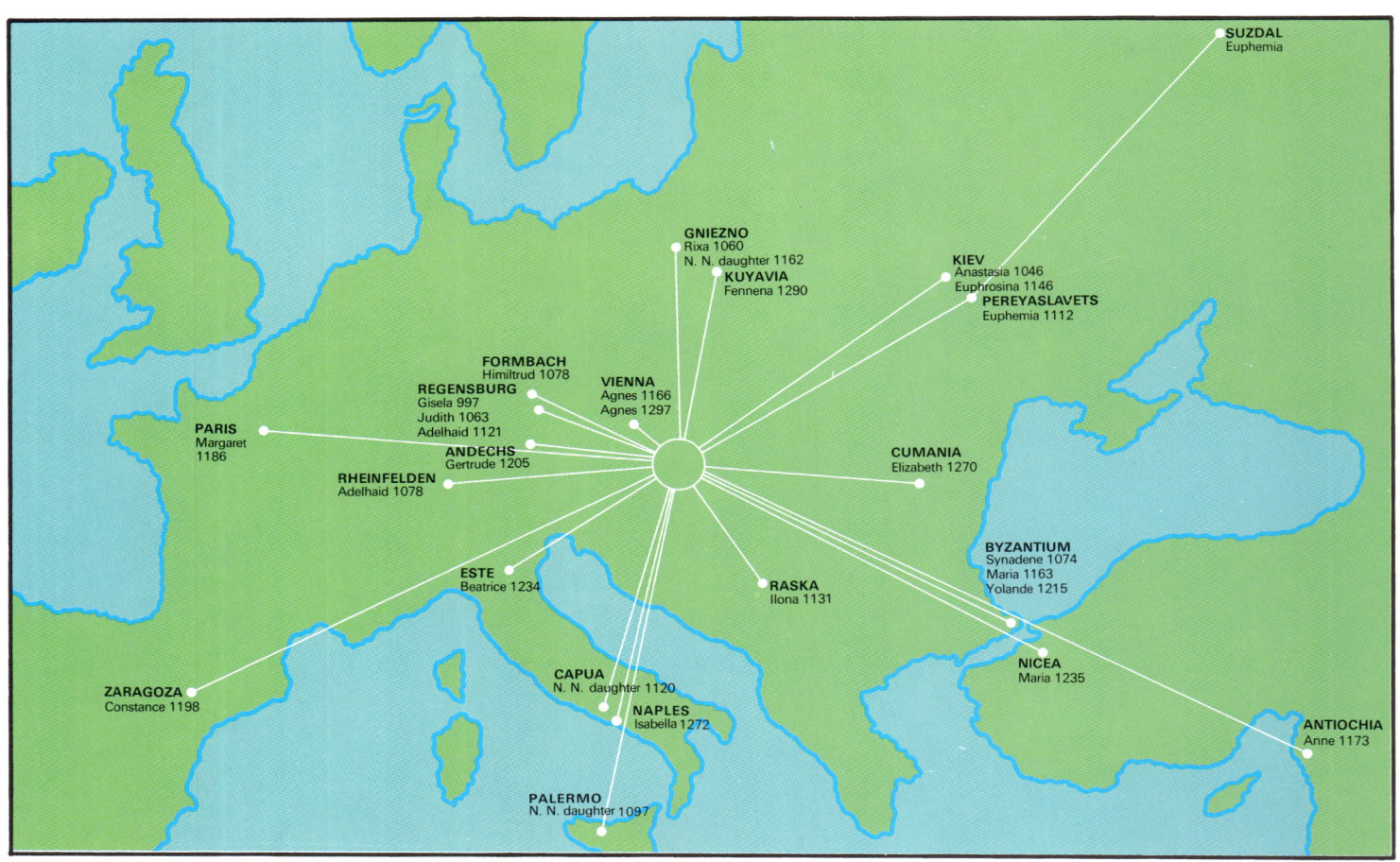

The House of Árpád and Europe—II.
The places of origin of Hungarian queens in the period of the Árpád dynasty (After Alán Kralovánszky)

the position they enjoyed as auxiliary troops in the age of the Conquest. During domestic conflicts, they supported an independent kingship, opposing foreign feudal dependency and the foreign knights and the claimants to the throne relying on them.

For a long time, the larger animals—horses and cattle—served as the most valuable resource and even as the standard of value among the Hungarians. The minting of coins instituted at the beginning of (Saint) Stephen I's reign—which was so successful that later the money of the first Hungarian kings was "counterfeited" in many places in Europe—transformed the economy and gave new meaning to precious metals, widening and magnifying their earlier role in hoarding. Though more than one king later increased his income with the endless deterioration of money values, the role of various monopolies became

the panning of gold in rivers) which was time and again newly regulated as to ownership and economic rights. Copper did not come to the fore accidentally. At times, our nearly monopolistic position in the production and export of this indispensable metal brought about enormous economic advantages, not only for the nation, the king, and the immediate producers, but even for the miners in their privileged situation.

It was not only the domestic growth that increased the size of the population but also the settlers of high and low rank apparently streaming into Hungary from every direction, who found relative safety and even-handed treatment in this tormented country. For example, we know about a quite large Ishmaelite population with their Mohammedan faith who could practice their religion in comparative freedom and were obligated to serve the king only in case of war and even then only against a non-Mohammedan enemy. Venice and Hungary, though often at war over Dalmatia, concluded an agreement permitting the free movement of each other's merchants.

The fact that in Hungary only the king dared collect taxes aroused admiration throughout the world.

In the six decades following the reign of Béla the Blind, certain motifs returned tediously as if on a merry-go-round: disputes around the throne, military campaigns with mixed success, the peaceable and combative marching of the Crusaders across the land, and all the rest. But on balance, everything was largely positive, particularly under Béla III (1172–1196), whose first wife was Anne de Châtillon and the second Margaret Capet. These two women introduced the French style at the court, where Frederick Barbarossa was received in a manner worthy of his rank. With the king as their example, the barons increasingly followed the fashion trends of Europe, which to no small extent contributed to Hungary's participation in world commerce. However, Béla III's son, Andrew II (1205–1235), was, in contrast to his puritanical and staid father, a rollicking, lavish, ambitious, and happy-go-lucky young man. He engaged in an ill-fated war on Russian soil and—the first Hungarian king to do so—he undertook his "own"

The grand coin from the time of Béla III. *This masterful impression, which is a striking example of medieval abstraction, places before us a ruler of the House of Árpád who was, in truth, unimportant, but who was made successful by circumstances and the economic strength of his nation. His companion on the coin is Anne Châtillon (of Antioch) whom, though of French descent, he brought with him from Byzantium. They shared a tomb in Székesfehérvár, and today they repose together in the Matthias Church, in Buda.*

The tomb of Béla III and his wife in the Matthias Church in Buda. *With the exception of the Habsburgs entombed in the Capuchin crypt in Vienna, there is hardly a Hungarian king whose tomb and corpse survive in an identifiable form. Though Stephen I was buried at Székesfehérvár, and the basilica there, which was later badly damaged during the wars with the Turks and subsequently razed to its foundations, became the most permanent burial place for royalty and also served as the coronation church, Ladislas I wanted to be put to his final rest at Nagyvárad, for instance, and Andrew I in Tihany. The royal tombs at Székesfehérvár, ransacked and most of them destroyed beyond identification, became the object of archaeological excavation in 1848 for the first time. It was then that the extraordinarily well preserved earthly remains of Béla III and Anne of Antioch were taken to Buda. The repeated explorations of their common tomb at Buda made possible those anthropological investigations and the preparation of those skull reproductions that revealed the striking resemblance between Béla III and the person portrayed by the Ladislas herm in Győr.*

Crusade. He did so purely on borrowed money, and he gave the long-Hungarian Zára (Zadar) to Venice instead of paying charges for ship rentals. He actually reached the Holy Land through Cyprus, but he ran out of resources before he could fight a real battle with the infidels. Returning in disgrace, he complained as follows in a letter to Pope Honorius III in 1218:

"When we were spending our time in regions across the sea in the service of the pilgrimage we had undertaken, we learned from frequent messengers beyond any shadow of doubt that the seed of dissension had spread

The abbey church of Ják. *Though with signs of much decay and reconstruction, the Ják and Ócsa churches serve intact as Catholic and Calvinist houses of worship respectively even today. The one at Zsámbék, damaged by an earthquake, is like a torso among the Romanesque provostal churches built at the beginning and in the middle of the thirteenth century. The church at Ják belonged to the Benedictine Order, the other two to the Premonstratensians; Ják and Zsámbék were definitely founded by some leading family, thanks to the benevolent wishes and economic power of local landowners. The Ják church is undoubtedly the most splendid edifice of the three, though it is apparent that the Mongol invasion interrupted its construction, which was then continued at a more modest level. Some of the heads of the full-length statues of the apostles are not the original ones. In all probability, the "decapitation" of these statues occurred in 1532, because of the rage felt by Turks besieging nearby Kőszeg toward representations of the human form.*

inexpressibly in our country. Consequently, shaken by this great danger and so much evil news and unable to bear the destruction of the tender shoot of Christianity in our country, we left the Holy Land out of necessity and not gladly. When we arrived in Hungary after passing through many dangers on the road, we had to experience even viler viciousness than we had heard of, which the members of the Church committed, as did the laity, so many and of such kinds that we do not considered it necessary to bring them to the attention of Your Holiness; after all, the enormity of the vicious deeds perpetrated could hardly have remained concealed from Your keen-sighted eyes.

Your Holiness should also be informed that when we arrived in Hungary, we found not Hungary but a country so tormented and bereft of its income from the treasury that we could neither pay the debts in which our pilgrimage had involved us nor restore our country to its previous condition even in fifteen years."

And so things came to pass. Andrew II reigned for seventeen more years. Meanwhile, his renowned Golden Bull came into existence in 1222, which sought to restore the shattered legal system by banning many acts of tyranny and not the least curtailing royal power, and authorized the nobles to oppose the king by force of arms if he or his successors should breach the Bull. And this was done by a ruler whose first wife, Gertrude of Merano, was killed by a conspiracy of chief nobles, who were shocked by the life of luxury she carried on with her foreign companions at the court. (The best known Hungarian historical drama, *Bánk bán*, by József Katona, relates this episode.) About 1221, Villard de Honnecourt, the French architect from Picardy, prepared Gertrude's tomb at Pilisszentkereszt.

Now it seemed as if the saying that 'as the tree is such is the fruit' was not confirmed. Among the children of the pleasure-seeking Gertrude and the happy-go-lucky Andrew II, Elizabeth, whom Louis IV, the Marquis of Thuringia, married, was later added to the line of saints in the House of Árpád. And Béla IV (1235–1270), succeeding his father, seemed forced to bear duties similar to those (Saint) Stephen had to grapple with.

St. Elizabeth of Hungary—Part of a panel series
in the Hospital of the Holy Spirit at Lübeck, c. 1420–1430.
*St. Elisabeth is the daughter of Andrew II and Gertrude, who
are major characters in the most widely known Hungarian
historical drama, Bánk Bán, by József Katona (1791–1830).
In this play, the mother is far from being favorably presented.
Elizabeth was born in 1207, in Pozsony or at Sárospatak.
(A marble basin claimed to be her bathtub was on display
at the Sárospatak Castle for a long time; actually, it was
a kitchen sink.) She was four or five years old when she was
betrothed to Marquis Louis of Thuringia and immediately
sent to his court, where she gained distinction for her
gentleness, kindness of heart, and complete lack of feeling
for protocol. Within a few years after her marriage in 1221 at
fourteen, she bore three children. In 1227, her husband,
whom she always loved passionately, went off on a Holy
Crusade but died while he was still in Italy. Ferocious
relatives expelled the widow from Wartburg Castle.
According to another version, she left the castle with her
children on her own accord. Though she was nearly
destitute, it was again precisely her philantrophy that made
her popular. The swiftness with which she was canonized
in 1235 so soon after her death in 1231 is almost without
parallel. In Hungary, her cult spread quickly, all the more
because, after all, her brother, Béla IV was king.*

Julianus, the Dominican monk, has already been mentioned. He deserves credit for two matters. First, he verified the existence of Hungarians who had remained in the distant Magna Hungaria, and second, he brought word about the approach of the "Tatars", who would swiftly sweep them away as well. Or did Julianus actually head directly for the Bashkirian Hungarians—the reason the king dispatched him—because he knew about the approaching danger from the east and, for this reason, wanted to unite the two branches of Hungarians that had parted company centuries ago? This much is certain: the leaders of the Mongol tribes, assembling in Karakorum, decided upon a general attack against Europe and entrusted its leadership to Genghis Khan's grandson, Batu Khan, in the very same year, 1235, when the holy crown of the Hungarian kings was placed on the head of Béla IV. The Mongols knew where they were going. Their threatening letter, addressed to Béla IV, already reached Julianus through Russian hands in 1237; in it they called upon the Hungarian king well in advance, apparently from their starting position, to surrender.

In the meantime, the pope urged Béla IV to eradicate the heresy of the Bogomils in the Balkans. However, he tried to prepare for the Mongol attack. If he sent word to the Bashkirian Hungarians late, he did offer shelter to the remaining people of the distant kindred Cumans who, defeated and pursued by Batu, were traveling the very same road the Hungarians had followed in times past during the age of the Conquest. However, when Batu Khan's army did, in fact, pour through the Verecke Pass into the Carpathian Basin, adequate forces could not be raised to oppose it. In addition, the half-pagan Cumans, who stood at a stage of social development and morality similar to that of Árpád's Hungarians about 895, were, at this time, viewed with alarm in Hungary and looked upon as the advanced column of the "Tatars." Their prince, Kötöny, was murdered in Buda, whereupon the Cumans, instead of helping, departed to the south of the country and even routed the forces of the Bishop of Csanád marching north against Batu Khan.

The country remained the easy prey of the Tatars—let us call them this now; after all, it is the notion of the Tatar invasion that is ineradicable from Hungarian memory. Even if some cities did not fall, and some of the population escaped into the depths of the marshes and forests, the devastation was enormous. After the battle at Muhi, where the Tatars' arrows killed most of the Hungarians retiring to the protection of their baggage wagons before hand-to-hand combat could occur, Béla IV himself fled to Dalmatia with his entire family. The Tatar horsemen even pursued him there, and he finally had to sail from the city of Trau (Trogir) on the Adriatic coast to the Island of Čiovo simply to save his life. Now we were at the receiving end of the lessons we ourselves had handed to a Europe farther west during the age of the marauding raids.

It is customary to say repeatedly that this was the first

Andrew II's Golden Bull, 1221 —The obverse of the seal depicts the king, its reverse the royal coat of arms. *Through his noted Golden Bull, issued in 1222, Andrew II tried to bring about and strengthen the authority of the law by ending the anarchy pervading the land even at the cost of his own royal power. The content of this fairly mandatory royal document, which was brought about by relatively "general pressure," later came to be interpreted as Hungary's first constitution, and efforts were made for centuries to deduce from it legal grounds for the prerogatives of the Hungarian nobility, dated to ancient times, the age of the Árpáds. However, the Golden Bull is itself nothing more than a particularly important royal document, which is why it bears a golden royal seal. Andrew II alone issued at least seven bulls of which only one has survived, the one from 1221. (Recently, a stroller happened upon the golden seal of one of King Matthias Corvinus's bulls in the sand on the banks of the Tisza river at Szeged and turned it over to a museum. Before that, only a single seal of this kind was known.)*

massive pagan attack on Europe against which the Hungarians cast their own bodies. Thus the western "investment" which converted the eastern Hungarians to Christianity began to bear fruit... Undoubtedly, the Carpathian Basin (and the Balkans) was the most western area the Tatars reached during their military campaign of several years. But the fact that their attack broke off here was not attributable to the scattered and weak opposition of the Hungarians. Then to what? At news of the death of Great Khan Ogedei, Batu, interested in the succession, turned his armies around and headed home.

Although word of new threats from the Tatars frequently arrived, a military campaign as extensive as that of 1241–1242 never occurred again. At the same time, the Tatar danger did not vanish for centuries. It was particularly Transylvania and its Hungarian (Székely) inhabitants that were to suffer greatly from the raids of greater or smaller Tatar forces which later invaded the country, often as allies of the Turks.

Béla IV built on the ruins. After the Tatar invasion, he promoted urbanization; he urged the nobles to build castles, which was a gamble on his part: someone who governed a castle would be readily inclined to oppose him. He recalled Kötöny's Cumans, who had not found peace

in the south either, and, in general, he advanced the resettlement of the depopulated provinces; thus the vigorous mingling of ethnic groups continued in the Carpathian Basin.

We know of ten children of Béla IV (by Maria Laskaris, princess of Nicaea). Blessed Kinga married Polish prince Boleslaw, Elizabeth Bavarian Prince Henry I, Anna Russian Prince Rastislav, Constance King Leo of Halicz, Blessed Yolande Polish Prince (Pious) Boleslaw. The elder Margaret—who was, perhaps, betrothed to a prince of Mačva—and Catherine died in Klis (Clissa) castle during the escape to Dalmatia. Taking a vow during the Tatar peril, the parents of the younger Margaret, promised her, in turn, as a bride of Christ and put her in a monastery. Later, however, out of dynastic interest, Béla, having no other maiden daughter, wanted her to marry the Bohemian king, Otakar II. The chosen fiancé was bewitched by the beauty of the young nun. However, Margaret turned down her parents' request; she was not willing to leave the virgins of the monastery on the Island of Hares above Buda and Pest, where she lived in servanthood performing the most menial tasks; she did not exchange her barren cell for the royal throne and the marriage bed. She also increased the number of saints in the House of Árpád, and Margaret Island in Budapest obtained its present name from her.

Of the two sons of Béla IV, Béla took the daughter of the Margrave of Brandenburg as his wife. Stephen, who was strong in military virtues, and rose repeatedly against his father as heir apparent and eventually occupied the throne as Stephen V for two years, took Elizabeth as his wife, a half-pagan Cuman woman, who accustomed her husband to the boisterous lifestyle of nomads on the steppes, perhaps embellishing his daily existence with women slaves and concubines. He was succeeded by his son, the minor Ladislas (the Cuman) IV (1272–1290), in whose name his mother and various factions of the nobility exercised supreme power for a long time. His wife, Isabella, was a princess of Naples, from the House of Anjou, a fact which foreshadowed no slight change in the history of Hungary.

Memorial for the 750th anniversary of the Battle of Muhi.
Made by architect György Vadász and sculptor Sándor Kiss.
Muhi, coming between the Bükk and the Tisza river, directly blocked the very best direction for advance followed by the Mongols, that is the route coming through the Carpathian passes which was used during the migrations for a thousand years. Everything else was wrong. Just as it was rather difficult to fight off the swift Hungarians with their light horsemen on an open battlefield during the period of marauding raids, so the defending Hungarian army, withdrawn into an encampment formed by wagons, suffered defeat in almost the only major clash of the Mongol invasion. How could it have been possible to stop a people from the Steppes precisely on a ground most resembling the area where their warriors grew up, conducted their drills, and from where they swooped down upon Europe? Later a few towns and fortresses were able to defend themselves here and there, but the Mongols triumphed in subsequent smaller open clashes in almost every instance.

A golden belt buckle from Kígyóspuszta—A goldsmith's masterpiece from the mid-thirteenth century. *On the buckle, bellicose knights, heavily armed and wearing armor and helmets, clash with their swords on ponderous and well-built steeds. The weapons and war tactics of the Age of Chivalry became more common in Hungary, too—of course, among those who could afford them – why not? they were the bigwigs!—precisely when the "Tatar," or Mongol, challenge again unexpectedly confirmed the many advantages of waging war with swiftly moving, raiding light cavalry armed with bows and arrows against the rigid and cumbersome strategy of the knights that sometimes put ceremony ahead of effectiveness. In the mid-thirteenth century, as in the time of marauding raids, philosophies of life too collided with the forces and implements of war.*

On the deeds of the Hungarians—
The first page of Anonymus's Chronicle.
*After a long period of controversy, we now
believe that Anonymus, the nameless
"P. magister," was Béla III's notary and that
he may have been the same person as
Master Peter, the provost of Óbuda. He may
have written his history after the king's
death, about 1200. It is also assumed that
he studied in Paris and that he may have
been born in the Zemplén region (Northeast
Hungary) where, at Szabolcs, the
conquering Hungarians first settled down
and which he knows so intimately. He
praises the beauty of the area so lavishly
and is so familiar with its place names that
the latter conjecture becomes believable.
Anonymus does not so much describe as
reconstruct, actually "give birth" to the
events of the Conquest, with only a few
based on sources and most of them
conveying viewpoints prevalent in his own
time. Accordingly, his work attempts to
justify historically the interests of the Vazul
branch of the House of Árpád, those of the
old clannish leadership class, against those
of the new and, in part, foreign nobles.*

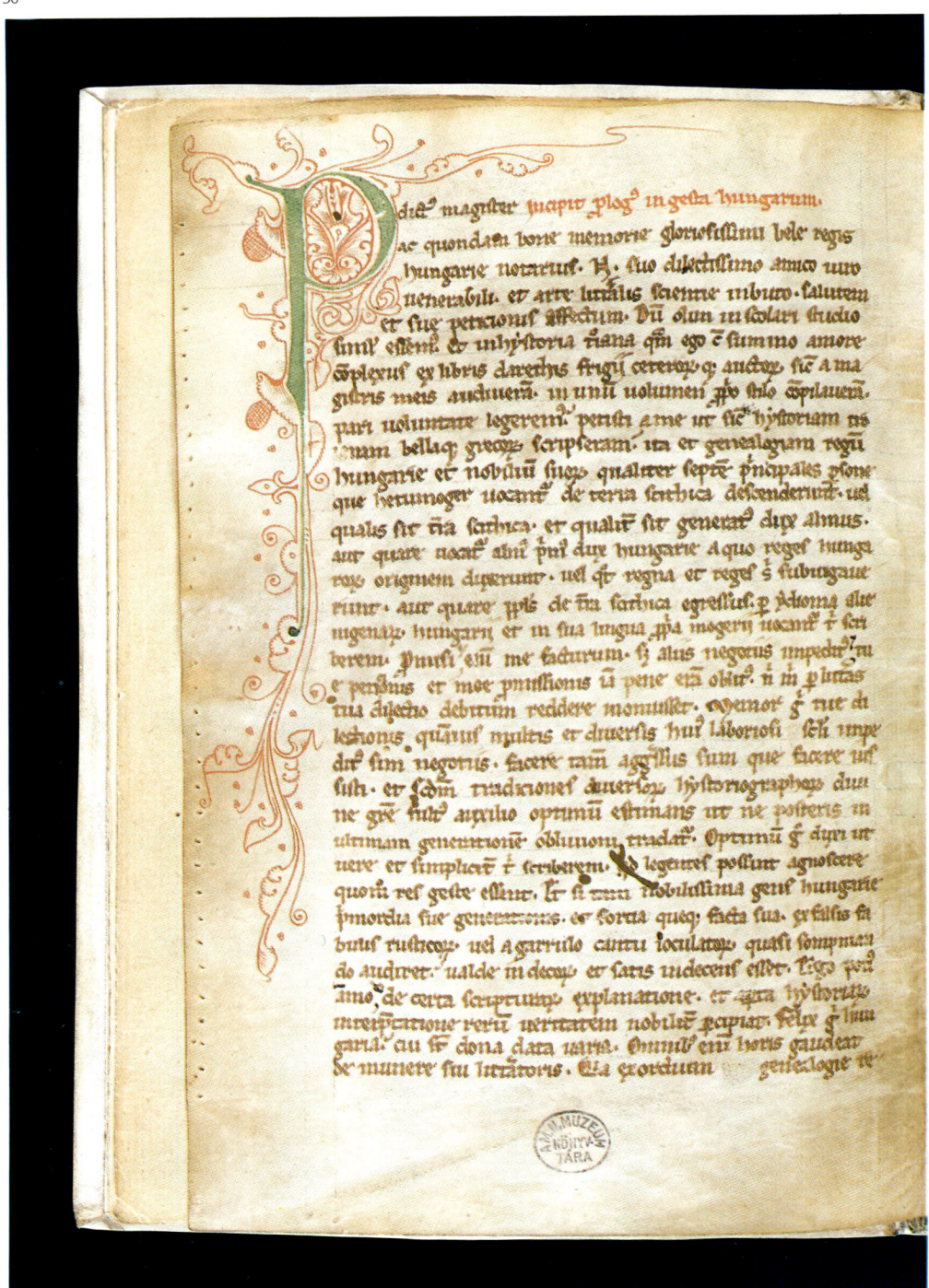

The logic with which the wise Béla IV strengthened the nobles' holdings and power in the interest of defending the nation flipped onto its wrong side: years, actually decades of feudal anarchy followed, a period of weak kings and powerful magnates. During this time, the Csák clan and then Máté Csák himself became so notorious that even at the beginning of our century, when the poet Endre Ady cried out against lordly "liberty" and despotism, he called the nation "the land of Máté Csák."

With the death of Andrew III (1290–1301), the male line of the House of Árpád died out without progeny. Nevertheless, the nation was still capable of greatness even in the state of disorder. A new dynasty was to make the remaining legacy flourish. It harvested another's planning.

However, before turning to this matter, let us say at this point—even at the cost of disrupting chronology somewhat—that the first canards of Hungarian history reach back to the distant past. These include the tales about the Hungarians' origin, for example, the emphasis laid on the Hun–Hungarian relation, which was not absolutely without reason but was very overdrawn. Later, the age of the princes and kings of the House of Árpád passed on two new exaggerated sources to posterity. One continued the predecessors directly; it raised the clan of Árpád to mythical heights, extending the tremendous merits of the most noted figures of the Conquest and the establishment and construction of the rich inheritance of Árpád, Géza, Stephen, Ladislas, Béla IV, and other outstanding rulers. But the creation of such canards is quite natural with young nations; we can encounter similar or greater ones in the history of many peoples.

The other canard, one that arose later, is "the doctrine of the Holy Crown." To the Hungarian royal crown which today, after its return from the United States, where it wound up in the wake of World War II, can be seen in a separate hall of the Hungarian National Museum and which originates undoubtedly in the Age of the Árpáds, even though its origin and age are highly debated, was linked during the course of later centuries to the notion that

The Holy Crown. *Though we do not know for certain whether this is the crown—if only half of it—that St. Stephen received from Pope Sylvester II at the turn of the tenth to eleventh century as a pledge of his Christian kingship, the legitimacy of Hungarian monarchs was ever since the time of the House of Árpád so definitely linked to this royal insignia assembled from pieces of earlier Byzantine and later Western goldsmiths' works that its sacral authority, its importance to sovereignty is unmatched in Hungarian history. Its possession occasionally was equivalent to the seizure of actual supreme power over the state; its absence prompted the charge of usurpation and cast doubt upon and made nominal the legitimacy of a reign, even if the ruler of the country possessed the proper military and political forces.*

this crown is not simply an embodiment of royal power but also of general political authority, of the legitimacy of rule.

As for the House of Árpád, whose male line ceased

in 1301, the facts about its marriage and dynastic relations are so numerous in this chapter not because we wanted to narrow down to the dimension of a family chronicle the history of a nation ruled by cursed and blessed kings in the eleventh, twelfth, and thirteenth centuries. The consistently exogamic matrimonial arrangements which prevailed in the House of Árpád before the appearance of its eponym, and remained so throughout, also meant that, in the end, not only did Árpád's blood not flow in the veins of the kings of the House of Árpád but hardly any Hungarian blood did so at all. As a result, the first ruling house of Hungary was engaged not only in constant political and power rivalries and alliances, but also in the closest physical and blood ties with the families of practically every neighboring country, with the ruling and leading families of all Europe.

THE FLEUR-DE-LIS
AND THE RAVEN

In the spring of 1300, the head of the Neapolitan branch of the fleur-de-lis House of Anjou, Charles (the Lame) II, the King of Naples and Sicily, and the "Cuman woman," Elizabeth, prepared his first grandson, Charles Robert, to go to Hungary. He obtained a bank loan in Florence for the first but not the last time. His family worries were not negligible: we know of thirteen of his children who reached adulthood, with a host of grandchildren; he had many whose future he had to see to.

On January 14, 1301, Andrew III of the House of Árpád died. In early spring, the crown rested on Charles Robert's head through the good offices of the Archbishop of Esztergom. However, it was not the authentic crown, for that one was not in the possession of the Anjou faction. The Archbishop of Kalocsa bedecked the Bohemian heir to the throne, Wenceslas, with that crown in August in Székesfehérvár. The latter, if we are correct, was twelve at the time. Charles Robert was older—by a whole year.

The next decade was continually filled with bitter strife for the throne, with the Holy Crown, meanwhile, turning up here and there (on the brow of Otto III, the Prince of Bavaria, for example). Charles Robert was crowned a second time in 1309, but still not with the Holy Crown; the final, truly legally binding coronation did not take place until 1310.

A panorama of Europe in the first decade of the fourteenth century... In France, it was the period of Philip IV of the House of Capet; the king crushed and dispatched to die at the stake the Knights Templar with whom, as with bankers, he had gone into heavy debt; he struggled with the papacy until his follower, the former Archbishop of Bordeaux, Clement V, transferred the seat of the papacy to Avignon ("the Babylonian captivity"). In England, Edward I wanted to acquire Flanders and Edward II, Scotland, in vain; the despotism of retainers replaced early parliamentarianism. On German soil, the ever more fictional "Holy Roman Empire," the institution of the prince-elector created a new form of power division and concentration; meanwhile, the Habsburgs, forced out from Switzerland but ambitious, were now only casting an eye toward the German–Austrian provinces. On the Iberian Peninsula, the Moors, having been driven out, tried in vain time and again to strike back. In Scandinavia, hardly anything that could affect Europe was happening. In Northern Italy, the city-states, despite the struggles going on within each and against each other, embraced an enormous economic power among themselves in both capital and control over commercial activity, and their economic position weakened only after the discovery of America. On Bohemian soil, despite constant political confusion, strong economic development took place in mining and textile industries. Poland was dismembered at that time, too, and it remained at the mercy of the Teutonic Knights for a long time. In Rumania, the Tatar invasion not only brought about years of destruction, it also put

A knightly ornament from the period of the Árpád dynasty
—A reconstruction. *At the time of its early kings, the Europeanization of the House of Árpád, Eastern in origin, was, in addition to its adoption of Christianity, represented by the invitation extended to illustrious foreigners and their acceptance into the royal court. Later, the members of the House of Árpád, increasingly mingling their bloodline through marriage, also took over many customs and ways of thought prevailing at the courts of the ruling houses of Europe. Thus the concepts and material accessories of the Age of Chivalry appeared. And though posterity called (Saint) Ladislas I "the chivalric king," that process lasted at least until the Anjou period, with many regressions along the way. The alternating red and white stripes were derived from the heraldic motifs of the House of Árpád.*

Moldavia under the rule of the Golden Horde for nearly a century. On Russian soil, the rebuke of the Teutonic Knights was successful but futile; after the destruction of Kiev, smaller principalities could exist only under Tatar supremacy, among which first the principality of Vladimir and then of Muscovy became powerful; in the western parts, large territories were in the hands of the Poles and Lithuanians. Byzantium was in its death throes; the Ottoman Turks had finally bitten off Asia Minor. In all of Europe—though toward the east to a diminishing degree —the development of cities and the increasing power of their middle class were apparent.

A cope clasp with the Hungarian Anjou coat of arms. *As early as the time of the Árpáds, the Eastern legacy of Hungarian art which dates back to the time when the Hungarians lived outside the Carpathian Basin—in other words to pagan times—was forced into the background, partly into the role of secondary motifs, by the strongly religious art of Western Christianity. At the time of the Anjous, European influence grew so much stronger that the more profane spirit of the chivalric age flowed into Hungary. This piece of goldsmith's work was prepared for the Hungarian chapel at Aachen (Aix-la-Chapelle) founded by Louis the Great. The figures of the three saints of the House of Árpád, Ladislas, Stephen, and Emeric, stand in the small Gothic niches above the Hungarian Anjous' coat of arms. However, it is not the founder of the nation but the chivalric king, St. Ladislas, who is found in the middle. Contrary to the view that this work originated in a Saxon workshop in Transylvania, its style and technique show Italian influence instead.*

Did the fact that with the House of Anjou, a western dynasty extended its rule over the Carpathian Basin for nearly a century represent a new stage in the Hungarians' incorporation into Europe? Or are we, by some chance, to interpret this differently? For, after all, did not the two Anjou kings, Charles Robert and Louis the Great, extend *Hungarian* influence instead, almost to every point of the compass? What occurred can be viewed either way. It is certain, however, that both of them depended on the sheltered Carpathian Basin and its human and economic resources. Alongside this fact, their line of descent was secondary.

Charles Robert, even after his third and final coronation, had to gird his loins against petty monarchs for a long time. Some oligarchies had as much economic and military power individually as he did. Fortunately for him, his adversaries were not able to form lasting coalitions. And they also slaughtered one another.

Charles Robert's greatest political achievement was the Central European "summit meeting" held in 1335 at Visegrád in the sumptuous Gothic palace which he developed on the bank of the Danube and which was protected by a powerful citadel and riverside fortifications. In addition to the Polish and Bohemian kings, the heads of several important principalities and a delegation from the Teutonic Knights attended the session. Among their far-reaching agreements, the one on economics was the most important. In it, they mapped out new roads and extended mutual advantages to one another. These were to the detriment of Vienna, whose title to staple rights harmed them all.

But how could the Anjou king who headed for the Hungarian throne from Naples with a loan from Florentine bankers have such prestige in economic matters

Visegrád. *The first stone fortress at Visegrád was a fourth-century* Roman castrum *that jutted out eastward toward the Danube from the later medieval castle. It was protected by a line of minor fortresses below, and Hungarians at the time of the Conquest also used some of its walls, building them up on the inside. Of all this, only the foundation walls remain. During and after the Mongol invasion, the upper and lower (or water-level) fortresses themselves formed the Visegrád fortification, which a wall running up the steep mountainside bound together. From the west, another wall—now gone—protected the early settlement belonging to the fortress. It was here that a magnificent castle was built in the age of the Anjous and then rebuilt by Matthias Corvinus. Its dimensions and sumptuousness as described in written works were later put in doubt, until diggings underway for a few decades have not confirmed the accounts of the ecstatic delineators.*

with his neighbors to the north? Well, at the beginning of the fourteenth century, mining and metallurgy continued to thrive in Hungary, especially the production of precious metals. As a result of the organization of customs stations, precious metal exchanges, and mints, the king became ever less dependent on the less reliable income provided by his landed estates. Charles Robert, at the town of Körmöcbánya (Kremnica), which he founded, began to mint that fleur-de-lis gold florin which thereafter retained such a stable value that it was recognized by its name, Körmöc gold, throughout Europe for five centuries as one of the strongest currencies. It was a veritable standard of measurement. Thus three hundred years after Saint Stephen a Hungarian monarch again succeeded—one can say for the second and last time—in issuing money that was well received in the international money market.

Charles Robert's son, Louis (the Great) I, during the four

decades of his reign (1342–1382), turned the accumulated economic capital to the uses of power. In the south, he more or less maintained control over Croatia and Dalmatia, and he renewed his efforts to keep Naples in the family's possession. In the southeast and east, he exercised feudal control along the Lower Danube. In the north, he inherited the Polish throne. The west was the only area where he could not extend the borders of his empire (which the lands under his authority could be called by now). In sighs of nostalgia we can occasionally hear even today: this was that beautiful period "when three seas washed the borders of Hungary" (the Baltic, the Black Sea, and the Adriatic). But irrespective of how illusory it was to call Hungarian this realm where the Polish throne involved only the person of Louis the Great and thus only a personal union linked Poland to Hungary, and, further, how shaky were the rest of the conquests with respect to feudal bonds (not to mention that at the time, the Polish kingdom did not extend to the Baltic Sea or even have access to it, since the Teutonic Knights ruled its shores)—in the light of this it is more proper to judge Louis the Great not on the amount of territory he ruled but on the actual accomplishments of his reign.

Undoubtedly, the economic power he inherited from his father was more than enough to carry on his military campaigns. The management of affairs improved in his court, and the results achieved in the Italian city-states, so advanced at this time, filtered through to it. Also Hungarian culture, which was then still strongly ecclesiastical in character but whose laicization pointed toward the Renaissance, derived significant benefits from the king's extensive international connections. Historians, miniaturists, architects, sculptors, and goldsmiths worked on his commissions. If only because he was preparing for the marriages of his three daughters, he had to make himself known in the courts of Europe. But when he died without a male heir, the fragility and high cost of his achievements quickly surfaced. It was mainly the tragic defense of the throne of Naples—deserving again only a Shakespeare's pen—that extracted a great price. On one of his journeys to Naples, Louis the Great carried gold coins equal to Hungary's six, and Europe's two years

spanned exactly half a century, he staved off only the severest fate, not deterioration. All the less so because—together with his brother, Wenceslas, who ascended the Bohemian throne—church concerns occupied his attention excessively: the Hussite wars and the anti-popes.

In the meantime, Sigismund fought two battles against the Ottoman sultan, the ravager of Byzantium rising high on its ruins, who was approaching the soft underbelly of Europe, the Balkans, as a dynamic conqueror. He lost both battles. This was sinister omen.

Louis the Great's gold florin—Obverse and reverse. *(The fleur-de-lis is the heraldic motif of the House of Anjou.) At the time of Louis the Great's reign, the two main conditions for the normal circulation of precious metals were whether the route for African commerce was open—which was dependent on the Crusades—and whether the enormous quantities of gold and silver mined in the Hungarian kingdom would accumulate at home or wind up "circulating" in commerce or through military expeditions. According to earlier opinions, Hungary's key position in the European market for precious metals lasted until the discovery of America, until cheap gold and silver (cheap because it was stolen!) poured into Europe from there. According to more recent perceptions, the most plentiful sources for precious metals in the Carpathian Basin had already begun to exhaust themselves somewhat earlier.*

of gold production, with countless silver pieces piled atop them. From the Hungarian viewpoint, almost all this treasure went up in smoke.

His daughter, the eleven-year-old Maria (1382–1395), succeeded to the Hungarian throne. Two years later, the ten-year-old Hedwig followed her father to the Polish throne. Later on, the two sisters shared their rule with their husbands. In 1387, at age sixteen, Maria took as joint ruler Sigismund of Luxemburg, the Margrave of Brandenburg. However, this event did not impede the decline. A rival king and his murder, oligarchical conspiracies, the imprisonment of the queen and her mother, the throttling of the latter, Maria's escape—the chaos lasted for years. When the young, twenty-four-year-old queen broke her neck in a fall from her horse, Sigismund had been the real ruler of the land for years and remained so for the next forty-two years. However, during a reign that

Sigismund's successors to the throne deserved, at least for a while, very little attention. In the southern borderlands, however, in the ever-increasing battles with the Turks, a general emerged who stamped his own individuality on the age more effectively than its crowned kings. With respect to his origin, János Hunyadi is held to be Rumanian—though his father's name was Vajk, an ancient Hungarian name—and he was also regarded as Sigismund's natural son. This is of little concern to us. His deeds qualify him. From a warrior of low rank he was to become the most eminent general of fifteenth-century Europe. At the end of his life, he owned two million hectares of landed estates. He spent his income almost exclusively on battles with the Turks. We shall not mention at this time all the battles he won and lost; let us merely recall why the bells ring.

In 1456, three years after he captured Constantinople, Sultan Mohammed II encamped and set off to besiege Nándorfehérvár (today's Belgrade). Hunyadi's relief army was a mixture of three elements. To the side of his mercenaries and the insurgent nobles, utilizing the lasting or rather the newly reviving aura of the Crusades, he also dared call to arms the common people, who had more than once rebelled against their lords. In the recruitment of Crusaders and then through all the battle engangements, Hunyadi's right arm was an impassioned Franciscan friar of strict morals, Giovanni Capistrano who was later canonized.

The Christian army gained a decisive victory. The wounded sultan was rescued half-dead from the battle by his guards. This triumph at Nándorfehérvár turned back

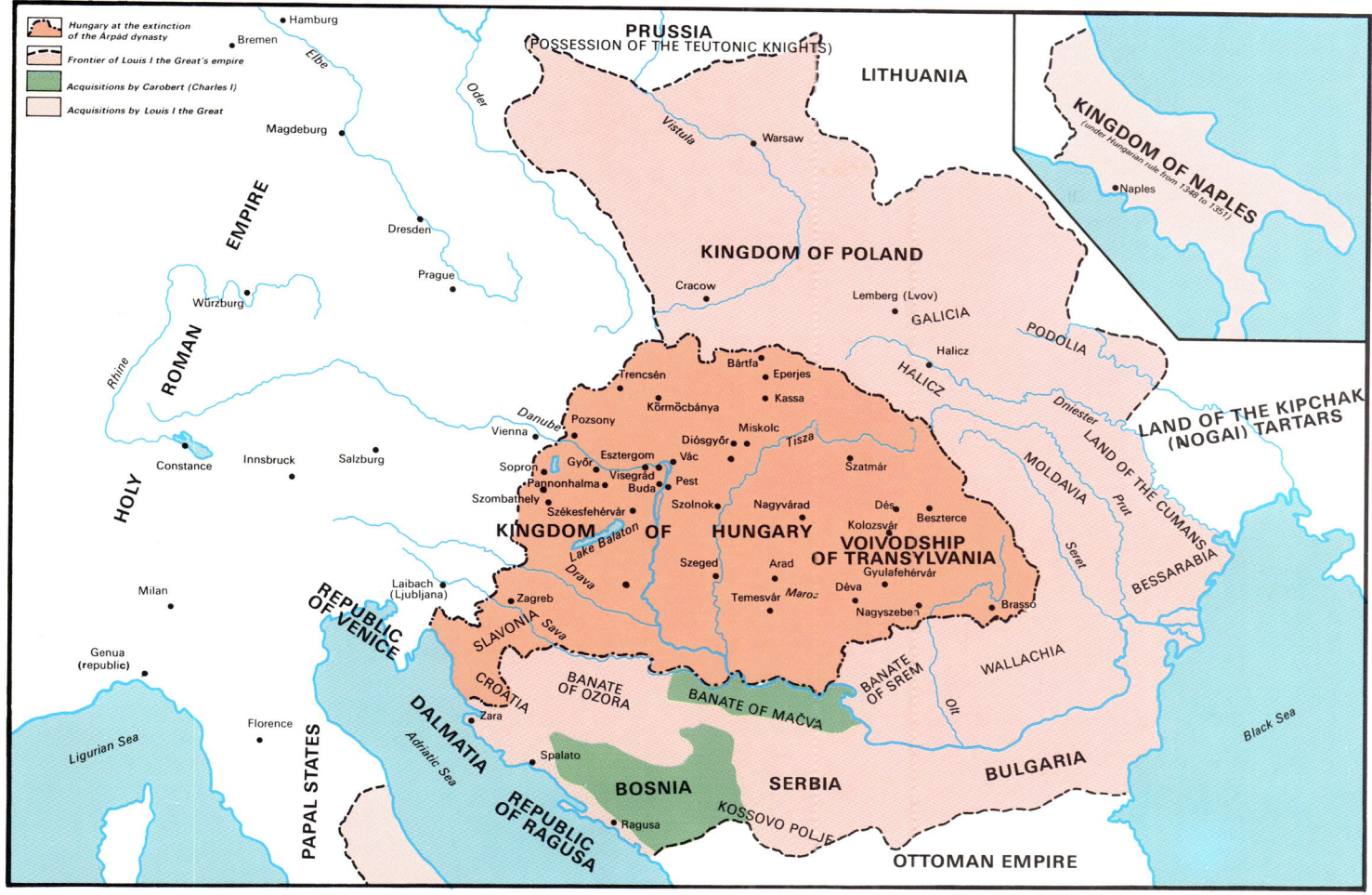

Hungary during the reign of Louis I the Great

for nearly a century the Ottoman expansion threatening Europe. This was an enormous advantage. It awaited exploitation. But often, only bells ring.

In Christian churches throughout the world, the pealing of the bells at noon still reminds people of the victory János Hunyadi achieved on July 22, 1456. According to one version, Pope Callixtus issued the decree. Actually, he issued this decree earlier and for another purpose. The pope had already given instructions on June 29 to ring the bells as a plea to the powers above to decide in our favor the impending battle, which he considered vital to Christianity. Still, the previous version is not totally false. For, as the pealing of the bells at noon turned from an occasional into a lasting event, a role was played in that transition by the universal joy that reigned after the battle, the celebration of victory.

However, barely a couple of weeks after the battle, the bells rang again for János Hunyadi: the death knell.

The Diósgyőr Castle. *After several earlier preliminaries, the spectacular build-up of this castle occurred at the time of Louis the Great, who from 1344 on, frequently hunted in this area, in the forests of the Bükk mountains rising above the castle; then from 1362 on, he apparently visited here for increasingly longer periods of time each year. After he was also crowned king of Poland in Cracow on November 17, 1370, he celebrated Christmas in this favorite place of his. It can confidently be said that the turning of Diósgyőr into a powerful and richly endowed fortress also reflected Louis the Great's policy toward Poland, it being located along the chief route leading to that country to the north. After two hundred years, when the Turks forced many landed and very powerful families in the south of Hungary to move north, the Perényis again reinforced Diósgyőr as well as Sárospatak. But while the former became a real border fortress, the Turks never reached the walls of the latter; even their occasional incursions did not spread farther north than Tokaj.*

The plague that broke out in the encampment carried him off too. That fall Giovanni Capistrano also died. The loss of the two forgers of the victory again plunged the country into anarchy. Two influential families vied for power around the weak king, and in one of the "episodes" of this war of changing fortunes, the king had János Hunyadi's eldest son, László, beheaded in 1457. It was a dreadful scene. During the public execution arranged with the assistance of the court, the executioner struck the youth's neck three times, but he remained alive. According to the custom of the age, he therefore had the right to an amnesty. Ladislas V, however, who was seventeen but already a debauched, neurotic lout, gave the signal: László Hunyadi was thrown down, and at the fourth blow his head fell to the ground. Fleeing, the king went off to Vienna and then to Prague. He dragged with him the younger son, Mátyás (Matthias) Hunyadi, as hostage. Do we see the hand of fate in the fact that the plague also disposed of Ladislas V in the fall of the very same year?

His successor was the hostage himself who quickly regained his freedom. In a romantic manner, the lesser nobility encamped in Pest chose Matthias Hunyadi Corvinus (1458–1490) as king below the castle on the ice in the middle of the frozen Danube, though hard bargaining preceded it at a session in the castle with the bands of nobles who held the country in their hands and were competing with each other.

The country had a national king once again, if this notion could have such a meaning at that time. Although the Hunyadi family acted as a guardian over the fifteen-year-old king for a couple of years, the young Matthias quickly proved deserving of the family's heraldic bird, the raven, which common belief considered to be a powerful and wise bird. Today, we most frequently mention Matthias's Renaissance court: its brilliance, richness, and soaring spirit. Italian tastes again transformed the Buda Castle and the palace at Visegrád, indeed, the entire country, so extensively that we can speak not only about imitation but about influences at work in both directions during the time. For instance, Janus Pannonius, raised in Italy and later Bishop of Pécs, was well known for his lyric poetry in Latin at all European centers of humanism. We know a great deal, relatively speaking, about this period, if for no other reason than that a good many leading humanists frequently turned up at Matthias's court, and some of them even settled there. His library, the Bibliotheca Corviniana, apparently developed into the best collection in Europe, but was, in any case, the first among the newly founded libraries.

Modern managerial practices controlled and imposed taxes on the Hungarian economy. The core of the

43

army—since Matthias had to pledge to order the nobility to take up arms only as a last resort—was the mercenary military force, the Black Army.

At first, Matthias wanted to continue his father's war in the Balkans against the Turks. But with his face to the east, he did not feel his back was secure. He competed for the thrones of both Bohemia and Austria: he wished to found a strong and powerful Danubian kingdom, in other words, an empire. However, his forces sometimes succeeded, sometimes failed in battle. And his marriages were unsuccessful. After the Bohemian Catherine of Podebrad, Beatrice of Naples was also childless. The latter—the suspicion is strong—was, perhaps, her husband's murderer. Either a sudden stomach ailment or a poisoned fig killed Matthias, while he was attempting to guarantee succession to the throne for his natural son, John Corvin, born of a Viennese commoner, and wanted to make him a prince and obtain estates and to muster supporters for him.

Matthias prepared against the Turks for decades in vain; he conducted most of his military campaigns not in the Balkans but in the north and west. "The proud bastion of Vienna groaned under the onslaught of Matthias's ferocious army," a poet still sang centuries later. However, Matthias lost what he wanted to achieve by this means. The power to be aligned against the danger from the east, against the rising Ottoman crescent, diminished instead of increasing.

Posterity mourned him and elevated him into a folk hero in its legends. Matthias was the Just One, who, walking the land in disguise, condemned fraudulent judges, shamed the greedy rich, and succored the poor; he made love to full-blooded shepherdesses and ingenuous maidens.

An "Apostle" found among the Gothic statuary in Buda. *At winter's end of 1974, in early spring, this author was present almost day after day at Buda Castle, at the diggings conducted by the late László Zolnay, as Gothic statuary (from the Anjou period?) was being uncovered, to add a new chapter to the history of Hungarian art. He dug some pieces of this tragic and victorious sculptural hecatomb out of the ground, out of the rubble with his own fingernails. This treasure trove of magnificent and originally painted statues, which could not have embellished some edifice for very long, come from the time of Louis the Great or perhaps that of Sigismund of Luxemburg. For some unknown reason, flung together not much later with all sorts of rubble, they wound up in a "grave." Was it simply because a new stylistic trend had arrived? Or were they sentenced to "death" for some other reason? to us, this verdict is fortuitous. After all this is why these statues did survive in their present form either intact or in fragments; this is why they did not fall victim to the Turks, who so zealously destroyed portrayals of the human form. Thus they demonstrate the richness of Hungarian art in the late Middle Ages, something that had been surmised but very difficult to prove until now.*

Emperor Sigismund—A painting by Pisanello (c. 1395?–1455). *Sigismund of Luxemburg, as coregent and king, was Hungary's monarch for fifty years (1387–1437) and German emperor for 27 years (1410–1437). He devoted his time and energy mostly to the defense of his external interests and the expansion of his own concerns: his relations with Rome, the Hussite wars, and so on. Thus, from this point of view his period was a continuation of the time of the Anjous. No small part of the economic and military power drawn from the Carpathian Basin served the ambitions of a foreign ruling house. This, however, at the same time represented the continuation and expansion of Hungary's integration into Europe, albeit not exactly to its own advantage. Pisanello may have met Sigismund in Italy in the early 1430s, apparently in 1433, when the emperor's crown was actually placed on his head in Rome. At the time Sigismund, who was in his fifties, was a splendidly virile figure. Four years later he was dead.*

Among the succession of pretenders to the throne who thronged eagerly, made lavish promises, and mustered armies to support their claims, Hungarian oligarchs, who had gained new power even before the death of Matthias, sent John Corvin packing and considered the Bohemian king, Wladislas II (1490–1516), of the House of Jagiello, to be more under their control. Wladislas even secretly married the widow, Beatrice, while the throne was not yet secure (at a later date, he considered this union void because, he said, he was forced into the marriage). This much more about him: he docilely disbanded the main support of the throne, the Black Army. With centralized power gone, the precariousness of the law,

Vajdahunyad Castle. *Vajdahunyad, in Transylvania, was the center of the Hunyadi family's enormous estates. János Hunyadi's father, Serb's son Vajk, obtained the formerly modest castle from the king, and the son, the great general himself built up the Gothic fortification, whose magnificence was unmatched in all of Central and Eastern Europe. After many and various kinds of destruction, it was expertly restored at the turn of the last century. And even though a blast furnace ejecting terrible pollution located nearby mars the view, Vajdahunyad is even today worthy of admiration in its original place. The building complex known as Vajdahunyad Castle which was erected in Budapest's City Park for the Millenary celebration of Hungary's existence in 1896, is a faithful imitation of its individual elements, and actually offers a cross section of the entire history of Hungarian architecture, representing its chief and eponymous parts.*

45

St. George—A statue by the brothers Martin and George de Coloswar, 1373. *(The statue reached Prague as a gift from Wladislas II; here we see a copy of the Prague original placed at the foot of the Fishermen's Bastion in Buda.) We know very little about its sculptors. They were born in Kolozsvár, and their father was a noted painter in the city in the mid-fourteenth century. Apparently, they made a study tour of Italy. They also prepared statues of several kings from the House of Árpád which stood in Nagyvárad, though only references, descriptions, and secondary representations inform us about them. However, the artistic quality and the technical skill embodied in the St. George statue in Prague indicates the high level of Hungarian art in the second half of the fourteenth century and the degree of loss that the Turks' condemnation of representation of the human form and their mutilation of statues caused during the time of their domination.*

46

János Hunyadi—A woodcut from the Brünn edition of the Thuróczi Chronicle. *János Hunyadi, who was regent of the country during Ladislas V's nonage, the 1440s, had to relinquish his position which made him almost equal to a sovereign when the king reached maturity precisely at a time when the Turkish threat again became acute. One of the fiascoes of his life is that although he tried on several occasions to bring the small peoples of the Balkans together against Ottoman expansion, the different degrees of their endangerment and their otherwise divergent interests made that collaboration transitory. The other shadow on his life is that whatever he achieved in property, power and organization at home was undermined by the jealous intrigue and counter power of his rivals, the different oligarchical families. It is a curious twist of fate that so to say at the cost of his older son Ladislas's death, his younger son Matthias acquired such prestige and such a posthumous rekindling of his father's reputation which helped him to mount the throne.*

the oppression of the serfs, and feudal anarchy weighed heavily on the country.

Again we come upon an age marked not by a king's name but first by a highly ambitious priest's, later by a popular hero's, and finally by a fanatical jurist's. Tamás Bakócz, the offspring of serfs—he was Bishop of Győr and Eger, and then Archbishop of Esztergom—was a true Renaissance figure. He was first Matthias's secretary, but later Wladislas's all-powerful deputy. Bakócz proceeded to Rome with wagons fully loaded with gold; he waited very patiently for the death of Julianus II, the great patron of the arts and Michelangelo's backer. At the conclave he was narrowly defeated by Giovanni De'Medici, who mounted the papal throne as Leo X. To compensate him for the failure and to get rid of him at the Vatican, the new pope granted Bakócz the right to announce a Crusade.

In Hungary, recruitment commenced, the army grew, predominantly with peasants. Swords were scarce, straightened scythes and flails abundant. Bakócz aimed at the papacy. The king hoped to gain a small military success, the nobles to clear the air. The people were driven by bitterness and not by faith or by zeal against the Turks. And it was not only the poorest and most defenseless serfs who were bitter. It was precisely the more united, the more

48

well-to-do serfs living in the boroughs of the Alföld, those who were already engaged in exports in addition to the production of goods that the nobles—almost as if they were competitors—attempted to force back. Thus they had more than just their chains to lose.

Surprisingly, the leader of the Christian armies was not some secular or church potentate, but a member of the lesser nobility in Transylvania, a Székely lieutenant, György Dózsa. The most zealous recruiters and administrators of his armies were the monks who belonged to a branch of the Franciscan order that followed the strictest regulations, the Observants. Most of them were of peasant origin. In their view, the laws of God did not support unequal distribution of property. Later, the highest church authorities launched an investigation against them, and they reprimanded and punished them. Still later, the first Hungarian Protestant ministers came from their ranks.

1514. The armies mobilized under the Sign of the Cross took arms not against the heathens but against their noble lords. All four corners of the country burst into flames. A bloodbath began. The manor houses of the nobility were ablaze, the magnates withdrew into their castles. where they were besieged and prepared to counterattack. John Szapolyai, the voivode of Transylvania—he was already a most powerful noble at the time of Matthias, and a major figure among the lesser nobility—was the military leader who suppressed the peasant revolt. He had Dózsa arrested—who had only gradually become the intentional leader of the popular insurrection. He had him seated on a redhot throne as "King of the Peasants," had a burning-hot iron crown placed on his head, and forced his lieutenants to eat of his flesh.

This was only the first act of vengeance. István Werbőczi, the jurist, composed his *Tripartitum (Hármaskönyv)*. This treatise marked out for centuries the framework of the

A shield of Matthias Corvinus's guard in Vienna. *In the early 1480s, Matthias's two main concerns were, with the Turks seriously threatening, to secure his rear from the west either through alliances or force and to arrange the succession of his bastard son, János (John) Corvin, to the throne, an opponent of the latter being Beatrice of Naples, the queen herself. In the end, he failed to achieve either objective; meanwhile, in the first half of 1485, however, he captured Vienna and then Wiener Neustadt two years later, when he also celebrated his taking complete possession of Lower Austria with this victory by holding a magnificent review of his troops. During these years, he moved about time and time again, holding court in Vienna and almost converting it into a second capital. Death reached him there on April 6, 1490—many suspected murder. His body was transported down the Danube to Buda and was finally interred in Székesfehérvár.*

The Philostratus Codex, *c. 1487–1490. (Matthias Corvinus's portrait is on the gold medallion to the left of center.) Enjoying luxury and culture equally, Matthias was a passionate book collector and customer. He purchased and commissioned codices. In the end, his world-famous library, which perhaps reached a thousand titles, was "declared protected" in vain; in the Jagiello period, thoughtless giving and lending depleted the collection. During their occupation of Buda, the Turks guarded what remained for a time, then carried off part of it to Istanbul. The rest were scattered later. Today, about 170 Corvinas are known to exist worldwide; of these, fifty are found in Hungary. The sudden surfacing of new Corvinas is not a rare phenomenon, and this sometimes depends on whether it can be ascertained through seemingly criminological methods where an individual book from the Corvinus library, carried so far away and its mark lost, originated and how it reached its present location. Today, no matter how much we would like to bring back increasing numbers of Corvinas to Hungary, the obtaining of the enormously valuable codices through exchange or purchase can seldom succeed.*

AD DIVVM MATTHIAM VNGARIAE
BO; AVSTRIE. Q. REGEM: PRINCIN
VIC. ANTONII. BON̄ TRADVCTIO. IN
PHILOSTRATVM LEMN. SOPHISTAꝜ
PRAEST. ET̄ PRIMIS PꝪATIO FOELĪCIP

ON E-
beſcat amph
us̓ ipꝼ poſte
ritas benefi
cio tuo Diue
Matthia: poſt
q̄ opera & uir
tute tua faꝯ
tum eſt: Vt
cum glorio
ſa uetuſtate
certare iam
audeat: Qd̄
ceteris preter
miſſis; ex bel
lo tantum ꝓ
alamannī co
ne incaput
excreſcere uideamur planius oſtendetur. Nā
cum profuſo. ſerenitatis tuę nomine ſuccen
ſi in Pannoniam uaueiſſemus: Compluraꝗ
uolumina Maieſtati tue ac Diue Beatrici fi
lioꝗ Ioāti fauſte indolis adoleſcenti dedicaſſe
mus: Dūm tranſ Iſtrum tua caſtra ſequumur
ea uictorie tuę ſigna & perpetua quidem mo

King Matthias Corvinus's coat of arms in the Matthias Church of Buda, from 1470. *Perhaps precisely because Matthias Corvinus was the first national king since the extinction of the House of Árpád, and thus making the question of legitimacy particularly important to him, but also because he built and decorated so extensively, the Matthias coat of arms is one of the most frequently encountered accessories in Hungary's history. As a signal, if not as ostentation, it is found on buildings and book covers, soldiers' shields, cannons, and religious treasures. Though it was Béla IV who founded the church for the use of German burghers living in Buda and Matthias is only one among a series of builders and rebuilders, the power of historical tradition fixes the parish church of Buda, the Church of Our Lady, as the Matthias Church because it was here that the consecration of his election as king took place—with an enthronement in lieu of a crown.*

relations between the serfs and the nobility. It is appropriate for us to note that, as a result of the high nobility's counter-interests, the *Tripartitum,* which favored mainly the interests of the lesser nobility, never formally achieved the force of law. Still, on the basis of custom, it became a determinative source of law, although life is always more powerful than law. The severity of Werbőczi's work dictated by the nobles' vengeance could not be effective on a broad scale. It sought to bind the serfs to the soil in vain.

Today, the name of Tamás Bakócz is mainly remembered by historians and by art historians through the Bakócz Chapel in Esztergom. Dózsa and Werbőczi, having become symbols of antagonism, remain fixed to this day in the consciousness of the nation.

Only nowadays can we truly measure how rich the Gothic art of the Angevin period in Hungary was. This knowledge is due, in part, to destruction. During the course of rapid changes in taste in the fifteenth century and enthusiastic reconstruction, a whole series of Gothic masterpieces wound up below the surface of the earth, under the ruins – no doubt through acts of barbarism. In the magnificent Renaissance royal place at Visegrád, archaeologists dug up from the Angevin period ornamental carvings, broken into small fragments, belonging to the foundations of the fountain structure dating from the age of Matthias Corvinus; in the Castle of Buda, their spades unearthed a veritable cemetery of statues from the Angevin period.

Esztergom, the Bakócz Chapel with its altar—A red marble sepulchral chapel, 1506–1507; a white marble altar, 1519. *Significant "royal" construction was already going on in Esztergom at the time of Géza. St. Stephen was born here. Later the town developed not as a royal residence but "purely" as the seat of an archbishop. Then it was in Turkish hands for a long time. Afterwards it took on a Baroque look. Among its many archbishops, Tamás Bakócz was the only one who not only toyed with the idea of becoming pope but very nearly succeeded (and if he had, Pope John Paul II would not have been the first Eastern European to sit on St. Peter's throne). In 1823, his magnificent sepulchral chapel built in a pure and mature Italian Renaissance style was dismantled into 1,600 numbered pieces and then transferred to its present location in the nineteenth-century cathedral of the archbishops of Esztergom.*

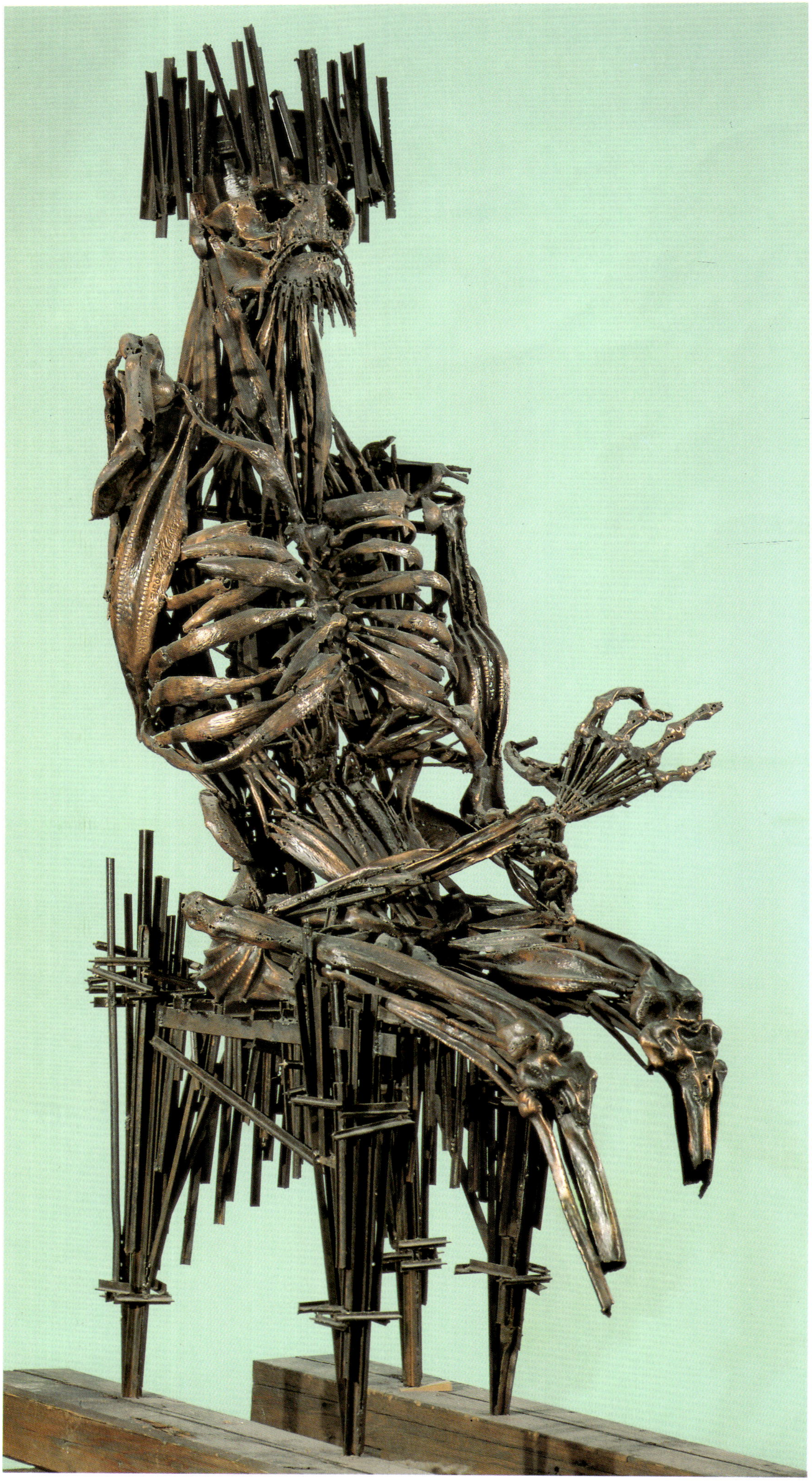

Dózsa—A statue by Tibor Szervátiusz. *Szervátiusz portrays the execution of György Dózsa Székely, the leader of the 1514 peasant uprising, which, according to authentic historical sources, was carried out as follows: the vengeful leader of the nobles, János Szapolyai, had the popular leader seated on a red-hot iron throne and had a red-hot iron crown put on his head; then he forced Dózsa's lieutenants to partake of his roasted flesh. It is hardly an accident that the above spirited representation of the infernal episode occurring at the end of the Middle Ages was actually created in Kolozsvár, Transylvania, from where sculptor Jenő Szervátiusz, the father (1903–1983), and his son Tibor (b. 1930) were forced to move to Hungary permanently.*

IN THE WAN LIGHT OF THE CRESCENT

Meanwhile, Columbus had long sailed to and already returned from the New World (1492); actually he had repeated the journey three times. The lines of power in Europe were also redrawn. As a result, the proud Adriatic declined into an insignificant waterway on the periphery of the Mediterranean; Dalmatian ports that had been resplendent city-states not so long ago became miserable fishing villages. Venice was experiencing its golden age, though a long agony awaited it. Replacing Italy, the Iberian Peninsula became the temporary center for the flow of economic power. What came to be called capitalism took its first steps on the backs of fat sheep and skinny peasants in England's textile industry.

In the meantime, Martin Luther posted his manifesto on the door of the castle church at Wittenberg (1517). This period is also called that "long sixteenth century" which arched from the middle of the 1400s to the thirties of the 1600s, which made wage-earners out of serfs in new centers shifting to northwestern Europe and gave birth to the Protestant ethic, and in which the citizenry, tolerated only in some places under feudalism, had begun to forge weapons for future victory.

We want to add two remarks to the preceding. A view over a longer time span would give them true meaning. One: in the wake of the discoveries and conquests overseas, surplus of precious metals suddenly replaced the scarcity of such metals in Europe, while prices and the terms of trade underwent great realignment. Two: the numbers of inhabitants in Hungary and England at the time of Matthias Corvinus were approximately equal. Today, the ratio is one to five.

The greediness of the Szapolyai–Werbőczi faction, which triumphed over the peasants in 1514, deprived the Fuggers of their mining concessions, who meanwhile "forgot" to pay the miners' wages. Then a miners' uprising followed that of the peasants—ending in defeat and vengeance. Is it any wonder that, after all this, there was not enough money for the war against the Turks, even though fortifications were falling in the south one after the other? The bells rang in vain; even legendary Nándorfehérvár fell in 1521. Five years later, in 1526, Suleiman the Magnificent decided to wage an all-out military campaign, at a time when the trauma of the brutal drowning of the 1514 peasant uprising in blood still deeply pervaded the country. However, because they were longer lasting, the nobles' more severe acts of vengeance were not their immediate physical reprisals but their stripping the peasants of their rights to movement and ownership, the strict subordination of the peasants to the landowner. Although the radical laws on this matter—like laws generally—were never completely enforceable, they nevertheless cast a dark shadow on Hungary for centuries.

The son of Wladislas II, King Louis II (1516–1526), then a twenty-year-old, puny-looking youth, was able to dispatch a total of twenty-six thousand ment to the south;

Louis II's armor. *King Louis II was born in 1506 and was already on the throne at age ten. This ill-fated young Jagiello—whose country, in addition to all its troubles, was damaged by his factional guardians—went off shilly-shallying to the battle of Mohács in 1526. Not in this armor, of course. But this chivalric armor, as a sheer anachronism, perhaps also bears witness to how slowly, at the advent of the age of firearms, the new weapons transformed the modes of waging war. The clash at Mohács was decided in no small part by the unexpected and devastating volleys of the Turkish artillery. Did not launching an attack while on the march against the sultan's army advancing on Mohács promise more than waiting in camp while the enemy also pitched their tents, rested, and devised its battle strategy calmly with all its fighting services and cannons?*

meanwhile, he waited in vain for Szapolyai's army of ten thousand coming from Transylvania. To this day, some still debate whether or not Szapolyai, who coveted the throne, was intentionally late. The Hungarian army did not attempt to block the strategically sensitive rivercrossings along the frontier; instead, it waited on an open field at Mohács and allowed the Turkish army with three to four times the number of troops and even greater fire power to advance. The defeat was disastrous. The archbishops of Kalocsa and Esztergom, five bishops, enormous numbers of nobles, and some ten thousand soldiers were killed. Louis fled, his horse stumbled in a swollen brook and buried the king under him. According to another version, enraged nobles finished him off. (His widow, Maria Habsburg, loaded the king's treasures on a boat and fled upstream on the Danube. Later, she energetically promoted the validity of her family's claim to the Hungarian throne; then she was successful governor of the Netherlands for a quarter of a century; she lived out her last years in Spain.)

"Mohács is the burial ground of our national greatness..." The conventional wisdom of the nation holds that Mohács was a reversal of fortune to the Hungarians like that of Waterloo and Verdun to the French and Wagram to the Austrians. Correctly, with reason? Not long ago,

The battle of Mohács—A Turkish miniature. *In the constantly burning wound of Hungarian historical consciousness, "the disaster at Mohács," in 1526, the following supposition arises again and again: if dissension and moral erosion in the nation had not been so great, if the large army led by János Szapolyai—later king—had not been "late" and had not pulled up so far from Mohács, then the fortunes of battle would have turned out differently. According to another view, a good decade remained even after the crushing defeat when it would have been possible to block the way of the Ottoman armies with proper joining of forces. In reality, the pressure of the Turkish sultanate's expansion through the Balkans and the Carpathian Basin toward Vienna was so great that in 1526 and immediately afterward, it was* already *and still* hardly avertable. *This miniature is an outstanding example of compressed, condensed delineation that was widespread in antiquity, and whose tradition was still being preserved by Turkish miniatures at the close of the Middle Ages.*

archaeologists stumbled across several of the long-looked-for mass graves on the battlefield at Mohács. In 1526, Louis II first ordered the mobilization of one-fifth of the serfs, then one-half, and finally all of them. And some time still remained... But, perhaps because of the ominous recollection of 1514, all this mobilization failed to come about. The bulk of the dead identified in the mass graves at Mohács turned out to be foreign mercenaries. Though the ranks of Hungarian leaders suffered enormous casualties at Mohács, the genuinely Hungarian military forces remained nearly intact after the battle.

Suleiman could still pillage unimpeded with his army; he reduced tens of thousands to slavery. He even entered Buda Castle, which was left undefended. And what Queen Maria had not carried off, he now loaded on boats, including the codices in Matthias Corvinus's library. After that, however, he evacuated the castle, then the entire country, and returned home. This Turkish behavior was only seemingly illogical. Suleiman the Magnificent wanted to demonstrate his power, and hereafter he appeared willing to accept a Hungarian ruler who was content to exercise sovereignty.

John Szapolyai (1526–1540), chosen to be king with full awareness of Suleiman's position, waged war with varying success against the rival Habsburg king, Ferdinand I (1526–1564), the brother of Queen Maria and Charles V, the Emperor of the Holy Roman Empire and King of Spain. Let us describe this period with three events. (1) Almost to the very day of the first anniversary of the battle, Suleiman again pitched his tents on Mohács's bloody

54

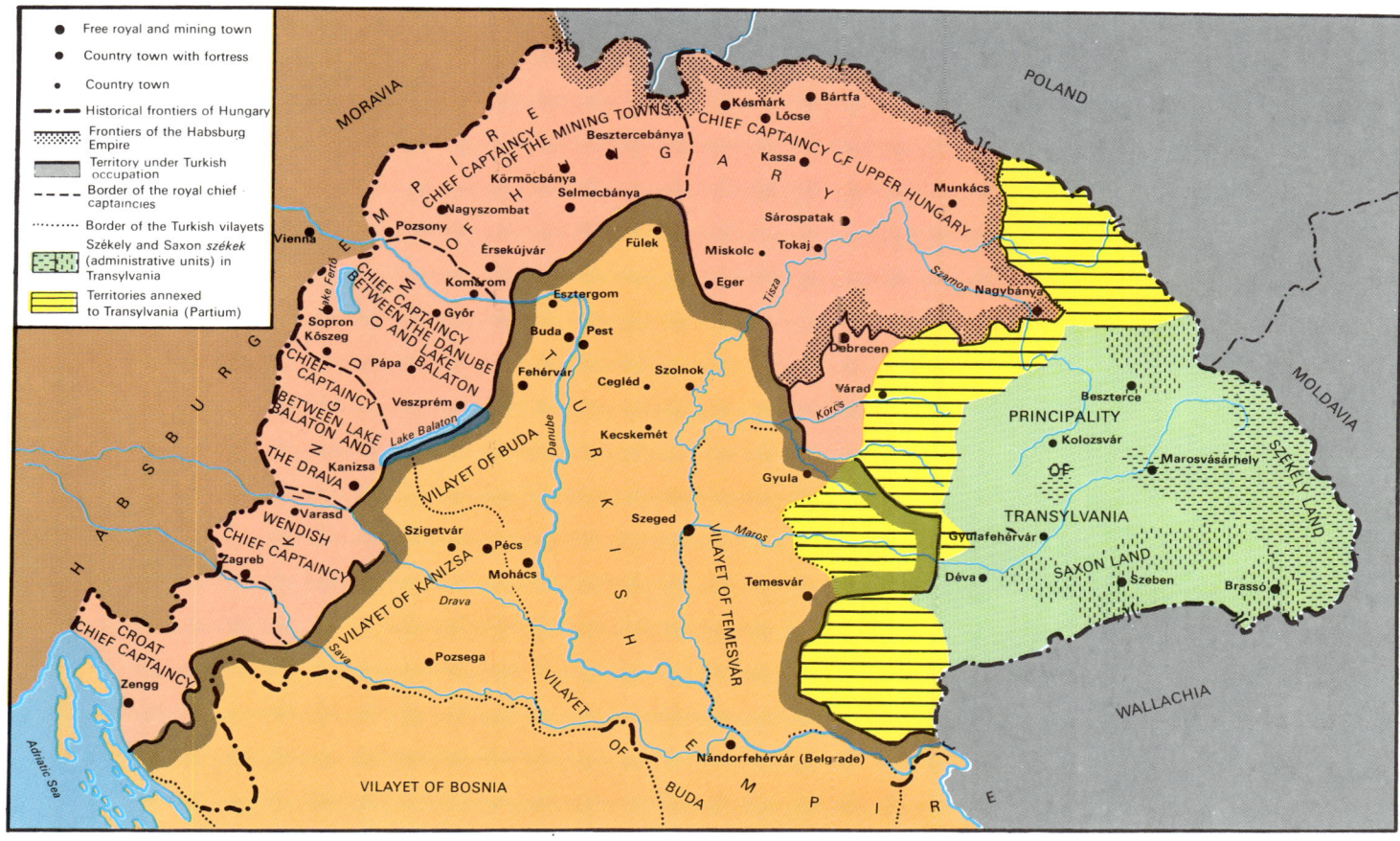

Hungary in the second half of the 16th century

fields, ordered Szapolyai, that is, King John I, into his presence, who paid homage to him there by kissing his hand. (2) In 1529, the Turks seized Buda by assault from Ferdinand I's forces but then handed it—together with the Holy Crown, which Suleiman had obtained in the meantime—over to King John. (3) The Fuggers, who had been recalled to the country, entered into contracts for the right to work the mines in Upper Hungary with one king and then another.

A decade and a half passed in this manner—meanwhile, the sultan tried to capture Vienna several times—then, in 1541, Suleiman again came to Hungary, apparently to assure Szapolyai's son, the infant King John Sigismund, of his support as guardian. A few hundred of the sultan's Janissaries, encamped below Buda, "strolled" into the castle and suddenly raised their flag. This is how the capital city of Hungary came into Turkish hands for a century and a half (1541–1686). The country, divided in two after Mohács, now split into three parts.

Its western and northern strip was a part of the dynamic Habsburg Empire; within this, it was a kind of border region of Austria's hereditary provinces, a buffer zone at the time of the Turks' deployments against Vienna, and a bridgehead for the hoped-for additional eastern conquests.

The middle triangle, the peak of which extended far beyond Buda, and which embraced the fertile Alföld, the eastern half of Transdanubia, some part of the central mountain range in the north, and the lower tip of Transylvania, was in time increasingly absorbed into the Ottoman Empire.

The Transylvanian Principality emerged quickly in what was Szapolyai's eastern kingdom; sometimes it was more independent, sometimes less so, though from the viewpoint of the future preservation of Hungarian national aspirations, it was of vital importance and was imbued with a predominantly Protestant character.

Let us proceed from the east to the west. Because his internal support was slight and unstable and the sultan apparently sided with him only so long as it lay in the interest of Turkish expansion to the west, John Sigismund eventually renounced the Hungarian throne and was content to occupy the throne of the prince of Transylvania. He was followed in this post by István Báthory (1571–1586), who was soon chosen king of Poland as well. Báthory, who was one of the most brilliant figures in Polish history, gained his most dazzling victories against the Russian czar, Ivan IV, mainly with Transylvanian and Székely military forces. On his death, Transylvania was again left to its own devices. Or quite the contrary, it could find even less respite under the immense pressure of the two rivals, but it was also tormented by its own "split personality." First, the hope arose that the Turks could be driven out with the help of the Habsburgs, and then, amid the vast shedding of blood and tears, the independent principality temporarily ceased to exist. Later, the sultan sent a royal crown to István Bocskai (1605–1606), who was once again turning to the Turks, though he did not pledge full allegiance. He remained prince, maneuvered, and gathered strength.

Here we must mention the main source of Bocskai's strength, who unfortunately died soon: the military forces of the Székely and the Haiduks. The origin and the settlement history of the Székely living in a part of Transylvania and essentially a Hungarian ethnic group are a long-standing source of controversy in Hungarian prehistory and history. This much is certain, that they arrived very long ago—perhaps not with the Árpáds but even earlier, or perhaps not long after them—on the southeastern as well as the southwestern borders of the Carpathian Basin, and there they supplied the border guards for the emerging Hungarian state. The autonomy of the troops in the southwest quickly faded; on the other hand, those in Transylvania preserved with varying success

through the length of the centuries their free legal status, which was comparable to the lesser nobility's, while efforts were made time and again to thrust them into serfdom. As a dreaded military people, the Székely were prepared to support militarily every leadership favoring or tolerating their freedom; in contrast, they resisted efforts to subjugate them in a series of uprisings. Meanwhile, they fell *en masse* as victims to the most various kinds of military reprisals; they fell—often as Turkish mercenaries—into the havoc created by the Tatar invasions of Transylvania as well as in the recurring epidemics. In the meantime, Saxons continued to move in and settle next to them, and Rumanian shepherds intermingled with them, who had for a long time been infiltrating from Moldavia and Wallachia, first taking cover in the hills and then settling in the valleys, progressively transforming the ethnic map of Transylvania.

Even hazier is the origin of the Haiduks, who had already participated in the Dózsa uprising. In all probability, they were, in part, Southern Slavs who withdrew to the north from the Turks, joined by drovers participating in the breeding and transportation of cattle and by runaway serfs. Supposedly this was how this marauding society developed, which willingly entered military service but was libertine even when measured by the standard of the age and which later, on settling down, amalgamated into a group of people stubbornly defending its Haiduk freedom—essentially the freedom of peasant life—and could almost be defined as a separate ethnic group. (Haiduks, apparently of the same origin, played a role in the history of the Balkans in the wars against the Turks.)

The dilemma of Transylvania—and not much less that of Royal Hungary—whether it was better to fight with the Turks against the Habsburgs or with the Habsburgs against the Turks, was interwoven by a religious schizophrenia caused by the particularly strong Protestantism in Transylvania and then by the Counter-Reformation rising in Vienna, not a purely

István Báthori—His tomb in the Mary Chapel of the Cathedral of Cracow. *Though it was really customary in this period for kings or heads of noble families who held themselves worthy of the crown to contract purposeful marriages and engage in wide-ranging activities, the career of István Báthori (1533–1586) was unparalleled; in Hungary he was "only" a Transylvanian prince (from 1571 on), but later he was also chosen to occupy the throne of the sovereign royal house of Poland (1576). However, more important than this mere fact is that, as a result of his ten-year reign and the strong central royal authority he exercised, the Poles themselves, who endure the bridle with difficulty, consider it to this very day a golden age in the course of a Polish history that was stormy and often grievously devoid of independence. Poles still keep Báthori's cult alive and hold on to his memory, and his tomb in the Mary Chapel of the Cathedral of Cracow is still greatly honored.*

The Bocskai crown—A Turkish work, early seventeenth century. *At the beginning of the 1600s, the Turkish court, waging war in distant Persia and torn by internal strife, gladly accepted and, apparently without being asked, helped István Bocskai (1557–1606), who had earlier belonged to the Habsburg faction, to oppose Vienna. After being chosen ruling prince by the Transylvanian diet or parliament at Marosszerda on February 21, 1605, he asked for a royal crown from Istanbul. After some hesitation, the sultan met his request. But by the time Grand Vizier Lalla Mehmed handed over the symbol of royalty, Bocskai was willing to accept it only as a gift. He remained a ruling prince because doing so did not cut the road to a possible compromise with Vienna. This was not the first or last decision that expressed the split personality characteristic of this period: a desire for maneuver bordering on the impossible.*

spiritual, religious division by any means. An unusual situation came about here. While it was not at all true in every case that everyone siding with Vienna was Catholic, and those siding with Transylvania were Protestant, the Principality of Transylvania itself, for instance, under Gábor Bethlen (1613–1629), presented a model of freedom of religion admired in and marveled at throughout Europe. The Turks, in turn, did not care very much about religious matters, and hardly pressed conversion to Mohammedanism; Christian priests functioned quite openly, and a large Jewish community, not Ashkenazi but Sephardic, existed in Buda. Religious intolerance and aggressive evangelizing under the aegis of a militant Counter-Reformation were confined to the Habsburg section of the country.

At the same time, Bethlen, tolerant at home and farsighted, fought very actively on the side of the Protestants on the international battlefields of the Thirty Years' War; on occasion he alone, it seemed, was successful on the frontlines, gaining breathing space for his German, English, Dutch, and Danish allies. (It was in his armies that that typical Hungarian light cavalry, the Hussars, emerged, which then also became an accepted branch of the military in foreign countries, for example, in France.)

About this time, the wandering of Hungarian students from university to university was particularly widespread, and the children of serfs were able to study beside the offspring of the nobility. While earlier we came across Hungarian names in the account books of Italian and then Cracow and Danzig (Gdansk) universities, now they could be also found on those of universities in Germany, Holland, and England (at Cambridge and Oxford). Meanwhile, Gábor Bethlen founded his own college at Nagyszombat (Trnava).

The Rákóczi dynasty was very successful in developing culture, particularly education, but less so in the military

and diplomatic field when ruling the Transylvanian Principality. Among them, György Rákóczi II (1648–1660), blinded by the example of István Báthory, began an unsuccessful battle for the Polish throne. For this, the sultan, letting his Tatar auxiliaries loose on him, taught him a grave lesson. Afterwards, drained of blood and crippled, the Transylvanian Principality, which was not only the defensive bastion of Hungarian aspirations to that time but also the place whose intellectual attainments radiated throughout Central Europe, lost its earlier role.

The Turks gradually extended their occupation of the country's middle region and reinforced it militarily. Though border fortresses existed earlier and would be found again later, the century and a half contemporaneous with the occupation of Buda embraced the period that came to be known as the Wars of the Border Fortresses. Located on the shifting boundaries of the Turkish and Royal Hungarian territories—at times wedged together like sawteeth—the border fortresses faced each other crammed with soldiers who were badly paid and barely held in check by distant company officers, who were reduced to looting, longed for military fame, and were fiery-tempered. The age was filled with breaches of peace, arbitrary raids, and romantic single combat: usually, neither war nor peace existed, sometimes easygoing, sometimes bloody and merciless showdowns occurred between defenders in the border fortresses and the Turks occupying the countryside.

Thus the people under foreign occupation lived in a hopeless situation, where they had not already been hauled off or had not escaped. Major campaigns decimated them, minor ones afflicted them; marauding soldiers often preyed upon their cattle; in the interest of repairing the damaged fortresses, they had to serve as thralls on both sides. True, the Turks allowed them to keep their prossessions and generally taxed them so that they would have some means left; after all, they had to have something to pay their taxes with on the morrow. They remained under a vestigial Hungarian administration; it was supplemented rather than supplanted by a Turkish administration and judicature. In the meantime, they also had to pay taxes to Hungarian landowners who had escaped from the occupied territory but showed up one after the other to collect the tax.

Nevertheless, the occupied part of the country was not crippled entirely. In the Alföld, the settlement system underwent realignment: the population of smaller settlements withdrew into market towns, or boroughs, surrounded by large uninhabited land. These towns achieved some measure of peace and independence by paying taxes jointly. And the export to the west of cattle raised in the open Alföld, if not undisturbed, continued unbroken. The herds were driven on foot from the Turkish section of Hungary to Austrian, German, and Italian cities; meanwhile, the sultan's deputies were content with the customs collected at crossings on the rivers Tisza and Danube; traders even achieved tariff reductions by bribing customs officials.

The Hungarian tourist is dumbfounded by the Turkey of today: awareness of the ethnic relationship between Turks and Hungarians is much more alive there than in Hungary. Turks consider the time after Mohács, the reign of Suleiman the Magnificent, to be their country's most glorious period, the time when their boundaries stretched the farthest. "Then," they say to us, "we ruled Hungary together, didn't we!" We view the situation differently. But the darkly painted picture of the Turkish occupation is not tenable either. The terrible destruction Hungary suffered can be put rather at the beginning and the end of the period, the times when the battles raged most fiercely. In the time between, the Turks' arrangements for a long-lasting stay were sensible. The tax rolls testify to good management. The bulk of the non-military buildings in Hungarian territories under Turkish rule were either religious—*türbe* (sepulchral chapels), *djami* (mosques), and minarets (towers attached to mosques)—or inns, baths, wells, and fountains. (It is worth mentioning that quite a few members of the highest leadership of the Ottoman state came, in time, from Hungarian children who were kidnapped and raised in a Janissary school.) The real standstill was caused by

Gábor Bethlen among his scholars—A painting by Géza Dósa (1846–1871), 1869. *The Transylvanian prince, born into the lesser nobility and also Hungarian king for a short time, is the most brilliant and most depressing example of that play-acting and political schizophrenia that forced Hungarian monarchs to depend on Turkish assistance in their struggle against the Habsburgs. As prince, he was cultured and farsighted, a good organizer of the economy who, however, wearing away between "two pagans for one country"—and also weighed down by his unfortunate personal life—left, in the end, hardly anything completed behind. Usually, he started off with vigor but his endeavors petered out and left behind no state structure that would endure. His character later became the basis for all sorts of depictions containing "mixed signals" and hidden or explicit allegories.*

57

Zrínyi's attempt to break out—A painting by Bertalan Székely (1835–1910), 1876. *The Zrínyis, partially of Croatian descent, bilingual, and owning estates in the Adriatic region as well as in Transdanubia (Western Hungary) were leading representatives in the wars against the Turks and for independence from Vienna for generations. Particularly significant was their interest in the through-traffic of cattle raised in the Alföld being driven on foot to markets in Italian and German cities. The essentially suicidal action of Miklós Zrínyi (1508?–1566), the surviving defenders' attempt to break out instead of capitulating, belongs among the most romantic and heroic military and defensive acts in world history. An epic,* Sziget Disaster, *by his great-grandson, the poet Miklós Zrínyi (1620–1664), perpetuates the memory of the "Hero of Szigetvár."*

the fact that the nation stepped out of the main current of European development for a century and a half to two centuries—this interim, in part, forever unrecoverable—and that many places of the country had to be repopulated with foreign settlers, thus significantly altering its ethnic character.

Arriving now at the third part of the country, the royal or the Habsburg third, the region of Upper Hungary, extracted a measure of profit, even though it was exposed to the struggles between Transylvania and Vienna and changed masters several times; for example, it benefited from the fact that many merchants traveled through this region to avoid the Turks. Western Transdanubia and Croatia were, on the other hand, borderlands, and they served as terrains and scenes for deployment in countless battles. True, Vienna—and this was no small disappointment to those who hoped the Habsburgs would act against the Turks—embroiled in other wars, entered into several disgraceful peace agreements with the sultan to protect its rear. But these agreements were fragile, and the interests of the Hungarian and Croatian nobles also thwarted them. The high command in Vienna paid the Hungarian troops

in the border fortresses especially poorly; it frequently sent to Hungary unreliable and pillaging merecenaries who were worse than the occupying Turks themselves.

We have mentioned different kinds of schizophrenia. Let us take one more splendid example, the case of two Hungarian nobles, a certain Maylád and a certain Nádasdy. "Maylád himself sided with King Ferdinand's faction, but in Transylvania, where his estates lay, this faction was driven back sharply, and it became apparent to everyone that Ferdinand's rule could not take root there. So, to hold on to his estates, Maylád wanted to support Szapolyai. The matter was quite different with Nádasdy, who was supporting Szapolyai at the moment. He was preparing to take a wife, and the estates of his betrothed, the immensely wealthy Orsolya of Kanizsa, lay in Western Hungary, in Ferdinand's part of the country. His interests dictated that he returned to the Habsburg camp. And the two nobles actually agreed at Berzence that Maylád would help Nádasdy cross over to Ferdinand's side, while Nádasdy would facilitate Maylád's switching over to Szapolyai..." Oh well, that is how things went...

And if, having broken the chronology, we have already returned to the 1500s, let us state that one of the most tragic episodes in Hungary's war history is linked to the year 1566. Its hero was a Croatian–Hungarian scion of the wealthy Zrínyi family which possessed huge estates from Transdanubia to the Adriatic: Miklós Zrínyi (the general, to distinguish him from his greatgrandson, the poet of the same name who, however, was also a noted soldier and as a writer not only penned verses but was also a superb author of military theory).

Miklós Zrínyi, under siege in the fortress at Szigetvár, which was surrounded by marshes, delayed from August 6 to September 8, 1566, the armies of the victor at Mohács,

Suleiman the Magnificent, who was heading for Vienna. At the end of the siege, the sultan himself died in his camp, though his leaders, keeping his death a secret from the army, ordered a last assault – supposedly, with the sultan "watching" the battle from his open tent fully dressed and seated on a throne. In this hopeless situation, Zrínyi burst from the fortress with the few remaining survivors without any hope of breaking out of the blockade. They all perished. But the Turks did not reach Vienna. At Győr, a major force of Austrian troops, standing guard with weapons at their sides, marched off as if they had carried out their duties well.

It is perhaps proper to single out precisely this pyrrhic victory from among the numerous deeds of the border fortresses. Of course, it is also certainly worth mentioning the heroic defense of Eger in 1552, when István Dobó, commander of the castle, drove from its walls a Turkish

The Császár Baths—The cupolas of a Turkish steam bath.
The beginnings of the bath culture using the thermal waters in Buda can be traced back to Neolithic times or even beyond. The advanced state of Aquincum's bathing life in the Roman period is quite obvious—at a place where thermal springs bubble up through the fissures in the limestone at every step at the base of the hills on the right bank of the Danube. A tradition holds that this is what drew Attila to winter among the ruins at Aquincum. Be that as it may, bath culture was continuous from the time of the Árpáds on.
It was natural, therefore, that because the Mohammedan religion prescribed the obligation to wash oneself clean, the Turks, who cultivated their bath culture everywhere and to whom the building of inns, baths, and places of worship was equally a kindly act—being proof of piety serving public welfare in the eyes of Allah—located their own baths on the long-known warm-water mineral springs in Buda. Apparently, today's Császár Baths were called by them the Veli bey baths. According to a surviving commemorative tablet, it was built in 1571–72 by the Bosnian-born Sokollu Mustapha, Pasha of Buda, the greatest Maecenas during the Turkish rule of Hungary.

army of 150 thousand with two thousand of his troops and the inhabitants of the city and its environs. But then, how shall we treat the second siege of Eger in 1596 when the Turks gained an easy victory?

On the basis of the first defense of Eger, the deed at Szigetvár, and similar sacred bursts of activity, Hungarian public opinion holds that—"for one nation between two pagans"—the obdurate and self-sacrificing battles at the Hungarian border fortresses impeded the further expansion of the Turks through Vienna and the Vienna Basin to the interior of Europe. However, let us also look at the dates: they can be decisive. On most occasions the Turks, when they came to Hungary with a combat-worthy main force, reached the southern border—the line of the River Drava and there Eszék (Osijek, the ancient Mursia, where the Romans had already built a bridge)—only at the end of July and in August. They had, thus, two months for battle, if any, and then, whether they wanted to or not, whether victorious or not, they had to return to their homeland. Perhaps, only once did the Turks actually manage to arrive below Vienna in mid-July.

The minaret at Eger. *After the first Turkish siege in 1552, Eger Castle, its military importance being recognized, was repaired and expanded for decades. In 1596, however, when Sultan Mohammed II himself arrived at its walls, it was not Hungarian guards who defended the castle but foreign mercenaries, who, unable to withstand a siege lasting barely a few weeks and considerably less aggressive than the one in 1552, forced their commander to request free passage for them. So Eger was lost. Eger is one of those Hungarian cities where the 91 years of Turkish domination left the heaviest traces. Although not many architectural remains from this time are found today—other than baths and a single intact minaret, the one found farthest north—we must all the more keep in mind what did not survive after the century of the crescent. Eighteenth-century reconstruction gave a predominantly Baroque character to the older sections of today's Eger.*

59

HEY, THÖKÖLY AND RÁKÓCZI

By this time the Turks had been the masters in Buda for a century and a half. What was the situation elsewhere in the 1680s? In England, a bloodless revolution took place against James II of the Catholic faction, and William of Orange was summoned from Holland to succeed him. In France, it was the golden age of the reign of Louis XIV, the Sun King. On the Iberian Peninsula, Portugal had recently regained its independence; the disarray around the Spanish throne quickly swept across all Europe in the bloody War of the Spanish Succession. Italy and Scandinavia were forced into the roles of supernumeraries. The Dutch were the newest beneficiaries of world commerce. On German soil, there was no trace of centralized power; Prussia admitted masses of French Huguenots. In Russia, the czarevitch, later Peter (the Great) I, the "western" reformer czar, marched toward power with youthful zeal; Cossack "pioneers" reached the River Amur in Eastern Siberia, where they clashed with the Chinese advancing to the west.

At the beginning of the 1680s, Hungary was no longer divided into three parts but into four. The fourth part was Imre Thököly's principality. Two forces were instrumental in the establishment of the latter: one was a peculiar power constellation, the complex and manifold collision between Viennese, Turkish, and Transylvanian aims and actions in the Carpathian Basin, and the other a capable individual who was successful both as a person and a soldier, though, in the end, his fate dragged him more than once as a victim to the wrong side.

In 1683, things "worked out" exceptionally well for the Turks: they had already reached Vienna in mid-July. The two Hungarian princes, Mihály Apafi of Transylvania and Thököly of Upper Hungary (his soldiers called themselves *kuruc*, after Dózsa's rebels who fought under the Sign of the Cross in 1514, although the word might be of Turkish origin), were both present—they had to be—in the camp of the besiegers, the Turks. However, by this time, the situation of the Ottoman Empire was shaky. Europe joined forces, and the united Polish, Bavarian, Saxon, and Austrian armies under the leadership of John Sobieski, the Polish king, raised the siege of Vienna and crushed the sultan's army.

During succeeding years, which were filled with chaotic wars in the Carpathian Basin, the Christian coalition continually gained the upper hand. The Turks, who three years before were besieging Vienna, were in 1686 unable to hold Buda against the regular army of liberation, reinforced by volunteers. The commander of the fortress, Abdurrahman Pasha, fell in a dogged battle. Of the 65 thousand soldiers of the victorious Prince Charles of Lorraine, every fourth one was Hungarian.

When in 1986, on the three hundredth anniversary of the successful siege of Buda Castle, the participants in an international conference of historians in Budapest debated the military events of 1686 and their background, the general opinion was that though the Christian forces had waged the military operations that forced the Ottoman Empire back to the Balkans not out of devotion to the Hungarians but in the obvious interest of all Europe, the recapture of Buda during their campaign was decisive and far-reaching in its effect: after all, from this time on, the Turks were increasingly on the defensive. This military victory made it possible for Hungary to be a part of Europe again after a century and a half, and the clogged arteries of development again opened for the nation.

Yes, but how did it come about? Hungarian military forces were present in the ranks of the liberators, but another, greater share served as Turkish vassals. Their existence threatened, the two small national principalities became the anemic satellites of the Ottoman crescent. Thököly's principality quickly crumbled, and though Transylvania's independence survived formally, it did not amount to much either under the waning Turkish crescent or between the claws of the two-headed eagle, the ambitious Habsburg predatory bird.

The complete liberation of the country would still require many more years, but the fate of the Turkish occupation of Hungary was already sealed. However, a decision about Hungary was also made—in Vienna. The Hungary cleared of Turkish rear guards became part of the Austrian Empire by right of armed conquest. It was a two-faced development... Vienna quickly prepared its plans. Within their compass, certain measures should have denoted progress: reducing the rights of the nobility, increasing those of the cities, and modernizing the executive administration and the control of trade. But they all bore the marks of royal absolutism.

From this point on, Hungarian efforts to achieve national independence became entangled with retrograde elements for about two centuries. Modernization measures that curtailed the nation's rights were often begun or would have been begun, and for this reason they were strenuously opposed. At this time, of course, the nation's body politic, conforming to prevailing conception of rights, included only the privileged classes: the nobility and the groups not formally of the nobility but possessing similar legal status.

Meanwhile, the government and the large landowners invited foreigners to settle in the regions depopulated by frequent military operations: Germans, Southern Slavs, and Northern Slavs. Even today, the rows of villages established by the state administration are easily identifiable through the symmetrical networks of streets that were laid out by military engineers. The spontaneous migration of people was also large. Slovakians, Ruthenians (Carpatho-Ukrainians), and Rumanian forest dwellers and shepherds moved down mainly from the impoverished valleys of the Carpathians into the interior of the basin. A large segment of the inhabitants in the growing cities were also foreigners: Germans, Serbians, Bohemians, Moravians, and others. In Pest, now liberated from

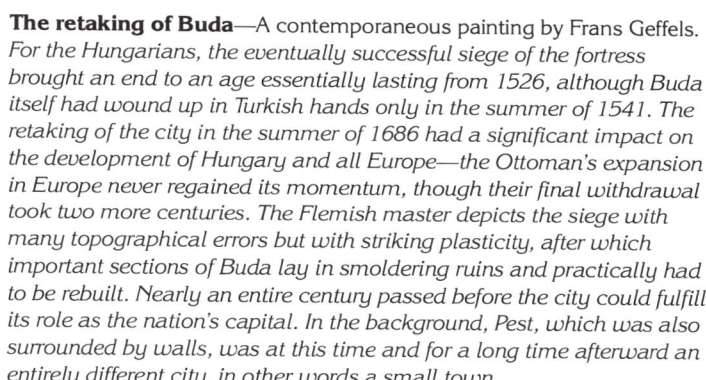

The retaking of Buda—A contemporaneous painting by Frans Geffels. *For the Hungarians, the eventually successful siege of the fortress brought an end to an age essentially lasting from 1526, although Buda itself had wound up in Turkish hands only in the summer of 1541. The retaking of the city in the summer of 1686 had a significant impact on the development of Hungary and all Europe—the Ottoman's expansion in Europe never regained its momentum, though their final withdrawal took two more centuries. The Flemish master depicts the siege with many topographical errors but with striking plasticity, after which important sections of Buda lay in smoldering ruins and practically had to be rebuilt. Nearly an entire century passed before the city could fulfill its role as the nation's capital. In the background, Pest, which was also surrounded by walls, was at this time and for a long time afterward an entirely different city, in other words a small town.*

the Turks, the Hungarian language was seldom heard during the first decades. Although Jewish communities were, to this point, mostly small and with their population and fate variable, they later gained strength and thrived. A good portion of the Sephardic Jews fled or perished with the Turks (after all, they had arrived with them), later waves of Ashkenazis followed each other from Moravia, Vienna, and then, in growing numbers from, the Ukraine, the border region of Ukraine–Poland–Lithuania, and Galicia through Carpathian passes to become the beneficiaries and leading promoters of modernization, chiefly of commercial and financial enterprises. Thus modernization activities serving the self-interest of Austria's absolute monarchy, but not always against Hungarian interests, set not only Vienna against the miserly nobility but also Hungarians against the nationalities in the Carpathian Basin and the strata entering the middle class, whom they looked upon as "foreigners."

It was at this time that the Baroque aspect of Hungary was established, which the cores of our cities and the majority of the baronial manor houses and the nobility's country seats display even today. Though the builders of Protestant churches could not shake off the influence of this style either, the chief inspirer and patron of the triumphant Baroque was the Counter-Reformation, whose vigorous development started after the division of the country into three parts and whose Austrian pontifical advocates found among the Hungarians such a zealous and educated promoter as Péter Pázmány, the Archbishop of Esztergom, a passionate and pungent preacher who reconverted to Catholicism in his student years.

Only today do we find out how many town houses and village churches turn out to be from the Romanesque or Gothic period under the plaster knocked off the main walls during renovation, though only the interiors of these churches could be converted into the Baroque style. And when we now uncover one Romanesque or Gothic feature after the other, we can measure the enormous magnitude of the reconstruction and remodeling that occurred after the Turkish period as well as in the nineteenth century.

But we have run a bit ahead in time. We must return to the *kuruc* movement, to the turn of the seventeenth and eighteenth centuries. After the recapture of Buda, Imre Thököly lost his principality and became a tragic figure: a pitiful tool, a Balkan pillager in the service of the Turks. At the end of his life, he lived in peaceful exile in Asia Minor. In Hungary, meanwhile, the youngest offspring of the Rákóczi family, Ferenc, became the prisoner of his own destiny.

Though he was to become the fifth prince of Transylvania in his family, the star of the young Rákóczi indicated, at first, something different. His father, Ferenc Rákóczi I, despite gaining the title of prince, could never exercise his supremacy; he died young. His widow bound her fate to Imre Thököly, and Ferenc accompanied his stepfather on military expeditions while a mere boy. He was

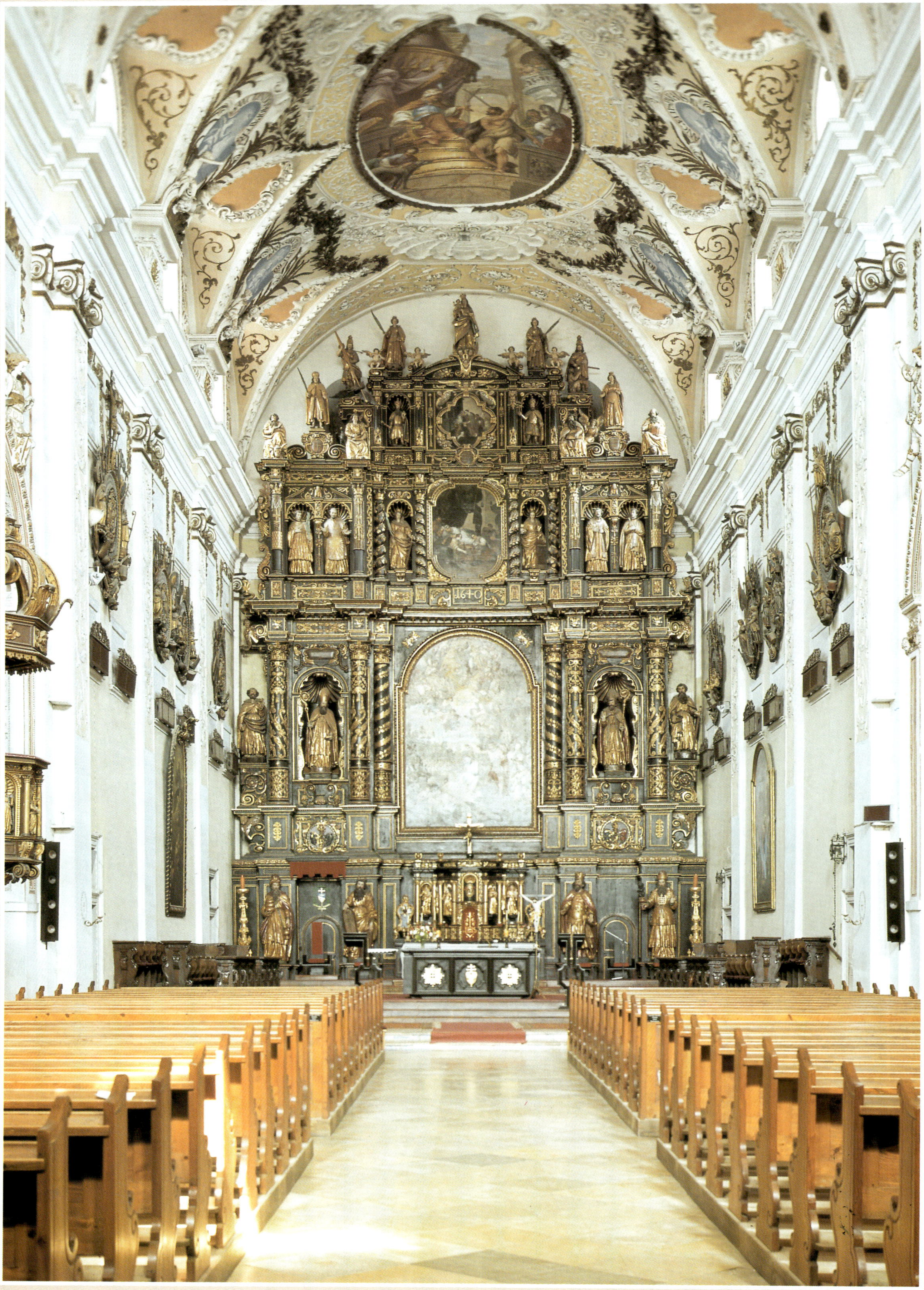

Péter Pázmány—A contemporaneous painting by an unknown artist. *Pázmány (1570–1637) was the chief figure of the Hungarian Counter-Reformation, a cardinal, the Archbishop of Esztergom, and originally a member of the Jesuit Order. His role in reconverting the nation's leading families was enormous—which also included the masses under their influence. In his sermons, he deliberately aimed at a popular vernacular so that many could understand them. Despite his activities in the Habsburg faction and in the restoration of Catholicism, he is deserving of respect. His aspirations had an inner trustworthiness throughout. As a Maecenas, he also furthered the access to culture of all Hungarians.*

Ferenc Rákóczi II—A painting by Ádám Mányoki (1673–1757), 1708. *This splendid portrait presents the self-confident ruling prince: the bold aristocrat, the handsome and pleasure-seeking man, at a time when the outcome of the rebellion still seemed to be very hopeful. That Rákóczi who, since his marriage broke up quickly and his wife became an Austrian hostage, fell lastingly in love with Polish Duchess Lubomirski during his exile. According to our well-founded suspicions, when he found time during the stressful conditions of the War of Independence to leave his court at Sárospatak to go hunting for a few days, he rode, in fact, across the Carpathians to his ladylove. We have no authentic portrait of the aged, exiled Rákóczi who became an ascetic in Rodosto (today: Tekirdag, Turkey) and immersed himself in theological analysis with an agonized cast of mind.*

The interior of the Jesuits' University Church at Nagyszombat. *Nagyszombat's emergence from the status of a small town can be attributed to the fact that when Esztergom was taken over by the Turks in 1543, the Esztergom archbishopric and chapter moved there (and remained there until 1820). Thus it was there that one of the chief centers operated by Austrian and Hungarian Jesuits first came into existence; then, under the impetus of the Counter-Reformation, Archbishop Péter Pázmány established first a seminary and then a university in 1635, with faculties in theology and philosophy. After Joseph II dissolved the Jesuit Order, the university was moved to Buda and then to Pest; it is the direct legal predecessor of the Budapest University of Arts and Sciences, which later took the name of Péter Pázmány and still later that of Loránd Eötvös.*

also present when his mother, Ilona Zrínyi, withstood the siege of the castle at Munkács by the Austrian Imperial forces for three years (1685–1688). Finally surrendering the castle—it is enough to refer to the dates to understand why—the courageous woman wound up in an Austrian cloister, from where her husband ransomed her for a captured Imperial general.

The boy's Jesuit tutors wanted him to become a monk—his million hectares of land would serve the Order well—but he, though deeply religious, freed himself from Austrian-Jesuit guardianship as soon as he reached maturity. Marrying quickly, he returned to Upper Hungary in 1694 and promptly became the hope of the Hungarian national resistance; he, however, fled from every political commitment. In 1697, he was called upon to become the leader of a peasant uprising that experienced initial success in the Hegyalja region. He was so terrified by the appeal that he rushed straight to Vienna. Still, the terrible state of the country just liberated from the Turks and the brutal reprisals against the recurring popular upheavals so upset him that he gradually altered his attitude.

The ancestry of one branch of his family tree consisted of the princes of Transylvania, which was extolled as the citadel of Protestantism, though he himself was a child of the Counter-Reformation (his father became a Catholic); on his mother's side, his great grandfather was the hero of Szigetvár, his uncle the poet Miklós Zrínyi; his grandfather, Péter Zrínyi, was called to Vienna with false promises and ended up under an executioner's axe. In 1701, when the War of the Spanish Succession, which had just broken out, made the circumstances propitious, he sent out feelers toward Paris. By that time he was ready for a leadership role. The ever suspicious Vienna pounced on him triumphantly. He was carried off, a death penalty threatened him, and he was able to escape from prison only through a romantic ruse and at the sacrifice of his

rescuer's life. He prepared to return to his native land from Poland with mercenary troops, but the leaders of a popular rebellion that had flared up again came for him. The country was soon aflame from east to west. The light cavalry of the *kuruc* captains, now flying Rákóczi's flag and proclaiming his call for recruits, raced as far as Vienna, striking blow after blow at the scattered Imperial forces (whose *labanc* appellation may have its roots in the word "lance").

Ferenc Rákóczi II was one of the most flawless and farsighted figures in our history. But was he really the prisoner of his own destiny? He was its master instead. He was the pampered scion of the aristocracy; he was zealous in his religion; he was well-read and a keenly inquisitive "intellectual," or if this term is anachronistic, then he was its prototype. He was a superb organizer. But it was also characteristic of him that even at the peak of the independence movement, he devoted only one or two days a week to the affairs of state and to the operational leadership of the war. He spent the remaining days at prayer, at increasing his erudition, at the hunt, or—the hunt serving as a pretext—with his paramour; but let it be said in his justification that his wife and two little sons were Austrian hostages and he was unable to free them.

The prince, whom, on the basis of the early military successes of the *kuruc* movement, first the Transylvanian and then the Hungarian Estates chose to be ruler, described the Hungary of his times with astonishing maturity. His writings, rich with Christian meditations, provide a profound and astute analysis of class relations and the obstacles in the way of his struggle posed by social backwardness and the country's inadequate development. By combining the incomes of the state and his own estates, he created an effective war economy. Its monetary system could function on a small margin, but, of course, only so long as it had the backing of gold reserves produced by victorious battles.

Mention should be made of the declining income from Hungarian mines. The huge quantity of gold and silver pouring in from overseas transformed the market in precious metals. The richest lodes near the surface were exhausted in Upper Hungary; treasure had to be dug from ever deeper down. Breakthroughs in mining technology could not offset this fact, something that could be observed, for example, in Selmecbánya (Banská Štiavnica); it was here that the first mining academy in the world was founded in 1721.

The new "gold standard" of the economy in the Rákóczi period was Tokay wine. It became famous during the Turkish occupation, mainly through the increased

The design of the mine hill at Úrvölgy—An eighteenth-century table decoration. *Research on the rich and colorful history of Hungarian mines and mining is hampered today by the fact that most centers of early Hungarian mining are now located outside the nation's borders, in Transylvania and former parts of Upper Hungary. Thus that history comes to light only slowly: the still completely manual operation with the chisel and hot-and-cold splitting, the increasing mechanization utilizing mainly water power, the determination of locations by means of a magnetic needle, and the details of the period after blasting in mines with gunpowder was introduced. The miners were everywhere predominantly of foreign origin, and so were often the mine owners themselves as well; and later the treasury of the mines, through the Habsburg monarchs, was also in foreign hands. Still, all this forms an integral part of the economic story and history of Hungary through the economic circumstances under which the exploitation of the mines was carried out and through the assimilation of no small portion of the miners.*

production of the distinctive *aszú*. However, "the king of wines, the wine of kings"—according to tradition, it was Rákóczi's ally, Louis XIV, who gave this flattering name to Tokay wine—had only begun its triumphal march. The prince himself gave Tokay wine made from his own grapes mainly as gifts, providing his diplomats with a supply so that they would "oil" their negotiating partners. He laid the foundation for its future successful export; the czar's court and wealthy Russian boyars soon joined the traditional purchasers, Polish and Baltic barons; for himself, however, he obtained only temporary and moral profit.

Rákóczi was incapable of overcoming two difficulties. He established good connections with two opposite poles in Europe, Louis XIV and Peter the Great, but, as soon as the international situation took a turn, neither French nor Russian interest was linked to having a Hungarian princeling "annoy" Vienna. On the other hand, the rebellious poor, the barefooted infantry armed with scythes and axes, the Haiduks, and the serf soldiers fighting for their liberation gave the *kuruc* army its real strength. Rákóczi recognized this fact—and he tried to secure its acceptance. But he also needed the support of lords and nobles—he was, after all, their prince—though their interests dictated something else. And the time had not yet come when the common people could prevail.

A war of varying success went on from 1703 to 1711. In part, Hungarians opposed Hungarians: among the *labanc*, the number of Hungarians attracted or forced to the side of Vienna was not small. And for the *kuruc*, they spent the last couple of years in hounded flight. Treachery

65

Scene of a battle between the Kuruc and the Labanc—A painting by an unknown artist. *In a country bled to death "between two pagans" at the time of the Turks, the Thököly uprising and Rákóczi's War of Independence extended continual warfare for decades. Battles never ceased in the entire Carpathian Basin; they surged back and forth endlessly, often like "blitzkriegs," and were fought by raiding parties of light cavalry, with the ransom and destruction inherent in them. Ferenc Rákóczi II attempted, though, to vitalize the economy by reforming the currency—by introducing copper coins from necessity—and by making his soldiers buy goods instead of simply requisitioning them. Still, the arrival of either warring side was often a scourge to inhabitants. The insurgents, who were called the Kuruc, were by no means all of Hungarian nationality, Ruthenian participation was especially significant—on the other hand, a large number of Hungarian field officers, commissioned officers, and enlisted men fought on the side of the Imperials, who were called the Labanc. The opposing sides thus often consisted of former comrades-in-arms and personal acquaintances. At times, all this was cordial; at other times, it lent a tragic hue to the battles, and it partly explained the frequent changing of flags: the treachery and desertion occurring back and forth between the two armies.*

disrupted their ranks, plagues decimated them, and the serfs were absent from and needed at the nobles' estates.

Rákóczi was forced into exile. He did not accept the amnesty offered—and German ducal rank. He went to Poland; he also met with Czar Peter the Great; then he lived in France, sometimes like an exotic and romantic figure at the Sun King's court, sometimes like a monk in the seclusion of the cloister.

The peace negotiations which led to the *kuruc* laying down their arms were conducted by the commander-in-chief, Baron Sándor Károlyi, whom the emperor then rewarded with enormous estates (taken from Rákóczi's) and the rank of count. For this, a curse

burdened his name—Hungarian public opinion considered him unequivocally a traitor for nearly three hundred years. However, according to more recent research findings and historical perceptions, Károlyi—with Rákóczi's knowledge to boot—reached an optimal agreement: in large part, the peace agreement provided what the rebels could not achieve on the battlefield. Of course, this was not more than the restoration of that legal state of Hungary and Transylvania that Vienna had revoked by martial law after 1686. The effort to gain national independence—again and not for the last time—proved illusory. However, in addition to the essentially complete amnesty—moral and material—the freedom of religion in Hungary was restored, and the Haiduks retained their privileges.

In 1717, Rákóczi went to Turkey, hoping to gain the sultan's support. But the international situation did not turn to his advantage at this time either. A little town on the shore of the Sea of Marmora, Rodosto, was designated as his abode (its Turkish name is Tekirdag). He lived there until his death, with a few remaining supporters, on a small pension from the sultan. One of his sons joined him for a couple of years; his wife looked him up once but only stayed for a short time—they had long been estranged. He studied theology and wrote treatises; he hunted and, for diversion, he passed his time with cabinetwork.

In 1906, the Hungarian nation solemnly brought his remains and those of his mother home to Kassa (Košice); the remains of Imre Thököly were taken to Késmárk (Kežmarok) at the same time. Rákóczi's house in Rodosto—a memorial museum today—is, like his grave in Kassa, a place of pilgrimage for Hungarians, whose admiration for him continues undiminished to the present day.

MARIA WITH A CROWN, JOSEPH WITH A HAT

"Let others make war; you, happy Austria, make marriages! To others Mars gives countries, to you Venus"—whoever may have carved the Latin original of this epigram, keen and not devoid of envy, this much is certain: the House of Habsburg, interested in and around many European thrones, could be most thankful for its dynastic ties, its adroit marriages.

In the early 1700s, Charles Habsburg was sitting on the wobbly Spanish throne, and when his elder brother died in 1711, he was urgently summoned to Vienna. This haste also had a role in the lenient provisions of the peace treaty concluded with the *kuruc*. With this Charles, who was III in Hungary and VI as emperor of the Holy Roman Empire, the male line of the once prolific branch of the House of Habsburg died out. In the twilight of his life, Charles was greatly troubled by this prospect. He urged rival, throne-hungry dynasties and all other interested parties to accept the line of succession through the female line of his family. Apparently, success crowned his efforts. Charles balanced with agreements and legal formulas whatever the Habsburgs did not bring off through matrimony. At least he closed his eyes in 1740 with an awareness of his achievement.

At the time, his daughter, Maria Theresa, was twenty-three, a blossoming young woman, awaiting the birth of her child. After Charles's death, contrary to every agreement and promise, almost everyone rejected succession through the female line; indeed, immediate attacks began to dismember the Habsburg Empire. It finally became clear that the peaceful deals were null and void, though by this time Maria Theresa had given birth to her first male child. In 1741, this barely six-month-old child was present in the parliament in Pozsony (Bratislava) when his mother asked the Hungarian Estates of the Realm to protect the throne. Many of the members had waged battle with Thököly and Rákóczi when young.

In times past, mention was often made of the generosity and chivalrous virtues of the gallant Hungarians on the basis of Maria's and the infant Joseph's dramatic act in Pozsony may have contained some subjective elements. Still, that was not the essential point. When at this parliamentary session the Estates pledged "our lives and our blood" in acclamation to rescue the Habsburg royalty that was looked upon with hostility not so very long ago, and they voted to supply military and financial assistance, the Hungarian nobility was acknowledging

the consummation of the 1711 peace agreement. On the basis of this treaty, the landowners' benefits were not curtailed, as a matter of fact they were strengthened. By then, the Vienna court was attempting to govern *with* them, not against them.

Simultaneously, because of the security based on law, the beginning of a relatively peaceful period, the momentum of reconstruction and its need for manpower, and commercial and economic developments (although restrictions of the classes without rights, particularly the serfs, remained, even increased somewhat; after all, Hungarian law proclaimed a permanent serfdom)—the period after the age of the *kuruc* brought a greater or lesser relief to the majority of the population and prosperity to the entire country. It was worth being grateful for this. And Maria Theresa not only made requests, she provided an antithesis: a wider international field of play within Hungarian independence. Her gestures to win over the Hungarians had, in part a real value and in part, a prestigious character. It was of unquestionable practical significance that from this time on, Vienna did not directly control Transylvania and other border regions; instead, by placing them under the authority of the Hungarian crown, the court controlled them indirectly.

In the War of Austrian Succession, which lasted for

67

Count Lipót Pálffy (1716–1773), a captain of the guards (in uniform). *The Hungarian Noble Guards, established by Maria Theresa, whose rather light duty tied its members mostly to Vienna, served as an educational institution for many Hungarian youths, principally at the end of the eighteenth century. From these young soldiers emerged many field officers in regular military service, several diplomats, and, oppositely, the group of Hungarian Guardsman Writers, whose most widely known member was György Bessenyei (1747–1811).*

Vitam et sanguinem! Our life and our blood!—A painting on a clock face, nineteenth century. *This is the famous "great scene at Pozsony," September 1741, which was endlessly narrated, described, painted, and mainly commented upon, but which never took place, at least not as it is shown here. It was earlier, on September 11, that the Hungarian Estates of the Realm pledged their loyalty to the young Maria Theresa with the above public acclamation—or something resembling it but, in any case, in the Latin language—while the empress and queen had the little heir to the throne brought to her only later, and presented him to members gathered at a parliamentary session on September 21. Since it is, after all, a part of the same tradition, let us add that those who shouted "Our life and our blood!" added loudly "But not our oats!" In any case, this much is true, that over and above the declaration of political loyalty, the not less urgently needed economic aid did not approach anything near the level of the common zeal.*

years—during which the Habsburg Empire did undergo some realignment but ultimately, its aggregate value was hardly impaired—Hungarian (and Croatian) hussar and infantry regiments decided the outcome of a whole series of battles. (Meanwhile, sometimes they had to fight against their own kind; after the *kuruc* period many became mercenaries seeking renown in the most diverse armies of Europe.)

And so Maria Theresa retained the Hungarian and Bohemian crowns and many of her titles and estates. At home, in Vienna, on the other hand, she could function only as the Archduchess of Austria. The prince-electors and Estates did not confer the crown of the Holy Roman Empire on women; and Charles VI never tried

to accomplish this either. The situation was extraordinary. Maria Theresa elevated her husband to the rank of honorary joint regent, the father of her increasing number of children, Francis of Lorraine, who was only Grand Duke of Tuscany, a title which he had to renounce upon his marriage. In 1745, he became Emperor of the Holy Roman Empire. In the Burg, however, for all practical purposes, it was his wife, increasingly strong-willed but otherwise good-natured, family-loving, and warmhearted, who issued the commands: absolutistic but also listening to a few outstanding liberal advisers, she made the decisions and governed; in short, she ruled.

With two faces. In principle, she was opposed to the ideas of the Enlightenment gaining ground at the time, but still, in practice, she implemented them in some matters. Previous dynasties and especially the ever stubborn Habsburgs, who believed they were anointed by God, viewed their subjects as mere living objects whose only legitimate destiny was to serve their rulers, but her father, Charles VI, manifested certain feelings of responsibility, while Maria Theresa accepted a dual relationship and commitment. She believed she was responsible for the peoples whom God placed under her crown for their own good, for their physical and spiritual well-being.

She seemed to treat the Hungarians favorably, from gratitude and by design. She founded schools and provided laws of education for them. She ordered Hungarian guardsmen to Vienna, whose members, from noble

families, not only served in the Burg in a colorful uniform and a cape of leopard skin, but also had the opportunity to improve their minds. It was an irony of fate that, on completion of their service, many officers of her guard returned to Hungary armed with the ideals of the Enlightenment, which the queen opposed in principle. The guardsmen writers of the eighteenth century represented a small chapter in the history of Hungarian literature.

In time, Maria Theresa secured the rights of the nobility without leaving the serfs completely defenseless; the fact that serfs could seek legal redress was a novelty. However, defining the norms of feudal services had on occasion an opposite effect; after all, there were landowners who previously had not demanded as much as the new law permitted; yet this, too, constituted a step toward restricting the autocracy of the nobles. Undoubtedly, industrial development enjoyed a great advantage in Bohemian and Austrian areas, while Hungary was forced to participate only as the supplier of raw materials in what was by now the "common market" of the Habsburg holdings lying mostly in Central Europe.

In the meantime, in addition to the traditional export of livestock, animal products—especially wool—and wine, the shipment of grain, almost entirely on waterways, slowly moved to the forefront. Its driving force was the fact that a more intensive agricultural economy had gained ground to the west of Hungary and that the Carpathian Basin supplied a grain of outstanding quality for bread—it was called "steely", or durum—and of great value in baking. Bread took on a better quality when this Hungarian durum wheat—the "corrective wheat"—was simply mixed with the soft wheat raised elsewhere. (The cultivation of "steely" wheat is a question of type, but its quality also depends on the time and conditions of the harvest: harvest time in the Alföld is generally drought-stricken, when the wheat continues to ripen to perfection uncut and then—until the age of the combine, which harvests and threshes

Eszterháza—A color etching by János Berkeny (1765?–1822). *Eszterháza's name has been Fertőd since 1950. The builder of the Baroque palace inclining to the Rococo was Prince Miklós (the Magnificent) Esterházy (1765–1833), who lived there in "the Hungarian Versailles" in a splendor surpassing that of royal courts. After his death, the center of the estate and household was moved closer to Vienna, to Kismarton (Eisenstadt, Austria).*

The Esterházy Madonna—A painting by Raffaello Santi (1483–1520). *This small-size masterpiece, presumably prepared in Rome about 1508, was a gift from the Vatican to the imperial court in Vienna; then it became a part of the Kaunitz collection, from which Miklós Esterházy purchased it. Anyone admiring the treasures of the Old Picture Gallery at the Budapest Museum of Fine Arts might think that this public museum acquired several old aristocratic collections mainly after 1945, perhaps through state confiscation. To the contrary, the Hungarian state bought the Esterházy collection back in 1871, and a series of subsequent smaller but also very valuable collections came under public ownership before 1945 through purchases or gifts. Aristocratic properties and thus art treasures were taken into public ownership only in exceptional cases.*

simultaneously—to dry stacked crosswise in ricks for weeks before threshing.)

Maria Theresa was the least clear-sighted in religious matters. But practicality did not allow her to fall into extremes here either. She partially withdrew her decrees restricting the Jews (it was in this period, however, that the characteristic German family names of Hungarian Jews originated; they were compelled to assume them at her orders). As for the Protestants, if she could not convert them, she tried to drive them from her realm toward Transylvania. Thus the traditional freedom of religious practices survived in Transylvania with such "extremes" as the Unitarians' success in almost eliminating God from their faith locally and as many of the Hungarian "Sabbatarians," followers of Jewish religious precepts for centuries, later becoming victims of Nazi persecution of the Jews.

After she stabilized her throne, the pressure of circumstances compelled Maria Theresa to found a Danubian Empire, where, after all, most of the dynasty's holdings were grouped. In this, her natural allies were the Hungarian aristocrats, who, through the storms of the preceding centuries, had been able to preserve much of their occasionally exorbitant wealth, and had, actually, been able to increase it. Now that commitments to the war against the Turks no longer burdened them, their mounting wealth manifested itself in the construction of country seats rivaling Versailles and the queen's Schönbrunn and in the amassing of riches among circles who steadily immersed themselves in a European aristocracy that hardly recognized national borders, intermarried indiscriminately, and assumed cosmopolitan traits. We should be pleased to find one aristocrat who spent at least a part of his domestic income at home or who eventually bequeathed his acquisitions to his homeland.

An example of the latter case was the Esterházy collection of paintings and art treasures, which was to form a basis for the Budapest Museum of Fine Arts and which was already substantial by this time. It was also to the Esterházy family's credit that Joseph Haydn served on their Hungarian estates for more than three decades; it was in Hungary that he composed and presented most of his works. Less praiseworthy was that Hungarian aristocrat who, when a prize for the person appearing in the most expensive costume at a Vienna ball was announced, attired himself in a painting of Correggio he had removed from its frame and cut into a dress. Legend also has it that when one of the Esterházys invited Maria Theresa for a sleigh ride and the weather unexpectedly turned mild, he had the road from Schönbrunn to Kismarton (Eisenstadt), a distance of a good forty kilometers, strewn with salt.

These two episodes are, perhaps, especially appropriate at this point: before the one that followed the death of Maria Theresa. The infant who, in 1741, had appeared with his mother in Pozsony ascended the throne as Joseph II (1780–1790). But did he actually ascend the throne of Hungary as well? He had been Holy Roman Emperor since his father's death in 1765. But by that time this title had lost so much of its importance that his powerful mother left it up to him to do whatever he chose with this rank. Still, Joseph's influence was slowly felt throughout the realm. This strange Habsburg was Hungary's king in a strange way. His ideas, which are called Josephinism after his name, represented an enlightened, yet extreme version of absolutism. Joseph II introduced a powerful centralism and governed by decree; he shattered every regional aspiration and feudal privilege in the name of his concept of a unified and effective empire. He dissolved the religious orders and appropriated their property.

Recognizing the strength of the Hungarian nobility's conservatism, he flauntingly refused to be crowned in Hungary; he had the crown carried off to Vienna and locked up. For this reason, he is called the king with a hat in Hungary. Passing judgment on this headstrong, yet Hamlet-like monarch has roused the emotions ever since his time. It is impossible to deny the boldness of his efforts

71

A portrait of Sámuel Teleki—A painting by János Márton Stock (1742–1800), 1787. *The special value of this portrait by the Saxon painter from Nagyszeben is that in addition to Transylvanian Chancellor Sámuel Teleki (1739–1822), it preserves in the background a likeness of Baron Sámuel (Bruhenthal) Brukenthal (1721–1803), the noted Saxon politician, Maria Theresa's adviser, and the governor of Transylvania who established an enormously valuable library and museum in Nagyszeben (Şibiu) with his vast wealth; it is the most outstanding institution of the Transylvanian Saxons. János Márton Stock himself was a restorer in this museum. A small statue of Joseph II appears as the third portrait in the picture. With their names or irrespective of them, the painting immortalizes personages who wanted to refashion Transylvania along the lines of Joseph II's reforms, those of enlightened absolutism. An ironic overtone is lent this painting by the fact that Brukenthal later resisted Joseph II's reforms, which also infringed on Saxon feudal privileges so strongly that the "king with the hat" relieved him of his high office.*

at modernization, his values outstripping those of his day. But he executed everything with grating callousness. He always considered himself so much wiser than anyone else that he could not brook interference or even listen to advice. And the forced Germanization of regions outside Austria deeply damaged whatever beneficial intention he had in mind.

Unsuccessful in his foreign policy and war against the Turks, Joseph II withdrew all his reforms on his deathbed, with the exception of his decree for religious tolerance and the one that alleviated the life of the serfs. Was he compelled to see the failures of his lifework? Did a Hamlet-like struggle with his own self overcome him? Or was he afraid that his successor would quash everything he had instituted? And therefore, he tried to save the savable?

HANG
THE KINGS!

O r behead them like the French? Belgium broke away from the Habsburg realm, and, although the dying king had withdrawn his decrees, Hungary also threatened to do the same. For this reason, the younger brother of Joseph II, Leopold II (1790–1792), hastily announced that he would follow his mother's path and not his brother's. A lengthy bargaining about the details of his course and the ways of dividing power commenced between the Estates and the monarch.

The Jacobin movement in Hungary, which ended in tragedy, was a part of this. Ignác Martinovics, a Franciscan friar, was the leader of a secret society faithful to the principles of the French Enlightenment but never able to win the masses over. This ardently capable and polymathic scholar and materialistic philosopher was an *agent provocateur*, a secret agent of Vienna. What did the court want from Martinovics? Nothing more than to exert pressure on the conservative aristocracy to take the wind out of the sails of a radicalism, made all the more dangerous because it was uncontrollable, through the sheer existence of the group he organized and recruited from a middle class longing for bourgeois liberty. And in addition, to "draw the badger out of the bushes", to establish the identity of the revolutionary, the seditious group. Though Martinovics was a figure full of ambition who indulged himself in double and triple games and gambled perilously, it still cannot be denied that, in his own blundering Machiavellian way he meant well. At times he deluded himself with the belief that he could induce the king to undertake reforms, at times with the idea that his undercover work was purely tactical and that he would ultimately have the upper hand. A split personality, he did not see the net he had woven for himself; he was even less able to retreat when his cause was fated to fail. And there was another change on the throne: the son of Leopold II, Francis I (1792–1836), was a decidedly retrograde ruler who immediately ended all ambiguity about the Hungarian Jacobin movement. He put its participants on trial and beheaded its leaders, with Martinovics in the fore. Four authors, the best of the Hungarian Enlightenment, were also among those given long prison sentences.

Leopold II had barely embarked on the war against revolutionary France; it was Francis I who deployed the troops. This is not the place to explore in detail how this war requiring so much Hungarian blood turned into the struggle against Napoleon, into an all European involvement. Perhaps it is enough to point out that Marie Antoinette, the French queen beheaded in Paris in 1793, was Maria Theresa's daughter; in touchingly naive letters, the mother warned her daughter about the frivolous life that undoubtedly had a role in the eruption of the French people's wrath. Barely seventeen years later, in 1810, the defeated and disgraced Francis I could save the savable only by giving his daughter, Marie Louise—thus Marie Antoinette's second cousin—in marriage to Napoleon,

whose first marriage had ended under tasteless circumstances. (...you, happy Austria, make marriages...?) It was of small consolation to the arrogant Habsburgs that by now Napoleon had been emperor for a long time, wanted to establish a dynasty, and had, for the most part, liquidated the achievements of the French Revolution.

Meanwhile, did the Hungarians cast wary eyes at Paris, as the Jacobin poet, János Batsányi, recommended they do? Maybe. We cannot even say for certain how they perceived it. No doubt, the French Revolution's swift and surging veerings aroused their interest and, indeed, their enthusiasm as well, though its real impact did not unfold then but a half century later. The changes in France rather alarmed the nobility. Later, Napoleon could, as emperor, again exercise magnetism with his imposing victories. Yet, not very many cherished the hope that Hungary's national interests could actually be realized through him. This Corsican was too greedy, his fortunes were too fickle! This opinion was also reflected in the fact that when Napoleon—the living legend himself—in 1809 entered Hungarian soil with his armies and in a proclamation (composed by Batsányi) called on Hungarians to break away from Vienna, his summons fell on deaf ears.

The year 1809 was a memorable one in Hungarian military history and social development. A call for the nobility to take up arms was issued for the last time. And the army of the Hungarian nobility, joining an Austrian force of similar strength, was annihilated at Győr despite its slight edge in numbers.

This humiliating defeat later served the progressive forces of Hungary as an important argument in support of modernization. Namely, it revealed how definitely obsolete was the legal system under which the nobility paid for its privileges by defending the homeland—in case of an *attack*—with their swords. For all practical purposes, the nation now terminated this "social pact" that was agreed upon very long ago and was so vaguely outlined. It no longer asked for "protection" from the nobles, who had turned boorish, had lost their military virtues, whose cast of mind was engulfed in cobwebs and their swords covered with rust, and whom the Corsican drubbed so ignominiously at Győr.

This verdict was entirely justifiable from a historical perspective. It is, however, worth mentioning that it was naive to expect twenty thousand insurgents who have just been mustered into an army from their humble village estates—and as many Austrians who, though regulars, were nevertheless demoralized—to break the neck and block the way of that Bonaparte who more than once had rolled victoriously with his veterans from one end of Europe to the other. The problem was not with the personal courage of the majority of Hungarian nobles entering battle at Győr. They fought hard, bled, died, and were routed—they did their duty. Their "crime" was not the defeat. It was that they did not sense earlier that time had passed them by. (Of course, I myself am biased. Namely, one of my ancestors and his brother, lesser nobles from Zala County, were there; saving each other's lives and that of their commanding officer, they distinguished themselves in that ominous battle at Győr.)

On the other hand, both the Hungarian nobility and the nation derived substantial profit from the Napoleonic wars for a long time: demand for and prices of agricultural products increased. At this time, the chief export items, in addition to wheat, were wool and tobacco. However, the conservative restoration which the Holy Alliance organized by Vienna imposed on Europe weighed ever more heavily politically on Hungary too. And with regard to the economy, war expenditures and defraying of debts with paper money, and the inflation of currency, particularly its frequent devaluation, once again sharply confronted

the ruler, who had returned to absolutism, and the Hungarians.

Among the latter, national awakening took a new direction. Writers—including those who had been imprisoned as Jacobins—stood at the head of that trend of the Hungarian Enlightenment which discovered our language. In our country, Latin was the traditional and second mother tongue of the nobility—Horace was a frequently quoted "domestic" poet, almost a family member in most country seats of the nobility and since the sixteenth century, the pressure to make German the official language of the state kept reviving. But could it be possible for Hungarian to remain the poor, tolerated third language in its own country! Let it take its rightful place everywhere! And if to this end it must be developed, then the writers will invent and form new words and make this language suitable not only for the national literature but also for the purposes of science and state life.

The desire for modernization had many roots. The cities and the middle classes were powerless, but they did exist. They could not stand in the forefront, but they could show their faces. While many of them had earlier traveled around Europe as soldiers, now, with the advent of more peaceful decades, it was the aristocrats who traversed the continent and had the opportunity to make comparisons. The best of them recognized the shocking symptoms of backwardness and the curse with which it depressed their own and the nation's prosperity. Many of the lesser nobles became poor: their ancient estates were broken up or disappeared from under them. They had to take on

The execution of Ignác Martinovics and his comrades—A water-color by an unknown artist. *On May 20, 1785, five leaders of the Hungarian Jacobin movement were beheaded on the Vérmező (Bloody Meadow) in Buda: Franciscan monk and philosopher Ignác Martinovics, 40, jurist József Hajnóczy, 45, Hussar Captain János Laczkovits, 41, jurist Count Jakab Sigray, 35(?), and jurist Ferenc Szentmarjay, 38(?). Two weeks later, jurist Pál Őz, 29(?), and law-student Sándor Szolártsik, 26, were dispatched in the same way at the same spot. Here it is also striking that among Hungarian intellectuals, the preponderance of interest in law and the professions was overwhelming for centuries. Later, the bodies of the chief defendants in the Jacobin trial who perished on the Vérmező were long searched for; finally, in 1914 systematic digging uncovered them with their heads placed at their feet.*

72

The experimental railroad at Kőbánya—An engraving by János Hofbauer (1803–1846) and Eduard Gurk (1801–1841), 1829. *Today, who knows anything about this curio of technological history? In the nineteenth century, notwithstanding every adversity and obstacle, Hungary again tried to catch up with Europe intellectually and technologically. As we look at the picture of this experimental railroad built in 1829 on Pest's city limits with nostalgia, and admire the viaduct and the elevated rail section resembling the aqueduct at Aquincum, we begin to understand how it was possible for Hungary to carve out by the end of the century a leading place for itself, for instance, in its milling machine industry and then in its electric machine industry, which served the rapidly developing electrification. World War I fatefully brought this development to a close. (For the sake of completeness, let us add that the first "real" railroad track running between Pest and Vác was opened in 1846.)*

official duties, and this was not just a new phenomenon in their lives; their participation in community life was also something entirely different from the time when they viewed the world through the protection of the sheepskin, or precisely for its protection (in other words, their letters patent of nobility traditionally written on parchment prepared from sheepskin).

The giant of this period, the first half of the nineteenth century, was an aristocrat with an athletic build and a noble, sharp-featured face, Count István Széchenyi. His father had already founded two of our major public institutions with generous donations, the National Museum and the national library that today bears his family's name. Széchenyi himself gave an almost extravagant sum for the establishment of the Hungarian Academy of Sciences. But this was only one episode in his life.

"Shall the waters of the homeland always flood with boundless rage its most fertile regions, and shall the arbitrariness of poison emitted by swamps always breed misery and death? Shall the peaks of the Severin and the crags of the Danube always block our communication with other inhabitants of the world? A single lean year plunge half the country into mourning in future as it so often has in the past? The small tax now levied upon the people become increasingly burdensome with the passage of time? Shall a permanent bridge never link the heart of the homeland, Buda and Pest? A national theater forever be denied to a people who, so to speak, possess nothing outside their own language? A better knowledge of agriculture never clothed in green our sunsoaked, barren plains and leaf-littered heaths? Manufacturing, fabrication, and trade never elevate the wealth of our country? The Hungarian forever remain unknown abroad? No, no! Our country, deserving of a more beautiful life, must cast aside this pity or these blemishes worthy of disdain." (*Hitel* [Credit], 1831.)

How numerous are the themes in just these few lines, in a single paragraph of his written lifework extending over countless volumes: improvement of waterways, a bridge, a stone theater, agricultural knowledge, industrial manufacturing, commerce. Let us look at just one of them: the flooding. The Carpathian Basin is an enormous flat-bedded "skillet" in which the streams all flow to the interior; the Danube is the only one flowing outward. And even with just the territory of present-day Hungary in mind, *half* its inhabitants live in such an area, and one-third of the agriculturally cultivated land—most of it the best—lies in regions that floods regularly destroyed in earlier times, before Széchenyi initiated defensive operations. Holland is the only other example in Europe of similar struggles between water and man, where the ocean is the enemy and where polder reclamation continues today.

But we also regard István Széchenyi as the father of inland steamboat navigation. And adopting the methods of MacAdam, the Scottish engineer, he organized

GRÓF SZÉCHENYI ISTVÁN.

Szechenyi nagy Magyarunk bár élete napja letüne
Szellemi kincsetben örködik honja felett.

Count István Széchenyi (1791–1860)—A lithograph by V. Katzler, 1860. *Although, as in other similar tragic moments in Hungarian history, suspicions of political assassination emerged, Széchenyi ended his life by committing suicide at the Döbling Neurological Clinic, which is located in a suburb of Vienna. This descriptive apotheosis prepared after his death seems to surround with encyclopedic completeness the elderly man broken in body and spirit with drawings of all the ventures which he established or in which he played an important role in initiating and developing. Oddly, however, his chief project is omitted from the circle of pictures, the one to which he sacrificed most of his wealth: the Hungarian Academy of Sciences, which still stands at the Pest abutment of the Chain Bridge as an institution and public building.*

Sándor Petőfi—A daguerreotype, 1847. *This daguerreotype, one of the first of its kind in Hungary, which was made with a photographic process discovered ten years earlier and which captured Europe so swiftly, was taken of Petőfi shortly before the outbreak of the War of Independence. Though it had to undergo extensive restoration on its discovery, it can be considered a faithful representation of the poet's real facial features and thus his characteristics, which were often over-romanticized in later portraits. His simplicity and his piercing and stern look are particularly identical with the elemental impulse found in his poetry. After this daguerreotype, the living Petőfi, the hero who fell on the battlefield at Segesvár, can no longer be distorted by the appropriations of posterity.*

the construction of a network of stone streets.
He promoted bank and credit enterprises and supplies
of money for the economy. He recognized the value of the
Balaton, the largest lake in Central Europe, which others
wanted to drain and put to the plow. He supported
horseracing as one of the bases for modern animal
husbandry. It would take too long to list his other
far-reaching ideas and accomplishments. Now it can also
be revealed that while, as today, the developed West
mightily protected its inventions, its technical achievements
from the East, the aristocratic Széchenyi, at the cost
of bribing a customs official, smuggled across the Channel
a gas appliance whose export was banned under
the imposition of the death sentence. On that occasion,
perhaps, of greater consequence to him than the risk of his
own life was the possibility that his arrest would have very
painfully affected his relatives and his friends in the most
exclusive circles of the British aristocracy and the court who
a few days eralier had gathered around him
so enthusiastically.

And yet, the life of this splendid man was nothing but
inner struggle, discord, and anguish. He had to struggle
until his death, not only with his country's backwardness
but also with blockheads or, perhaps, the very hotheaded.
His rash and sinful relationship with his older brother's wife,
an Englishwoman named Caroline Meade, cast a shadow
on his youthful period; he won his great love only after
many years, after her husband's death, though this greatly
desired, patiently awaited, and late marriage failed
to succeed. And in connection with Széchenyi, too, we
must mention his Hamlet-like character: his journal is
crammed with doubts, terror, and thoughts of death.

Younger than he by a decade and more radical (perhaps
merely apparently so) was the, in fact, *déclassé* Lajos
Kossuth, a member of the gentry who built first a provincial
and then a parliamentary career for himself. With him—and
the dispute about Széchenyi and Kossuth still the subject
of heated debates today—we arrive at the Hungarian
chapter of the 1848 wars of independence in Europe.

In the middle of the century, youthful parliamentarians
—delegates' secretaries and deputies—law students, young
writers, and other intellectuals introduced into Hungary
the ideas that roused a whole series of capital cities
between Paris and Prague even to the point of revolution at
the end of winter and in the spring of 1848. Lajos Kossuth
played a paramount role in these events. When speaking
of him, we must mention the special merging of social
roots, character, and possibilities he manifested. He spent
the years of his youth in Zemplén, the locale of Tokay wine,
and, holding office in the county's administration, he bore
a lion's share in suppressing the uprising resulting from an
outbreak of cholera in 1831. The embittered and
impoverished serfs of Northern Hungary held their own
masters responsible for the epidemic, believing blindly that
wells disinfected with chlorine had actually been poisoned.
The army suppressed their rebellion, and bloody reprisals,
executions, and mass floggings followed.
At this time, Kossuth, displaying more than a modicum
of courage and executive ability, protected his own class,
though he increasingly perceived the symptoms and
consequences of stagnant social development in Hungary
in the rebellion.

He was an Adonis and a magnificent orator. When his
career in Zemplén County came to a standstill, he sought
a new arena for himself in Pozsony (Bratislava). Exchanging
the provincial forum for the national, he discerned with
great sensitivity the shortcomings of the press and
the deficiency of information, the paralyzing effect
of censorship. First his parliamentary reports—*handwritten*
in the beginning—constantly obstructed by established
authority, and then his ever-widening publicist and political
activities increased his prestige and circle of followers.
He helped organize the boycott of Austrian goods and
the development of domestic industries, based, lacking
capital, on national zeal; while engaged in these,
he promoted the wearing of national attire by women.

And thus, that Kossuth was maturing whose leadership
role seemed to become almost unmistakable in 1848–49.
He was already the chief political factor when the concrete
role he took was still narrow in scope.

In Hungary, the sparks of ideas flying back and forth
between Vienna and Pest—and Pozsony, where Parliament
was in session—detonated the popular movement on
March 15, 1848. Even though the uprising would be terribly
fiery and seething, the road was, in the beginning, still open
to constitutional resolution. Compelled only by
the obstinate and perfidious attitude of the court in Vienna
and swept along by the innate laws of radicalization,
the Hungarians arrived at armed conflict and then the act
of dethronement at the parliamentary session in Debrecen.

"What do the Hungarian people want? Let peace, liberty,
and harmony prevail!

1. We want freedom of the press, the abolition
of censorship.
2. A responsible Ministry in Buda and Pest.
3. An annual parliamentary session in Pest.
4. Civil and religious equality before the law.
5. A National Guard.
6. A joint sharing of tax burdens.
7. The cessation of socage.
8. Juries and representation on an equal basis.
9. A national bank.
10. The army to swear to support the constitution,
our soldiers not be dispatched abroad, and foreign
soldiers removed from our soil.
11. The freeing of political prisoners.
12. Union with Transylvania. Equality, liberty,
and fraternity!"

These were the *Twelve Points*. Instead of going into
the details as to what the demanded cessation of socage,
in the given period of Hungarian feudalism, really meant or
why the union with Transylvania, which earlier had again
been forced under the rule of Vienna, was judged
necessary, I would rather call attention to the degree
to which the imprint of place and time is felt in the drafting
of this dramatic proclamation: the fervid haste,
the makeshift formulation that occurred in the heat of the
moment. The twin of the *Twelve Points* is Sándor Petőfi's
"National Song", written in the course of the night of March
15, 1848, which opens on this high-sounding note:
Rise Hungarians, your country calls!
The time is now, now or never!
Shall we be slaves or free?
This is the question, choose!
To the God of the Hungarians
We swear,
We swear, we shall slaves
No longer be!
The "National Song" could only partially fill a role as
the Hungarian "Marseillaise" in the 1848–49 War
of Independence, because neither then nor now was truly

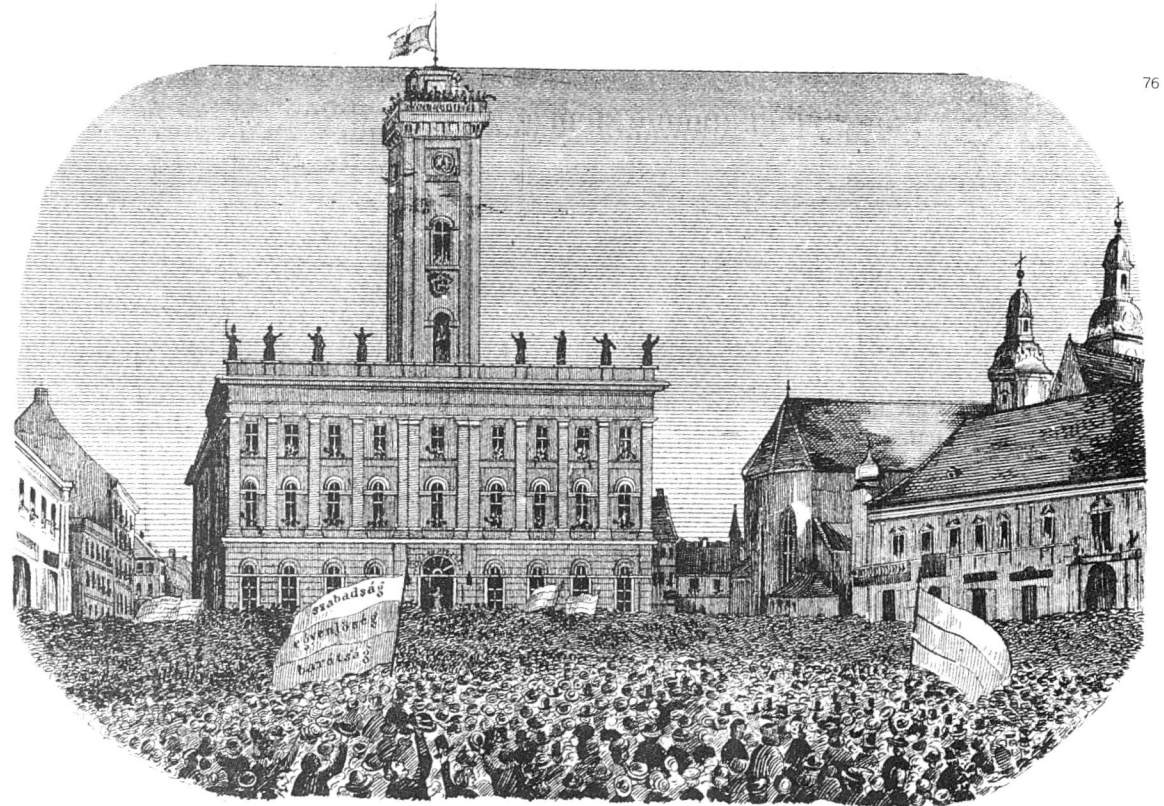

The inhabitants of Pest submit a twelve-point petition to two city councils—An engraving from the March 25, 1848 issue of "Képes Újság." *The result? The Council's minutes say: "In the name of Pest's inhabitants, the undersigned are pleased to inform the Hungarian nation officially that what led to bloodshed among the citizens of other countries, reform, was achieved in Budapest by agreement in a peaceful and lawful way within 24 hours. Namely, the City Council having been informed by the voting citizenry that the city's citizens and inhabitants wanted to discuss the serious issues of the time with the Council, it opened to the people on March 15, 1848, at 3 p.m., the doors of the council chamber that have been locked for centuries; and having understood the people's lawful requests, the members of the Council with one heart and will made those patriotic wishes their own, most of which already existed and were being cherished in their hearts; indeed, at this public meeting, the Council signed and put in the form of a request to Parliament those twelve points which, in large part, the nation had advocated so frequently through legislation since 1790."*

good music composed for it. So, when actors and zealous patriots recited it, the crowd could speak mainly the refrain aloud with them but not sing it.

The *Twelve Points* and the "National Song" are the two texts with which revolutionary Pest indicated that there was no longer a time lag between word and deed.
If the abolition of censorship was present in the first point, demonstrators seized the best-known press in Pest, and, immediately printing the prose and poetic proclamations, they flooded the streets with leaflets. In Buda they freed the "political prisoner" Mihály Táncsics from jail, which was such a notable act of the 1848 bourgeois revolution because Táncsics was a forerunner of the still non-existent Hungarian proletariat.

We shall continue to follow only the main currents of events. The Habsburg Empire became, inflamed or glowed on the verge of flaring up, and the king, Ferdinand V (1830–1848), or rather his councilors acting in the place of the sick and undistinguished monarch, at first easily—too easily—assented to the formation of a responsible Hungarian government, in which both István Széchenyi and Lajos Kossuth occupied posts as Minister of Public Works and Transportation and Minister of Finance respectively. The Prime Minister was Count Lajos Batthyány, who did not really want a post so open to many pitfalls but

who, precisely because of his well-known unparalleled integrity and composure, enjoyed wide confidence.

Were fire and water being mixed in this government? Well, Széchenyi and Kossuth had never disagreed about major goals, only about paths leading to them. Széchenyi was afraid of a sea of flames, whose spread he considered unstoppable; he believed that the barriers that Kossuth would have ignited by throwing firebrands at them could be removed by argument and patience. Széchenyi liked to argue and could do so, Kossuth was able to inspire. But soon there was no need for arguments. Inspiration, on the other hand, became indispensable ammunition, supplementing gunpowder occasionally. But it is not certain that all this vindicates the inspirer against the arguer...

When Vienna came to its senses, it did not attack frontally. Exploiting the fact that Croatia, which was directly dependent on the Hungarians within the Habsburg Empire, would have itself liked more independence from the Hungarians even as we did from the Austrians; the court, thus offering something that did not, or did not directly belong to it within this peculiar system of state law, mobilized the Croatians. However, their forces invading from the south did not reach Pest. The hastily mustered Hungarian army, which consisted mainly of territorials, dispersed and routed them. But since they fled to Vienna and not home to Zagreb, their pursuers also headed in this direction.

They did so all the more because an uprising was occurring in Vienna at the beginning of October. If not the king himself—even Petőfi was to "recommend" this only in a later poem—the rebels did hang the Minister of War on the street. The first responsible Hungarian government, which, in fact, was a coalition balancing various tendencies, resigned. The Committee of National Defense replaced it. Lajos Kossuth was its leader. However, the Hungarian army, though it did cross the national border, came to a sudden halt before Vienna. Not before the enemy. For a time, caution and the fiction of constitutionality gained the upper hand. And when the situation at home continued to grow more radical—and in the meantime, the displaced court tried to turn the Serbians as well as the Rumanians against the Hungarians—the Hungarian army which eventually moved ahead to relieve a Vienna besieged by the reorganized Imperial forces suffered defeat.

At the end of 1848, the court compelled the incompetent Ferdinand V to resign. Francis Joseph I (1848–1916), his nephew, who was sixteen years old at the time, took his place, even "stepping over" his heir-apparent father. Though at the time of succession to the throne he was in the clutches of his bigoted and dictatorial mother, it can be said of him now that he was to fill a determinative role in the region for sixty-eight years.

Kossuth's recruiting speech at Cegléd, September 24, 1848

A drawing by Franz Kollarz (1829–1894). *Vienna's armed intervention in the fall of 1848 radicalized the leaders of the Hungarian revolution and compelled them to mobilize military forces quickly. Kossuth's tour to organize a popular insurrection in the Alföld went as follows: Cegléd and Nagykőrös on September 24, Kecskemét on the 25th, and Szolnok on the 26th, a very demanding pace given the state of transportation at the time. The popular orator was in his element; the captivating man won over more followers—and this was decisive in shaping the public mood—among patriotic women than among men subject to mobilization. The speech at Cegléd formed a milestone in the development of a foundation for the revolution. According to tradition, the peasant leader György Dózsa also delivered his manifesto at Cegléd, in 1514, and the country towns in the Alföld were the centers of a wealthy peasantry that showed certain marks of a developing middle-class mentality. Kossuth tried to get the great masses in agrarian Hungary to commit themselves to the support of the War of Independence.*

Who was being verified at home by later developments, if, indeed, the quest for verification can really have any meaning in a revolutionary situation? Victorious in Vienna, the Imperial forces soon launched attacks on Hungarian soil as well and occupied both Buda and Pest.

Then, although battles of varying success went on almost everywhere in the country, the 1849 spring campaign essentially produced victories for the Hungarians. In Transylvania, the Polish General Bem provided brilliant leadership; he was the impassioned itinerant soldier of Central European revolutions, who was to close his life in final exile in Aleppo as a Turkish pasha, a convert to Mohammedanism. The Hungarian commander-in-chief of the army, Artúr Görgey, became, perhaps, the most frequently and most widely controversial general in our history, although no one could ever question his personal courage and military capability; however, his temperament did not make him very suitable to lead a *revolutionary* army. His obstinacy and vanity embroiled him in an inevitable rivalry with Kossuth, who, in many respects, had a similar temperament. The friction between the political and military leadership of the revolution was ceaseless. Meanwhile, the army itself was not unified; it was rent by generals of divergent character, cast of mind, political views who sought to outvie one another.

Thus the domestic situation was both encouraging and troubling. For a time, the nation successfully supported with paper money—called the Kossuth banknote—an economic lifeline for uniforms, food, and munitions for the armed forces that was not bad under the prevailing

The capture of Buda Castle on March 21, 1849—A painting by Mór Than (1828–1899), 1850. *During the seesawing battles that took place in the 1848-49 War of Independence from Vienna to the end of easternmost Transylvania, Budapest—at this time, still Buda, Pest, and Óbuda—fell to the Austrians without direct combat. However, the rebel army, organized with a new vigor by the government that had fled to Debrecen—when the Imperials evacuated Pest without a battle—commenced its siege of Buda Castle at the beginning of May and carried it successfully on the 21st, not without great casualties. After a mere seven weeks, the enemy marched in again in the middle of July, apparently without effort. Though the inhabitants of the capital played a large role at the beginning of the movement for independence, on the Ides of March in 1848, and later also provided many soldiers, the three cities themselves appeared to endure the changing events of the war impotently.*

circumstances. In the newly established war industry, jack-of-all-trades Hungarians worked competitively—the Székely Áron Gábor created a cannon factory almost out of nothing—and so did industrial and manufacturing families that had recently immigrated but were quickly becoming Hungarians at heart. The personal participation of Jews in Hungary in the War of Independence was extensive and not only in the sense of a material sacrifice.

But history repeats itself. The conflict of interest between the noblemen and serfs had already appeared in the Rákóczi period. The law had already declared the liberation of the serfs. True, but the court in Vienna had also accepted this law. Consequently, this achievement had only a slight connection with the issue of national independence. On the other hand, many of the less important services of serfs remained in place to which the law did not apply; their survival or abolition continued to be the subject of debate. The destitute peasant, the cotter, gained nothing worth defending.

Francis Joseph I's Olmütz Constitution was prepared. In some ways it put Hungary in a situation similar to that which was characteristic of the time after the Turks, when martial law prevailed. It, however, declared the equality of rights for the minorities in the Habsburg Empire. The Hungarians should have done at least that much as well. Or would not even this have satisfied every natural desire of the non-Hungarians living in the border provinces of the Carpathian Basin?

In this situation, the dethronement proclaimed in Debrecen after extensive debate was a daring leap forward. Kossuth became regent; his government, however, had moderate tendencies and was open to negotiation. Was the dethronement both a severance and a search for compromise? But no one was left to negotiate. A few weeks after the act of dethronement, the Czar of all the Russians, Nicholas I, offered armed assistance to the Austrians. At their meeting in Warsaw, Francis Joseph I publicly thanked him by kissing his hand.

The czar's army, made up mainly of Cossacks, forged ahead, not without forced delays but enjoying superiority nevertheless, against the Hungarian forces caught between two fires, who sometimes fought magnificently, but sometimes were demoralized. By now, a decision enunciating the rights of nationalities or any other endeavor would have been futile. Kossuth resigned and fled to the east. On August 13, Görgey, invested with full powers, surrendered with the main Hungarian army to Russian troops at Világos, in Arad County.

As with Count Sándor Károly's act in 1711, we are again pierced by doubt: was Artúr Görgey a traitor or not? To this very day, volumes that would fill a library and dozens of dramas addressed this question. Let us lay down some arguments and facts. The Hungarian forces kept decreasing and weakening, both in morale and equipment. The dethronement turned many away, Cholera was destroying the czar's troops, but an epidemic is hardly selective. General György Klapka, who withdrew to the powerful fortification at Komárom with his own garrison troops and with the mass of people joining them, put up resistance even after Világos, and obtained complete

The surrender at Világos—A painting by István Szkidzsák-Klinovszky (1820–1880?), 1851. *In mid-August 1849, a fate no longer avoidable overtook the Hungarian revolutionary army. Even so, more favorable terms could have been obtained for its forces. Gaining full power upon the withdrawal of political confidence from Kossuth, the stubborn and vain Görgey actually laid down at Világos, near Arad, not only his arms but symbolically also those of the remaining scattered forces before the Russian armies that took part in the intervention, and not before Haynau who had also been maneuvering and was encamped near by; in doing so, he based his hope on the chivalry that Russian field officers had displayed to that point. The hope and promises however proved to be, one can say, unofficial, with the exception of the one that personally affected Görgey's destiny, the amnesty offered him. Of course, the individual and mass reprisals following Világos were acts of vengance carried out by Austrian Imperials. It was no accident, however, that Czar Nicholas earned the name of "Europe's gendarme" in his own day and in posterity with a series of interventions against revolutionary movements.*

amnesty for himself and all his men when he finally capitulated. Görgey trusted the amnesty promised by the czarist generals; however, the Austrians disregarded it after the surrender, to the disgust of Russians with finer feelings. There might have been a corner of the country—for example, the Tihany peninsula stretching into Lake Balaton – where the remaining insurgents, barricading themselves, could have made the siege so costly that they might have won terms comparable to those gained at Komárom.

Generally, in history, we call it fruitless to raise the question "what would have happened if...?" But it is a tragic fact that whereas Görgey capitulated with his main army on August 13, the Austrian Council of Ministers instructed the military régime on August 16 to undertake negotiations with very favorable terms; however, when news of Világos arrived in Vienna, a new order calling for severe reprisals replaced this decision.

The czar's army marched out of Hungary. The Austrian Field-Marshal Haynau had command over life and death in the country. On his orders, the death sentence was carried out on October 6 in Arad against thirteen generals by a hangman or—out of mercy—by a firing squad. Perhaps, weighed against the great numbers of other

The execution of Lajos Batthyány—A lithograph by Louis Noeli.
The family of Count Lajos Batthyány (1807–1849), the president of the first responsible Hungarian government, was well-known from the beginning of the 1500s. He himself was an enlightened and rational manager of his own vast estate and a supporter of measured opposition and progress through compromise. On the Ides of March 1848, he was ideally suited to provide assurances to those rallying around the Vienna court and those supporting Kossuth. He occupied his otherwise reluctantly accepted office only as long as the path to compromise manifest in his appointment was viable; he resigned in mid-September once and for all, and then, when he later returned to political life as a representative, he was, to the end, a supporter of moderation and a compromise with Vienna. His execution was a judicial absurdity, the product of intimidation and brutal vengeance.

victims, it is somewhat unfair for us to mention the Arad Thirteen so frequently; the day of their martyrdom is a day of national mourning, although another hundred or so died and thousands were imprisoned, while tens of thousands drafted as common soldiers had to serve unpredictable numbers of years in the godforsaken spots of the empire.

On October 6, 1849, the Austrians also executed in Pest Count Lajos Batthyány, the former Prime Minister who had,

however, counted on being a moderating element to the very end. It is a question for psychologists to answer why Francis Joseph I afterwards kept the painting of Batthyány's execution in the Burg apartments so that he could look at it every day. Was he so imbued with hatred toward him? Or was he repenting in a peculiar way? Both are plausible in an emperor with such a strange character.

Haynau, who was also called Hyena of Brescia because of his earlier atrocities in Italy, created an atmosphere that even Vienna soon could not stomach. The emperor relieved him. On his last day, in his wounded fury, in a schizophrenic and capricious manner, Haynau ordered immediate executions and performed unexpected acts of mercy at the same time. His name and portrait were so well known, so widely spread throughout Europe at the time that when he traveled as a private citizen, English longshoremen recognized him and beat him up. At the end of his life—again a strange turn—he bought a village estate in eastern Hungary and lived there as a meek landowner. Not so long ago, a researcher collected fantastic tales about him and his family still being told by people living in this area. In them, Haynau is a Dracula-like vampire.

THE COMPROMISE AND
THE MILLENNIUM

The rest: a dead silence? After 1849, the Bach period—named after the Austrian Minister of Interior at the time—brought on a new version of absolutism that tried desperately both to preserve existing conditions and to open the way to unavoidable development.

For years, Hungary wore the black veil of mourning, haunted prisons, wrote pleas for mercy, hid fugitives—and dreamt. It staked its hopes on developments taking place outside the country: in the Italian movement of Garibaldi, around whom vagrant freedom fighters in Europe had again gathered for a time, and in Napoleon III, who perpetuated the famous and notorious name of the Corsican (and only that).

Legends proliferated. Most of them involved the poet Sándor Petőfi, who, with the rank of major, was an adjutant of the diabolically clever Polish General Bem and who most certainly perished in the last of the more significant battles, at Segesvár, in Transylvania, impaled by a Cossack's lance. But the nation was not willing to accept his death. Like false czars in Old Russia, false Petőfis appeared throughout the country. He was also thought to have been hauled off to Siberia. We have not come across his grave to this day, and the enigma of his death is still being investigated.

Lajos Kossuth and his emigrant staff, going from country to country, attempted to rally support or at least to evoke expression of sympathy. There was no lack of the latter. The former regent's tour of England and America were especially successful. His oratorical skills sparkled, his manly profile was engaging; his best attributes asserted themselves. When he finally settled in Turin, Italy, the peoples' tribune became a living and very frequently speaking monument, a national idol. He spent his days as a polymathic naturalist; he corresponded about spiders and mosses, and worked on his memoirs. It was a holiday for him when growing numbers of guests and even delegations from the homeland called on him; he was the oracle in Hungary's domestic disputes, and he acted as an

unavoidable counterpoint or at least a basis of reference for a series of political tendencies. An exile of the nation, he was still the everpresent *paterfamilias* to whom people sent first-baked bread to slice and newly drawn wine to taste. They solicited his opinion in legal matters; they asked him to be a distant witness at weddings, to be a godfather—and they paid increasingly less attention to his real views.

Austria fought a war first with France and then with Prussia—without much success. In the south, its interests in Italy were crumbling; from the northwest, Bismarck pressed it hard not to meddle in German affairs, even if it had been doing so for five hundred years. In recompense, let it expand toward the Balkans instead. (World War I was to develop out of this—or shall we not be in such a hurry?) But the peace terms were surprisingly lenient compared to the serious defeats Austria suffered in the battles. In the middle of the European power map, a need existed

81

The Kossuth Memorial Statue in New York, *1928. Kossuth and his fellow exiles, whose escape route, like Ferenc Rákóczi II's and his followers', led first to Turkey, tried to arouse sympathy in Western Europe, and obtain the support needed to resume the war. Their finally unsuccessful endeavors took two main paths. On the one hand, public opinion was, perhaps, most receptive in the English-speaking countries, the British Isles and the United States, which had come into existence by gaining independence from the British. On the other hand, the 1849 exiles cast their hopes in the national struggles going on in Italy, in the development of Garibaldi's independence movement. (Kossuth himself lived finally in Turin until his death.) In America, the aura Kossuth obtained through his personal tour after the failure of the War of Independence was revived by the emigration that carried wave after wave of human beings to the New World at the turn of the century and even after World War I. Though this emigration was chiefly rooted in economic factors, it was invigorated by patriotic nostalgia, and the "1848 state of mind" and the Kossuth cult seem to exercise some influence to this day.*

The Austro-Hungarian Monarchy in 1914

Frontiers of the Austro-Hungarian Monarchy
Frontiers of the Kingdom of Hungary
Border of the co-dominions
Border of the provinces
The occupied territory of Bosnia and Herzegovina

for this formation that divided the Germans, curbed the Slavs, and kept a tight rein on the emerging smaller national powers of Central Europe. By the middle of the nineteenth century, the land of the Habsburgs could have already been carved up and partitioned. Self-satisfied with his dynasty's and his own mission, why should Francis Joseph I see that only the need of others for the monarchy he ruled prevented this from happening.

Kossuth was on the move for years; he made plans in or at least kept watch from Turin for decades. His exile could even be viewed as the high point of his life.

Ferenc Deák—A painting by Bertalan Székely, 1869. *Ferenc Deák (1803–1876), a descendant of a family of medium estate-owners in Transdanubia (Western Hungary) and a law graduate, was a matchless figure both as a human being and as a politician. Unmarried, he spent his life in hotels and as a wandering guest in mansions and manor houses in the provinces. His knowledge of the law and his cast of mind put to shame the countless refined and crafty lawyers of the time as he sought the framework, form, and formula for the compromises he served so stubbornly. His authority was fantastic not only in the narrower political sphere but also in all intellectual areas. No one can cast doubt on his moral integrity. His character is preserved by hundreds of anecdotes; he was, after all, a most witty conversationalist and debater. His written lifeworks are concerned with law and publicism, but the volumes of his writings represent an exceedingly small fraction of the tremendous intellectual activity he displayed in his political life every day.*

82

Queen Elizabeth—A painting by Gyula Benczúr, 1861. *She was one of the most beautiful women of her time, and her enigmatic sadness only enhanced her sex appeal. Her love-marriage could not possibly succeed, at least not for the other party: her husband was ultra-conservative and, though a king, petty bourgeois in his outlook and conduct of life and pedantic and small-minded, contrasting sharply with the sensitive and freedom-loving nature of the accomplished Elizabeth. In addition, she was a neurotic who transmitted to her son Rudolph, the heir to the throne, her melancholy temperament and her disposition to suicide, which lay hidden in her family and herself, together with her liberal frame of mind open to modernization. It was only his mother's serious vein which was unfamiliar to the tragically-fated heir apparent.*

Count Gyula Andrássy (1823–1890)—A painting by Gyula Benczúr, 1884. *He was considered to be one of the handsomest men of his time, in whom an athletic build, physical courage, and keen intellect came together. He was one of the very few Hungarian politicians who occupied for a considerable period of time one of the three "common" ministerial posts in the government of the specifically structured Austro-Hungarian Monarchy. In addition to his German orientation, he strongly resisted the transformation of the dual and thus bipolar Monarchy into a triple one—the favorite idea of Francis Ferdinand, the new heir to the throne—in which the fulcrum and triangle made up of Austrians, Czechs, and Hungarians would have come into being with Vienna's primacy unchanged. Romantic speculations about his having had an affectionate relationship with the queen cannot be verified and are very likely untrue.*

The Millenary Monument on Heroes' Square in Budapest.
Its construction began in conjunction with the celebration of the Millennium of the Hungarian Conquest in 1896 at the eastern end of what was then called Sugár út, where most of the festivities had taken place. The monument was fully completed only in 1929. The seven Magyar chiefs are arranged at the base of Archangel Gabriel's statue, which symbolizes victory, while at the sides the following historical personalities were represented originally: St. Stephen, St. Ladislas, Coloman Beauclerc, Andrew II, Béla IV, Charles Robert, Louis the Great, János Hunyadi, Matthias Corvinus, Ferdinand I, Charles III, Maria Theresa, Leopold II, and Francis Joseph. First in 1919 and then after World War II, the Habsburg monarchs were removed, and later István Bocskai, Gábor Bethlen, Imre Thököly, Ferenc Rákóczi II, and Lajos Kossuth replaced them, demonstrating the realignments occurring in historical esteem.

István Széchenyi, whom Kossuth, in an ebullient moment, called the "greatest Hungarian" was completely crippled by the débâcle of the revolution that he had so long foreseen. Before he shot himself in the head in an asylum in the outskirts of Vienna (1860) after so many death plans, his mind sometimes cleared, sometimes plunged into the hell of madness. But to him, clear-sightedness was the greater hell. Was this what drove him mad? The duty beyond fulfillment?

In its war against the French (1859) and the Prussians (1866), Austria's armies fought bravely but with poor equipment: with muzzle-loading rifles and in snow-white uniforms that made them easy targets, even though the camouflaging field-gray had already been invented by then. Francis Joseph I, whose chief merit was his conscientiousness as a state official and whose chief ambition was to place the needs of the armed forces in the

The historical tarot card game—A painting by Arthur Ferraris (1856–?). *Under Ferenc Deák's half-length portrait in the Liberal Party Club are shown Kálmán Tisza (1830–1902) and the players and kibitzers participating in the "general's" tarot card game, including: Károly Eötvös (1842–1916), the "voivode," lawyer and author, the successful defender of the Jews at Tiszaeszlár charged with "ritual murder of children"; Mór Jókai (1825–1904) and Kálmán Mikszáth (1847–1910), two princes of prose fiction who were also publicists and members of parliament; Baron Frigyes Podmaniczky (1824–1907), who as city planner was noted for his contributions as the manager of the Opera House and the National Theatre and as the president of the Metropolitan Public Works Council; Lajos Csernátony, journalist, publicist, among others. Kálmán Tisza, landowner at Geszt, István Tisza's father, was prime minister from 1875 to 1890. This was an unprecedentedly long span of time! During the period was fashioned that "prewar peace" which was conducted in a good-humored and wily but aggressive manner, and when the major issues were settled not in parliament but at casino tables. At the time, political and intellectual life and the élite were still not separate entities.*

forefront, chose one bad army commander after the other. It is an irony of fate that in both of the aforementioned wars, one or another Hungarian field officer played key roles who were, to the end, faithful to the court and the ruler, but incompetent. It was the military fiascos in which they also participated that actually cleared the way for the Compromise of 1867.

The lessons of war demanded of Austria the same thing as the bourgeois development did: modernization. And it became clear at this time that what remained of the realm, though it had many smaller and larger centers of gravity, had two major ones: Vienna and Pest. Neither could really prosper without the other. The bridge that would again span the chasm springing from the events of 1848–49 was being built from both sides. Austria lagged behind the more western parts of Europe, and Hungary behind Austria (and the Czech and Moravian areas). They had to take steps. Expansion toward the Balkans was not possible if the Hungarians were only pacified militarily and administratively. The structure based on state law which was brought about in 1867 had a thousand ramifications. The Age of Dualism began. The name that embodied this oddly balanced edifice was the Austro-Hungarian Monarchy.

In Hungary, Ferenc Deák, a stocky and jovial member of the gentry, had a lion's share in its formation. His ornamental epithet was: "Sage of the Nation." What he devised with Vienna after many starts and stops, deals, retractions, and mutual compromises was a dual governmental structure whose political carrying capacity varied and whose domestic laws continually took shape in the course of subsequent difficult disputes and conflicts, and always did so late. However, the limit to economic possibilities and dimensions the structure gave birth to was hardly perceived for decades. The "happy times of peace" commenced. It lasted for one, one and a half generations, which, however, meant a century.

In the *K. und K.*, the *Kaiserlich und Königlich*, structure, Austrian and Hungarian foreign and military affairs were conducted jointly; a joint Ministry of Finance was added to them; the other ministerial departments were separated (Hungarians bore 30 percent of the common expenses of the Monarchy); the various other parts of the realm were connected to one or the other of the two parts in complex and diverse ways. The joint Foreign Minister was Hungarian for an extended period of time, but generally, it was not Hungarians who directed the joint affairs. And occasionally, the joint expenditures, the customs union, and the segregation of Hungarian units in the army and the subordination of the official Hungarian language of command created daggersdrawn conflicts.

But let us linger awhile in the "honeymoon." According to a romantic view, the language of the heart played a great role in the Compromise of 1867. As early as 1854, Francis Joseph I had married his first cousin, the sixteen-year-old Bavarian princess, Elizabeth. In the marriage that began with true love, grew bitter later, and finally ended in separation without divorce, the life of this extraordinarily beautiful young woman, who longed for emancipation and possessed an intellectual bent and a warm but melancholy temperament, was so embittered by her overbearing mother-in-law, the Hungarian-hating Archduchess Sophia, that Elizabeth—if only out of spite—became increasingly sympathetic toward the Hungarians. She learned their language and studied their history. She came into personal contact with them. The extent of the intimacy in her relationship with Count Gyula Andrássy, who was considered to be one of the most attractive European statesmen of his time, is uncertain. (In 1849, he was Görgey's adjutant; he was an organizer of the exile; in 1851, he was sentenced to death *in absentia* and hanged symbolically; he returned home under an amnesty; he was Prime Minister from 1867 on and thus the second responsible Hungarian prime minister; appointed to head the joint Ministry of Foreign Affairs, he became probably the most successful politician in foreign affairs in the Dual Monarchy, in a way, however, that his successes, reflected in the strengthening of the Monarchy, originated in his

Ferenc Liszt giving a concert before the royal couple in Buda castle. *A whole series of East Central European artists—mainly musicians and painters, whose language is international, after all—participated in the lot and afterlife of Ferenc Liszt (1811–1886) in that they were often identified as being of Austrian, if not German, nationality. In addition to the drawing power of the Vienna-centered Austrian and then the Austro-Hungarian Empire and its role in absorbing and then sending artists on to other European countries, another circumstance interposed itself, the fact that despite their ethnic origin, many Hungarian, Czech, Croatian and other artists (and scholars) born in territories controlled by Austria used German as their mother tongue or had forgotten their own native language, or, perhaps, rarely used it. Nor did the character of their family names serve as decisive proof, and the national motifs present in their works were even less so. The by now sometimes distasteful debates about the true national origin of these artists could definitely be determined only when they themselves cast the vote in the matter. Only late posterity has discovered the startling modernism of the music of Ferenc Liszt, who constantly claimed he was Hungarian, albeit in broken Hungarian, and whose virtuosity made him truly famous. He was Richard Wagner's fatherly friend, but his real heir was Béla Bartók, Wagner's complete opposite.*

exploitation of growing—and ultimately dangerous—German orientation and alignment.) It is certain, however, that Elizabeth greatly respected the wise Deák's human disposition and his political ideals, and she gave many signs of her regard. At the time of the Compromise, Elizabeth was still a wife, not just an empress and queen; in the summer of 1868, after a ten-year interval, her fourth child, Maria Valeria, was born.

In the final analysis, the Compromise, the creation of a dual state, which represents a relationship of higher degree between two countries than a personal union does, was a historical necessity (with economics at the bottom of it all) whose foundation could not rest upon accidental human factors, even though they could influence details in a substantial way.

From abroad Kossuth passionately opposed Deák and his work. There was much truth in his prophecy that by tying themselves to a Monarchy doomed to destruction, the Hungarians were heading for disaster. But was what came to pass with World War I really predestined? And what else could have been done during the intervening half century? The hope of active revolutionary changes slipped away. The passive resistance that developed to such a masterly extent during the Bach period, the obstinate daily confrontation with the foreign state power became such an obsession that its effect is felt even today; for example, the ways of outwitting customs, of smuggling goods across borders, of concealing income and not paying taxes, of distilling brandy clandestinely, of deceiving administrative bureaus at every step by Hungarian citizens are not thought of as immoral actions but as downright honorable national exploits. These are, however—let us not

The New Banquet Hall
A part of the royal palace
in Buda, 1912. *The 1867
Compromise was not merely
an act or the beginning of
a process of power and rule
within state structure and
politics. In the multipolar
Austro-Hungarian Monarchy,
the role of the Hungarian
capital grew continually.
Pressure kept increasing on
Emperor Francis Joseph to
live more in accord with his
royal title and move his court
to Buda and to Gödöllő for
more extended periods
of time. In keeping with
the spirit of this view,
the rebuilding and restoration,
the expansion, and much
other construction reflecting
the tastes of the time went on
for decades at the royal
palace in Buda.*

quibble—negative virtues; a developed economy, a national future can hardly be built with them.

Meanwhile, a substantial amount of uncommitted capital accumulated in Europe, which, at signs of domestic consolidation in the Monarchy, headed for Hungary —mainly from Berlin and Vienna. The eye seemed dazzled, seeing all and even more than Széchenyi, amid so many grievances, recommended, dreamed of, urged, and also initiated now materializing one after the other. Instead of singling out data on the length in kilometers of roads and railways being built and other numbers filling statistical columns, I should like to make apparent the developments that emerged during the last third of the nineteenth century and at the turn of the century.

In the 1960s and the 1970s, the number of highly reputable Hungarian businesses celebrating the centenary of their founding was striking. Behind most of these enterprises were hidden an unwritten *Buddenbrooks*, by Thomas Mann, *Forsyte Saga*, by John Galsworthy, *The Thibaults,* by Roger Martin du Gard, and *The Artamonovs' Business,* by Maxim Gorky.

Now classicism tempestuously repainted cities that had taken on a Baroque character after the Turks and then the style of the Art Nouveau and eclecticism, while farther out on their periphery, the zone around the factories and workers' colonies displayed the bleak sootgray of classical capitalism, of the original accumulation of capital. A large number of sturdy but airy public buildings existing even today—railway stations, post offices, army barracks, schools, offices, banks, and museums—wear the indelible marks of the period.

According to historical geography, the picture of nature that had unfolded before the eyes of Árpád's Hungarians in the Carpathian Basin altered in its basic features only at this time. Through a thousand years, vegetation and riverbeds remained virtually unchanged. However, Széchenyi, back in 1846, broke ground for his gigantic project in flood control and regulation of rivers. But the actual continuation of the venture could occur only

after 1867. And in it, the landless cotters, who had gained hardly a thing from the liberation of the serfs, found employment for decades; they were agricultural laborers by this time. The construction of railroads and cities also required tremendous amounts of raw manpower at their worksites, where even the simple machines used to build the Suez and chiefly the Panama Canal were lacking. For example, in the course of Hungarian development, which was one-sided and gaining momentum while retaining many outmoded practices, large estates used enormous steam-powered machines to plow their fields, thus supplanting the old shallow-working shoe of the plow, and the deeper turning of the soil suddenly increased the average yield. But landowners did not import the harvesting machines already in use throughout Europe; harvesting was still performed with a hand scythe on a sharing basis, thus guaranteeing a yearly livelihood earned in kind to the greater part of the agrarian population. On the other hand, threshing was carried out with modern machinery.

It is an old accusation that the Monarchy condemned Hungary to be an exporter of agricultural products and that industrial development remained the prerogative of Austria, Bohemia, and Moravia. This is partially true. But the natural

The Parliament. *With its back to the Danube and facing the statues of Ferenc Rákóczi II and Lajos Kossuth, the neo-Gothic lace-trimmed Hungarian Parliament was also the offspring of the inordinate self-confidence that pervaded the Millennium. It was built between 1885 and 1904 according to plans prepared by Imre Steindl (1839–1902); among the designer's models were the Cologne Cathedral and the Houses of Parliament on the Thames in London. Not directly across from it but still forming the counterpart of the huge block of Buda Castle on the right bank of the Danube, the edifice, very controversial for the extravagant scale of its exterior and its interior decoration, immediately dominated the cityscape. Unfortunately, on occasion during the course of time, its solemnity has had only a slight impact on the representatives in session; its honorable chambers have witnessed ugly scenes. Damage in World War II and the wear and tear of time have made continual restoration necessary for decades.*

The royal family at Gödöllő—A lithograph, 1871. *Elizabeth's first journey to Hungary turned tragic: her first-born daughter Sophia became ill in Debrecen and died suddenly. But the otherwise very sensitive queen stayed ever more gladly in Buda after the Compromise and coronation in 1867, and especially in Gödöllő, in the former Grassalkovich palace, which had been rebuilt as a royal summer residence. (Count Antal Grassalkovich was such a noted builder that the history of Hungarian art differentiates a distinct "Grassalkovich style" within the Baroque.) Later, as Elizabeth became increasingly estranged from her husband, to the point where the family seemed to disintegrate, she preferred to go south, to the Mediterranean region, most frequently to the Island of Corfu, instead of Gödöllő.*

endowments of the Carpathian Basin are really the best in this region. And with equitable terms of trade, the large agricultural surplus is so valuable that only a very profitable industrial export could compete with it. If we examine the complex question of grain production, we encounter an instructive example. For centuries the export of grain flowed from Hungarian soil, while water mills floating on the Danube ground flour mainly for domestic consumption, and so did numerous mills throughout the country driven by water, wind, and animals. But at the end of the century, a pool of steam-powered mills already handled the substantial export of flour. The domestic machine industry meeting the demands of these steam-powered mills—with new inventions, like the roller frame and the flat sifter—grew into an important segment of export and a leading branch in manufacturing, whose prosperity spread into other areas and gave an impetus to the ironworks as well.

Following London, Budapest built an underground railway. The electrical engineering industry also became a leading branch of Hungarian industry. It became the chief supplier of Southeast Europe. And in this branch, numerous inventions sprang up and were quickly put to use, like the transformer. At a time when electrical power stations individually serving their own exclusive limited districts were functioning worldwide by the thousands, Hungary was the first to link them with long-distance transmission lines. In this way, the differing peak loads and the interruptions caused by industrial mistakes could be bridged.

Two spectacular events framed the period from which we have already departed occasionally. Not until 1867 could the Hungarian royal crown be placed on the head of Francis Joseph I, who had been emperor since 1848, and that of Elizabeth, who had been empress since 1854. Apparently at Elizabeth's urging, Francis Joseph returned the coronation gift customary on such occasions to the donors, the Hungarian people, by presenting it to the disabled soldiers of the War of Independence as a dramatic gesture of reconciliation. An enormous body of literature treats the Hungarian ambivalences of this period: after all, they were finally crowning that emperor and king who, at an early age, was responsible for Haynau's carnages but who, although a Habsburg, now extended the promise of a special upturn to the Hungarian nation.

In 1896, Hungarians put on the Millennium of the Conquest. (At this time, the remains of Kossuth had been resting in native soil for two years.) Externals were dazzling; the gala attire of the Hungarians sparkled and glittered: panther skins, capes of leopard skin thrown over shoulders, pipings, shakoes, plumes studded with gems, boots with spurs, dress swords, heavy decorations on heavy chains; regimental music and fireworks were inexhaustible. The most faithful picture of the character of the celebrations and of the whole atmosphere of the Millennium is not reflected by the Millenary Monument, whose construction was started on this occasion and which can still be seen in its largely original condition in Heroes' Square in Budapest (the Habsburg rulers were later removed from its gallery of statues and replaced with anti-Habsburg heroes of liberty from our own history). More characteristic than this is the Vajdahunyad Castle (today an agricultural museum) next to and behind the monument. This is every bit a special "neo" construction, which unites, jammed together, the motifs of several of the most characteristic monuments in the history of Hungarian architecture.

FROM SARAJEVO TO TRIANON

But first from Mayerling to Sarajevo... Incidentally, the writer of these lines is not surprised if someone summarizes Hungary's history in a way that, reaching the middle of the nineteenth century or even beyond that, it still holds in reserve half of its fixed length. Is this due to the pressure of accelerated time? To the glut of events? That history, moving on foot or horseback until this point, has now boarded a steam locomotive or an airplane? That the number of sources is increasing? That the charm of propinquity enthralls—the participation of our grandfathers, who died only yesterday or are still living here and there, in the events, and the direct impact of bygone events on our individual destinies? Still, let us try to hold to our own condensed endeavor and its differently proportioned course.

Before the turn of the century, the economy of the Austro-Hungarian Monarchy, which for decades had lived within its given borders, was comparatively stable and dynamic—its money, for example, was sound; however, its political structure was shaky and its society full of tensions. Even bourgeois developments had not reached fruition; a whole range of rights to liberty and rules of democratic procedures was lacking. The labor movement was already rumbling about establishing its own much more far-reaching objectives. The ideal of internationalism, proletarian internationalism, loomed seductively like a utopia, behind the whirl of fulfilled national and minority aspirations.

The relations between the Hungarians and the nationalities in the Carpathian Basin within the Monarchy were simultaneously characterized by the belief that those relations were regulated by a sound law of nationalities, that ample opportunities for emancipation were available to Slavs and other ethnic groups, including Jews (many of the most radical representatives of the struggle for the nationalities studied in Budapest, they lived or found self-awareness there; their movements took root there, they published their newspapers there), and that the tectonic force that always rent the Monarchy asunder ever more catastrophically could be sought in these very relations.

That characteristic feature of the economic development that, despite the tremendous dynamism, the Monarchy, the Carpathian Basin, and particularly its border regions were incapable of providing employment for their growing surplus of workers has to be probed separately. Though one of the keys to that dynamism was precisely the availability of a large, cheap, and placid labor supply, the sea of the unemployed was such a burden alongside the rapid acquisition of property, ostentatious wealth, and wasteful consumption accompanying prosperity that it was difficult to tolerate. Thus came to pass the phenomenon about which Attila József later wrote: "a million and a half of our countrymen tottered out to America." For a long time, official agencies tolerated this emigration as accomplices or encouraged it illegally. Even today we still do not know the exact number of emigrants. And the results would vary widely if we were to consider only the Hungarians, then include the nationalities, or the emigrés from the pre-Trianon (before 1920), or post-Trianon state, or if we were to deduct those who returned later. In any case, the loss of population was enormous. (But let us provide some figures: according to present calculations, the number of individuals leaving what were then Hungarian territories—some possibly making the journey more than once—with the intention of emigrating to America by all accounts reached 1.2 to 1.3 million between the 1870s and World War I. About one-fourth or one-third of them were Hungarians, and the rest other nationalities; however, at least one-third of the emigrants eventually resettled in Hungary.)

The assessment of this massive emigration, as a result of which separate Hungarian settlements and big-city colonies—sometimes ghettos—came into existence in the United States, Canada, and several South American countries (some emigrants did not master the official language of their new country for generations)—this assessment is almost entirely negative to this very day. This is the case even though there was no European country at the level of economic, technical, and demographic development at which we ourselves arrived at the turn of the century that did not also undergo the same experience. Today, one of the causes of the economic dead end in numerous Third World countries is precisely the fact that the Wild West, the great open spaces, the pampas where the temporary "human surplus" could emigrate are no longer to be found anywhere. For Hungary, however, it is a great benefit, both economically and morally, that no matter where we may find ourselves in the world, we encounter Hungarians, kinfolk who are to some degree, preserving their Hungarian character and their consciousness of their origin. And they also visit the old homeland frequently.

Let us now approach the internal strains of the Monarchy from an entirely different perspective. The only son of Queen Elizabeth's four children, the "ill-fated" heir Rudolf, was born back in 1858. He was his mother's child. His nervous system was rather vulnerable; he had an intellectual bent, he was eager to become emancipated, he was on friendly terms with scholars (among them, the great zoologist, Alfred Brehm, the author of *The World of Animals*); he was repelled by the court and also by his father's coldness, dogmatism, and rigid sense of duty. Naturally, a bad marriage was arranged for him. He knew about his father's petty love-affairs: about his almost cohabiting relationship with the actress Katherine Schratt, whom Elizabeth the wife herself recommended as a "substitute," about the back street of a back street that posterity learned about only recently: his fifteen-year relationship with the beautiful Anna Nahowski, who bore

István Tisza—A painting by Gyula Benczúr (Ede Balló's copy). *Count István Tisza (1861–1918), whom the period's greatest poet, Endre Ady, called "the wild man from Geszt" in his rage, was prime minister for a year and a half between 1903 and 1905 and for four whole years between 1913 and 1917; thus he headed the Hungarian war cabinet almost to the very last. He was a born party leader, who possessed such an effective political personality that he was able to defend the old order with elemental force. In 1914, he opposed the declaration of war, not because of principle but because of his belief that the Monarchy was unprepared. The principle that "force breeds force" must be seen at work in the fact that as early as 1912 a member of parliament already made an attempt to assassinate him with a revolver. And when unidentified soldiers shot the former prime minister to death in his own home on October 31, 1918, other assailants were, so to say, also on the way to make an attempt on the life of the hated count.*

several children during this period, during her husband's complete absence. And Katherine and Anna: they were easygoing silly-minded, domesticated petty bourgeois, the direct opposites of the refined, indeed decadent Elizabeth. And what kind of companion did Rudolf require? Several kinds also? After all, in addition to his flirtations at the court, he kept returning faithfully to a notorious Viennese prostitute, a popular but not exactly intellectual coquette. Then, half blind, he fell into little Marie Vetsera's net. At the time of their short and stormy relationship, Rudolf was a developed personality, to the extent, one can say, knowing his unsettled frame of mind. There was not the faintest hope that his father, aging but enjoying remarkable health, ever intended to hand over to his only son any real part of his power. Even if measured by the standards of an heir to the throne, Rudolf performed his third-rate duties indifferently enough; he preferred

to spend his time hunting, and following and promoting research in the natural and social sciences.

And he conducted publicistic activities. He wrote articles. Under a pseudonym. In the liberal, in the opposition press. Was it some kind of Oedipal rebellion against his father? His Majesty's Opposition within the family? A youthful caper? Something more serious, perhaps. Rudolf truly viewed the future of the Monarchy differently.

It is true that after several years of disinclination his father too was forced to acquiesce to Christian Socialist Karl Lueger becoming the mayor of Vienna. The times mandated it. And besides, Lueger was a confounded left-winger but a bigoted Catholic and a rabid anti-Semite. At best, Francis Joseph I made involuntary concessions. Rudolf would have liked to go forward. Toward a republic.

Mayerling, January 1889. Do Baroness Marie Vetsera and Rudolf die a shared death of their own will? To this day,

"PANEM!" (BREAD!)—A painting by Imre Révész (1859–1945), 1899. *Actually, agrarian society in Hungary has from the liberation of the serfs in 1848 to 1945 been profoundly fragmented, and the ownership of land very disproportionately distributed. Just one of the consequences of this was that as long as it was possible village people emigrated across the ocean by the hundreds of thousands, and land-distribution and agrarian-socialist movements arose at home time and time again. At the same time, it is a peculiar fact that though the use of simpler harvest machinery had spread to many agricultural regions of the world since the nineteenth century, harvesting by hand remained the sole method in Hungary until the middle of the current century. The reason for this was that it was the only way the landless agricultural workers could obtain the grain crop that in a way guaranteed bread and a minimal subsistence for them each year.*

efforts are being made to explain and unravel the secret of this tragedy in various ways. There are a thousand versions, ranging from the most simple romantic love death to the emperor himself ordering the murder of his son, whom he had cast out of his heart, together with his lover, because he was a political rival. Let us mention the version maintaining that the political assassin was a German, an agent of Berlin; after all, Rudolf's anti-Prussianism was widely known. The truth is not exactly simple but, in the end, quite prosaic. His father, in a peremptory manner, ordered Rudolf, who had long been nursing thoughts of suicide, to break with his love. There was no outlet or popular support for Rudolf's political ambitions. His mood grew ever gloomier. The syphilis that did not spare even him tortured him increasingly. And in the hunting lodge near Vienna, an

incompetent midwife botched an illegal abortion on Marie Vetsera, who had become pregnant after only a few intimate liaisons. Rudolf—this is what we think—to ease the demise of the gradually hemorrhaging Marie, shot her in the evening and then himself in the head at dawn. The Hungarians knew him as a friend and mourned him as a martyr; romantic legends sprang up about him, about a "good prince" who had been murdered.

September 1898. Luigi Lucheni, an Italian anarchist born in Paris and a guest worker in Switzerland—he was that, although the expression itself was not yet known then—was indecisively rummaging about among crowned heads and similar parasites because he was convinced they all had to be slaughtered. While running amok, he, almost by chance, thrust his sharp-pointed and dagger-like file—he did not have the money for a dagger—directly into Queen Elizabeth's heart in Geneva. He struck down the most blameless of the crowned "spongers" in Europe, the one who, if she had been asked, would, in all probability, have agreed with most of the anarchistic principles espoused by her assailant. Her life, which she lost so senselessly, had indeed been a complete burden to her for a long time. Death was a deliverance.

Archduke Francis Ferdinand, a cousin from a collateral line, took Rudolf's place. The new heir to the throne was arrogant; he had ravenous appetite for politics and was not exactly an indecisive character. Although he also offended the emperor with his morganatic marriage, and the emperor him by barring his children from succession to the throne, their views contained many kindred features. But Francis Joseph I did not share power with him either. He increased Francis Ferdinand's sphere of influence in minute portions only.

With the military occupation of South Slavic Bosnia and Herzegovina (1878), which took place to impose a burden on Turkey, the sick man of Europe, but worked against Serbia, the sharp turn toward expansion in the Balkans put the Hungarians in a delicate position. Our agriculture benefited. But the growing number of Slavs in the Monarchy caused anxiety, and military action led to the shedding of blood—mainly that of the fanatics—and the ranks of the Hungarian forces took station even less willingly in the garrisons of the hostile and wild southern provinces than in the north, in Polish Galicia. This is the way we saw it. At the same time, in the Balkans—and not just there—the greedy expansion of the Monarchy and the recent annexation of the Slavic population produced ever sharper rebuffs—and so did the Hungarians' active role and expanded participation in these events which brought them the benefits of usufruct.

At home, the Kossuth ethos of oppositional sentiment faded; the flames of the spectacular fireworks of the Millenary celebrations blazed up and then died out. Kossuth's two sons returned from exile, but one of them soon fled to Italy again, to become an engineer there; the other son, Ferenc Kossuth, could have become a major political personality, but did not have a personality. A whole series of significant laws were passed; apparently, the couple of decades following the Compromise were truly a new age of reform. High-speed mechanical presses poured out newspapers, the country became a secular state, and public education was made more mundane and practical. Bourgeois equality before the law evolved; a bourgeoisie has also existed, but only a small fraction of the population could achieve the status of a citizen. The framework of parliamentarianism was similar to Western Europe's. But it could have been filled out with real meaning only on the basis of more modern suffrage. With regard to this issue—and such things have happened before—Vienna would yield, indeed would have liked to allow more than the dominant social classes in Hungary were willing to accept, or bear. Sometimes Vienna made the effort to rule by military governance but then the spirit of the Bach period haunted the scene—on both sides: in the organization of opposition, of passive resistance—sometimes constitutionalism was again brought forth from the repository of instruments.

The lack of land and the fact that the larger part of the areas newly reclaimed and protected from floods and made cultivable wound up in the hands of the old landowners, and the bulk of the benefits from the periodic agrarian booms were also theirs, produced agrarian socialist organizations. The greedy new industries also nurtured the labor movement, whose noted organizer, Leó Frankel, was one of the directors of the Paris Commune in 1871, returning to Hungary after its collapse.

At the turn of the century, a political personality of a greater stature finally appeared on the scene: Count István Tisza. However, he emerged from the conservative wing. His aggressive activities filled with intrigues are explained, in part, by the fact that after the turn of the century a purblind political jungle war replaced the reconciliation of ideas, principles, and programs in the Hungarian Parliament. The members of parliament discovered obstructive tactics and developed them to a superb degree:

the parliamentary "slow-down strike," which crippled the almost unformed bourgeois state mechanism to the point of paralysis with an endless prayer wheel of speeches, frequent roll call votes, etc.

And all this occurred at the time when Francis Joseph I, forgetting the humiliations of the not-so-distant Prussian–Austrian War and ungrateful to the court of the Russian czar who saved his trone in 1849, entered into a most binding alliance with the voracious German Empire. The Austrian-Hungarian relationship, which reached its latest nadir in 1905, was of vital importance to the development of the military forces. Amid the violent internal turns and struggles of the next, brief decade, Vienna and Budapest reached many compromises in the interest of the survival and functioning of Dualism, but the question of the army was the area in which Vienna made the fewest concessions.

Nevertheless, at the beginning of the 1910s, a wing of the Austrian high command did see clearly that the Monarchy was too weak to face the major clash that threatened. Perhaps it was this that supplied the background for the notorious Redl affair; possibly, this head of the Austrian spy agency who was "unmasked" in 1913 and forced to commit suicide was not a traitor to his country but a clear-headed skeptic. Among the leading Hungarian politicians, the one who, perhaps, best sensed the dangers of an early entry into the war was the one who, it must be added, had done so much to reforge the Monarchy: István Tisza, who was then serving as Prime Minister of Hungary for the second time and whom the greatest Hungarian poet at the turn of the century, Endre Ady, hated so much because he saw him as a true adversary among the numerous contemporary politicians of small caliber who, precisely because of the range of his visions and determination, bore an extraordinary responsibility for the destiny of the nation. But Tisza's resistance was able to delay the entry into the war for only two weeks.

The military maneuvers in the southern region, which Crown Prince Francis Ferdinand viewed in June 1914, were extremely provocative. It was purely fortuitous, on the other hand, that the half-amateurish assassination attempt made against him succeeded on the second try; even his unfortunate wife died with him. At most, the Serbian student, Gavrilo Princip, accelerated events with his pistol shots at Sarajevo. The assassination was not the cause.

It is not our task to trace the events of the next four years in detail. World War I was what it was. Almost every part of Europe, as well as other regions, participated in it; consequently, our picture of it is as various as the participants. Despite all preceding events suggesting something else, the war atmosphere, indeed its hysteria, seized the majority of Hungarian public opinion; Hungarians believed that they would be able to hail their victorious forces by the time leaves fell; hundreds of thousands sang, "Halt, halt there, beastly Serbia!"

Serious blunders by the army command, particularly in the beginning, accompanied the Monarchy's participation in the destructive war with its prolonged seesawing but frequently stationary fronts. Francis Joseph I, who, he said, "weighed everything, considered everything" (his portrait prepared at this time was distributed throughout the Monarchy, showing him lost in deep thought, his royal face buried in his hands), often chose key commanders on the basis of order of prestige and subjective attachment; this colorless

A battlefield scene—A painting by László Mednyánszky (1852–1919), mind-1910s. *Like all European countries, Hungary welcomed World War I with almost wholehearted enthusiasm. Its people became aware only slowly of the modern savagery of this prolonged and mechanized war of life and death—and the inevitability of Hungary's defeat. In their poems, Endre Ady, abstractly from a distance and Géza Gyóni from up close, being on the front, began to stir up sentiment with the authenticity of the horrible events experienced personally against the war, which the painter Baron László Mednyánszky also contributed, as above, with extremely moving protrayals of his on-site experiences, so that those who were not suffering at the fronts would finally wake up to the brutality and hopeless tragedy of the battles.*

emperor-bureaucrat had extremely little feeling for talent—and casualties remained tremendously heavy to the end. It was a lamentable act of honor how the Hungarians, as well as soldiers from recently annexed Bosnia, distinguished themselves in bloody battles with their military skill and personal bravery.

For Hungarians, the most painful memories were the circumstances and defeats in battles fought on the Russian front, in Galicia, for the fortifications at Przemysl, then in Brusilov's steam-roller offensive, and finally in the Italian and Slovene Karst region, on the plains of the River Isonzo. In the memory of entire generations were indelibly imprinted the scenes and events of brutal and bloody battles, the bayonet charges at Gorlice in Southern Poland, the blockade of Przemysl, and the horrible trench warfare at Doberdo in the Karst region, then in Italy, now in Yugoslavia, where every incoming round was made even more dangerous by stone fragments.

From among the manifold consequences of World War I, we shall emphasize four without heed to order of importance.

1. The Monarchy collapsed. Not only did Hungary, as well as the newly created Poland, secede, but three "successor states" also came into existence in a semicircle: Czechoslovakia, Rumania, and Yugoslavia.

2. Lenin's revolution in Russia began, after so many utopian plans, to form a living socialism.

3. The United States' acceptance of responsibilities in Europe made it into a decisive factor of power in world politics.

4. The inconsistencies and abuses of the series of peace agreements sowed the seeds of World War II.

Prophecies boding ill were futile. Hungarians realized too late how strong and deep-seated the activities of the nationalities were. When in 1920 at Versailles, outside Paris, the new borders of Hungary were laid down after long but one-sided negotiations in the Trianon Palace, the territory of the Hungarian nation was mutilated into a third its size, and its inhabitants shrank to two-fifths their former number. Though the Entente Powers dictating the peace terms did not agree to every one of the most extreme recommendations and requests, the Rumanians, who gained all of Transylvania, would have gladly advanced farther west, all the way to the River Tisza; among the Czech and Slovak politicians there were those who wanted to establish a dividing corridor between Austria and Hungary cutting through West Transdanubia and Slovenia right down to the Adriatic, and also a Czechoslovakian port on the Adriatic coast; Yugoslavia, made up of Southern Slav peoples, would have definitely liked to possess, if not Szeged perhaps, then Pécs and its environs, and to this end it founded the short-lived Baranya Republic.

What was happening to us? and how could what did happen happen the way it did?

THE RED AND THE WHITE

Destiny granted undeservedly to Francis Joseph I that the ruins of the Monarchy would not bury him. In 1916 he moved down into the crypt of the Viennese Capuchins, next to his wife and son. He did not outlive his third heir-apparent, another nephew of his, Charles (I as Austrian emperor, IV as Hungarian king). But this was of hardly any significance by now. Charles could have even been a genius—which he was not—everyone everywhere was fed up with the Habsburgs. And the need for a monarch was experienced only in those countries in the region, like Rumania and Yugoslavia, which felt the need for this traditional requisite to national legitimacy between their new state boundaries because they were still not nations and awaited establishment.

A revolutionary wave naturally followed the loss of the war, which led to such extensive loss of life and property that society, and not just the political system, was affected. (One of the first victims was Count István Tisza; assassins gunned him down.) Nevertheless, the Hungarian revolution maintained proper order, at least to the extent that at the outset (in October 1918), Hungary was "merely" a bourgeois democracy. Its leader, Count Mihály Károlyi—from the branch of the Károlyi family that we already know from the events of 1711—was a radical left-wing aristocrat who himself was soon to distribute his estate among the landless. But while the confidence in the Károlyi government at home was not slight, it had to cope with gigantic tasks. The ragged, bitter soldiers streaming home from the collapsed fronts encountered people sunk in misery at home; nearly every family was mourning someone lost in the war or wanting for a prisoner of war to return. The radical changes in Russia had won over many of the prisoners, and thousands and thousands of them still remained in Russia, voluntarily fighting alongside the Red Army of the young Soviet state on the battlefields of the civil war.

Károlyi would have liked to see a democratic and constitutional evolution to take place, and, meanwhile, he himself also gradually shifted to the left; but his temperament was too weak for the post of "trusteeship in bankruptcy" that he inevitably had to fill at the head of the nation. He carried out the act of dethronement

Lines of demarcations — Neutral zones (November 1918–March 1919)

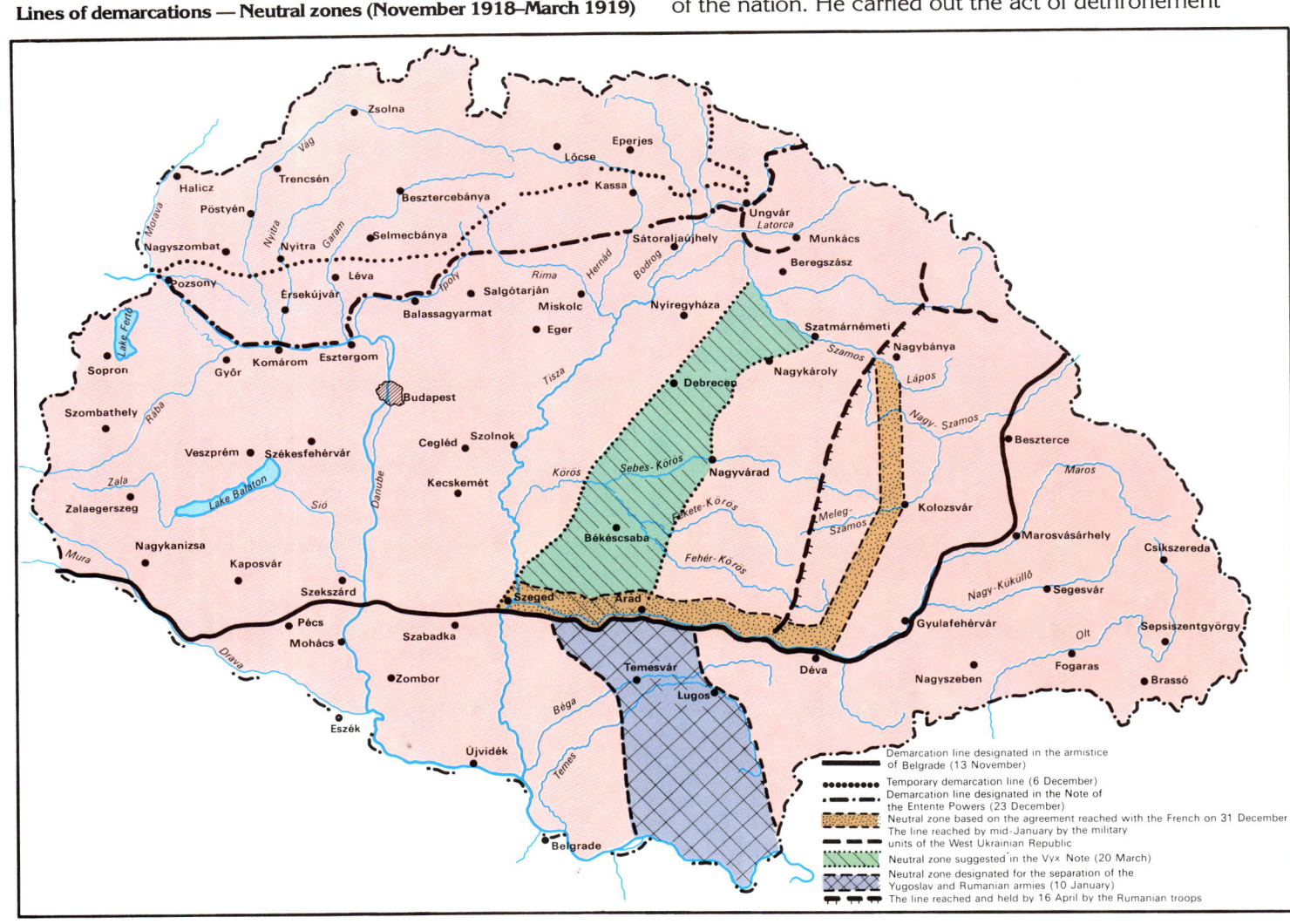

Demarcation line designated in the armistice of Belgrade (13 November)
Temporary demarcation line (6 December)
Demarcation line designated in the Note of the Entente Powers (23 December)
Neutral zone based on the agreement reached with the French on 31 December
The line reached by mid-January by the military units of the West Ukrainian Republic
Neutral zone suggested in the Vyx Note (20 March)
Neutral zone designated for the separation of the Yugoslav and Rumanian armies (10 January)
The line reached and held by 16 April by the Rumanian troops

The election of Mihály Károlyi as president of the republic (November 16, 1918). *The fate of Count Mihály Károlyi, a landowner, a liberal, and then a leftwing politician, was tragic on more than one count. He was the leader of the nation during the transitional period after it collapsed at the end of 1918; he had received his very limited power from the Habsburgs and handed it over to the Communists. Later, the question of the extent to which he retreated from and gave way to Béla Kun and his supporters of his own accord was the subject of heated debate. During the nearly thirty years he spent in exile, he became increasingly radical in his views. In 1946, he was welcomed home with all solemnity, but a real place in the political life of the nation never developed for him. He resigned his ambassadorship to Paris as a protest to the Rajk trial. He was certain about the falseness of the charges against Rajk, yet his old commitments put him in a schizophrenic situation: he moderated his protests, and withdrawn from politics, he died in 1955. His remains were brought home in 1962.*

and became President of the Republic in January 1919. Though no peace treaty had been concluded, the armies of the "successor states" pressed forward to the lines of demarcation that Trianon largely sanctioned later. Then they marched on. The Entente's local emissaries and the distant central bodies were firm, but only with the Hungarians, who in their eyes unambiguously signified that defeated side which they did not believe capable, after achieving independence, of true revival, of breaking out of the shadows of a past tying it to the Austro-Hungarian Monarchy. On the other hand, they did not act with sufficient firmness in dealing with the states of the later Little Entente. (An exception was the clash between Rumanians and Serbians in the south, in the Bácska region, over a contested—and till then Hungarian—strip of land. On this occasion, a French force separated them. The result of this incident was that Szeged and its environs also came under the occupation of French colonial—Senegalese—troops...)

The growing pressure from the left and the threatening and indeed the ensuing loss of territory undermined the Károlyi régime. The communists led by Béla Kun, uniting their party with that of the social democrats, forced Károlyi to resign. The Hungarian Soviet Republic came into being on March 21, 1919, with a bloodless assumption of power. It lasted for 133 days.

Today, it is possible to analyze calmly the kind of errors rooted in objective and subjective causes that Kun—who was later one of the leaders of the Comintern in Moscow, who wrestled arduously with the idea of the People's Front, and who, in the end, was a victim of Stalin's despotism —committed on the way after the seizure of power and its organization, which began with not inconsiderable success, when Soviet Hungary linked itself so quickly and buoyantly to the trend of world revolution which the war created and which, at the time, augured much wider expansion. Instead of distributing land, he nationalized the large estates and thus, by giving priority to supplying the cities and by issuing compulsory requisitions for food products, he alienated the peasant masses; the measures taken against the actions of the opposition, the counterrevolution, were inconsistent; the broad view impairing the revolution's trustworthiness alternated with compulsory measures that appaled the middle classes, and so on. All this is true. However, this is not the issue. The Hungarian Soviet Republic, then and there, did not have a chance. Not a chance from the moment it became evident that the hoped-for, swift-moving world revolution had come to an abrupt halt at its very inception (the third revolutionary experiment of the Soviet type, the Bavarian, was even more fragile than the Hungarian), and that the Soviet Red Army could not break through on the Ukrainian front into the Carpathians to provide the assistance that Béla Kun and his supporters requested.

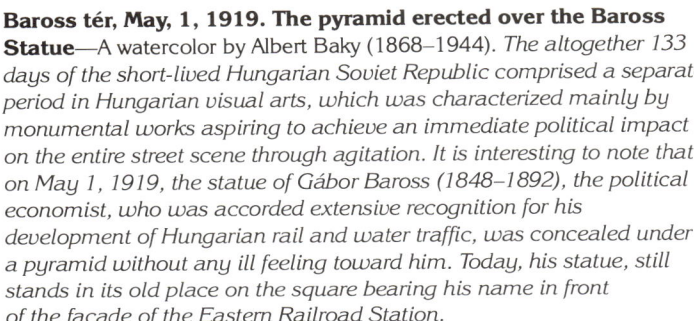

Baross tér, May, 1, 1919. The pyramid erected over the Baross Statue—A watercolor by Albert Baky (1868–1944). *The altogether 133 days of the short-lived Hungarian Soviet Republic comprised a separate period in Hungarian visual arts, which was characterized mainly by monumental works aspiring to achieve an immediate political impact on the entire street scene through agitation. It is interesting to note that on May 1, 1919, the statue of Gábor Baross (1848–1892), the political economist, who was accorded extensive recognition for his development of Hungarian rail and water traffic, was concealed under a pyramid without any ill feeling toward him. Today, his statue, still stands in its old place on the square bearing his name in front of the façade of the Eastern Railroad Station.*

Don't hesitate!—A poster by Jenő Erbits (1893–?). *When the Hungarian Soviet Republic recruited a new army to face the assault of intervening Czech and Rumanian forces, mobilization posters were created in the distinctive graphic style that developed within the leftwing workers' movement. The "heroic realism"—let us call it that—represented by this poster later took several forms. One version became the official style of the far right, for example in Nazi Germany; another version, on the other hand, later flourished temporarily under the name of socialist realism.*

Yet the beginning was encouraging. Within days a Hungarian Red Army came into existence that included young workers rallying to the call-to-arms and fighting shoulder-to-shoulder against the Rumanians in the east and the Czech interventionists in the north, as well as professional and reserve veteran soldiers who were ready to enter battle under flags of any color to preserve the integrity of the country. The two most outstanding leaders of these armed forces were Jenő Landler, a Socialist and then a Communist lawyer, a former antimilitarist and antiwar strike leader, and Aurél Stromfeld, an élite member of the Monarchy's army staff. But the Entente, which if it did not trust Károlyi and his entourage, trusted Kun and his associates even less, rendered ineffective successively everything that had been achieved by military means.

And that ever-growing group of politicians and soldiers who saw the white and not the red as Hungary's future color organized in Vienna and assembled in Szeged. The Entente looked upon them with suspicion, too, but considered them by far the lesser evil. A conservative, maybe a slightly liberal restoration but strictly without

the Habsburgs—this sounded much more acceptable to influential French, English, and Italian political circles than a "experimental" workers' state.

The legacy that forced Károlyi to capitulate to the Communists also swept Kun and company away. There was no power that could reconcile Hungarian public opinion to the loss of territory which the nation had already suffered and which still threatened it. In August 1919, a Social Democratic government took shape for a few days. A large band of leaders of the Soviet Republic fled to Vienna by train.

Wearing the feather of the white crane on their field caps, detachments of commissioned and non-commissioned officers quickly headed from Szeged in two prongs toward Budapest, which, meanwhile, had been occupied by Rumanian troops under the Entente's authority. A brutal sequel followed the reprisals upon which the military forces of the by-then royal Rumania had already embarked. Executions, torture, corporal punishment, and anti-Jewish pogroms marked the detachment's passage to the "sinful" capital, the main seat of the Hungarian Bolsheviks. Counterrevolutionary terrorism far surpassed the terror of the revolution in both the number of victims and cruelty.

The gray eminence of the white turn-about was Count István Bethlen, the owner of a vast estate in Transylvania.

However, a soldier was needed as a leader. Why was it that among the countless commissioned officers it was a sailor, Rear Admiral Miklós Horthy, from Nagybánya—the long-time aide-de-camp of Francis Joseph I and the commander-in-chief of the Austro-Hungarian battle fleet at the end of the war—who

therefore costly development. For example, several railway lines ended up a stone's throw from the Hungarian border; thus, they were lost to us, but, on the other hand, they could not really be utilized on the other side along the edge of the successor state either.

Though Karl Marx employed this phrase in relation

The entry of the National Army into Budapest on November 16, 1919—A copper engraving by Géza Wágner (1879–1939). *When Miklós Horthy of Nagybánya entered Budapest at the head of his notorious white-plumed troops, and had himself named, after a few months, on March 1, 1920, the regent of a kingdom without a king, its commander-in-chief, with the support of his military forces, for a time he seemed to be the captive, the hostage of his far-right officer detachments. Later, when, as a precondition to prospective loans from the West, Horthy had to consolidate his counterrevolutionary government, it was of no small concern to him to fend off and keep his early supporters under control, who were in part monarchistic and in part even more nationalistic than he was.*

came to the forefront? He was senior in rank among the officers assembled in Szeged. In 1918, he displayed determination following the sailors' revolt at Cattaro (Kotor). He was the descendant of a pure-blooded Hungarian medium landowning family; he could not, it is true, really boast about possessing any outstanding abilities, and he spoke Hungarian poorly, and was a Calvinist... If only he would have arrived aboard a gunboat on the Danube! But, attired in a dark-blue sailor's dress cape, he entered Budapest on a white horse at the head of his detachments in November 1919. And thus began that period when Hungary was a kingdom without a king, and its ruler a sailor, even though the country had no outlet to the sea. However, the Entente accepted this strange situation, in fact supported it. It withdrew the Little Entente's and its own forces, naturally only from between the borders drawn in Trianon. Thus further dismemberment of the country was averted, and if it did remain somewhat restricted, its national sovereignty was restored.

However, when we examine the new borders, two of their characteristic features emerge. 1. Several million Hungarians remained outside the nation's borders. Some of them were inseparably melded with other nationalities, but immediately on the other side of its borders were found regions made up entirely or almost entirely of Hungarians with which large numbers of non-Hungarian inhabitants would not have been turned over to Hungary. 2. The new boundary lines practically crippled several areas. Many Hungarian cities close to the border but more of them beyond it in the successor states were stripped of a substantial part of their gravitational centers and economic and population bases; consequently, they were either sentenced to slow decline or condemned to a forced and

to Czarist Russia, the Austro-Hungarian Monarchy was once also called the "peoples' prison." Sometimes it really deserved this name. However, what replaced it became some kind of "peoples' cotenancy," a compulsory temporary accommodation which, with requisite goodwill and compromises, could have been equipped with every modern convenience. Instead, the former "prison inmates," nursing grudges against each other, ruined the jointly used furnishings so that nothing would remain for the other party. A real catastrophe resulted. Rivalry over the ruins of the Monarchy and mutual suspicion and hatred muddled human contact and severed the most rational regional economic relations (exchange of commodities, transport, public health, etc.). Every small state in East Central Europe aspired to national self-sufficiency, though their production structure supplemented each other's very closely—it was precisely this that supplied the economic setting that made it possible to hold together somehow an otherwise most heterogeneous Monarchy!—furthermore, these states were forced into and shipped to distant and costlier markets. (It was at this time, for example, that the Hungarian flour-milling industry collapsed.)

The following is not an evasion but an explanation of the fact that the chief and, at times, the only rallying cry heard during the quarter century of the Horthy period concerned the enlargement of the country, rectification of its borders: "Dismembered Hungary is not a country, undivided Hungary is heaven." But if national borders had followed the true ethnic borders more closely, then who would have actually listened to Hungarians with large estates who employed only non-Hungarian field hands on lands that had ended up in a foreign state? Thus again, the harsh illogic of the borders rendered the grievance nationwide.

Those who resettled so that they could remain within Hungary's borders only enhanced the prevailing mood—they were predominantly state officials and people in the middle levels—and they were obliged to live for years in rail cars pushed onto the siderails of shunting depots.

From the very first moment, Horthy and his White Army made efforts to revise the borders. The sole, small success, as it happened, was achieved in the west. The city of Sopron and its environs had been awarded

stopped emphasizing this—he was faithful to the oath that bound him to the Habsburg throne. He proved this by legally reestablishing the institution of royalty. But why did he not go further? A significant proportion of his military and political base wanted him to do so. So much so, that Charles, who, driven from the country, had fled to Switzerland, twice entered the country at summons from the monarchists and with their complicity, claiming the throne lawfully for himself. His second attempt was

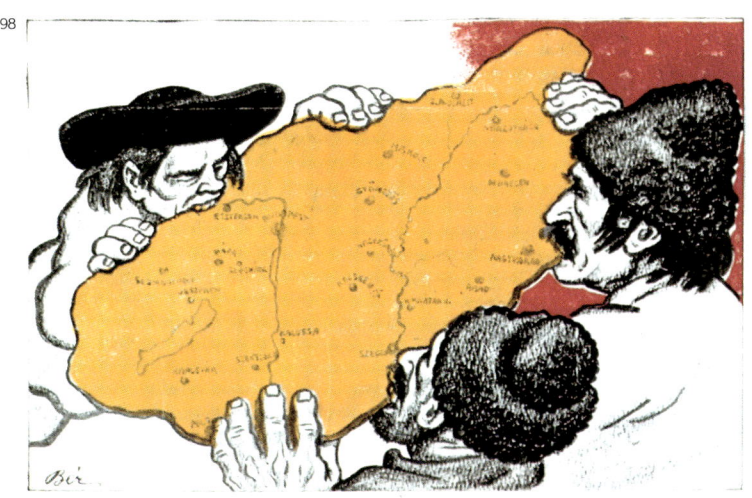

Justice for Hungary!—Irredentist postcards. *In the beginning, Horthy's Hungary wanted solely to correct the unquestionably misconceived and unjust territorial provisions of the 1920 Paris (Trianon) peace agreements through the revision of national borders in ways that benefited Hungary. Instead of reconciliation and cooperation in reducing the significance of the borders, it opted to the end for national, political, and ideological—and military—opposition. The many kinds of irredentist and revisionist propaganda it carried on did not recoil from crude devices that wounded the self-esteem of neighboring peoples (whereupon, of course, the neighbors replied in kind).*

to Burgenland, Austria. But a guerilla-like assault forced the weak Austrian troops to flee, and later it became possible to put the question of the region's future to a local referendum. Sopron remained Hungarian, and thus gained the name of City of Loyalty. But this action attracted attention not so much because it succeeded but because it typified how much the peace treaty failed to establish future political security and, instead, meted out punishment for the past. In what way? Even if we consider ridiculous the fact that the former national territory of Hungary had also been mutilated for Austria's benefit, that does not wash away the enormous responsibility of Hungarians for World War I. Though a significant segment of the inhabitants of Sopron and its vicinity was German-speaking, the majority of them were not, however. And at the time of the plebiscite, even a part of these favored belonging to Hungary.

Horthy had to tack about. The detachments that had raised him to the peak of power with such strong, bloody hands became too much for him. Their brutality and independence compromised him in the eyes of the Entente and the European bankers and even the citizens and capitalists indispensable to the consolidation of Hungary. Horthy was a military man, but he did not want to establish a junta. He would not share power. Not even with a king. Seemingly, or according to his statements—he never

noteworthy on account of the fact that it was, perhaps, the first hijacking of an airplane in the world: loyal supporters, former pilots, stole a plane and conveyed him to Hungarian soil from Switzerland: a daring air feat at the time.

At the head of an army joining him in Transdanubia, Charles IV reached the city limits of Budapest, where Horthy stopped him with a small army consisting, in part, of hastily armed university students. The Entente unanimously supported Horthy, and an English war vessel coming up the Danube took the captured Charles IV aboard and carried him into exile on the Island of Madeira. (He soon died. His son, Otto, is today a well-known political personality, as a citizen in Western Europe.)

Foreign countries had to be pacified once and for all—and also runaway inflation at home. Count István Bethlen was the unruffled father of the consolidation. Count Pál Teleki was the first prime minister—he, too, was an owner of a large estate in Transylvania, and otherwise an important geographer who was chiefly an authority on ethnic groups and economic geography; as such he participated, by invitation, in the first demarcation of the state borders of modern Iraq in 1924–25. Then Bethlen himself became the head of the government.

In the mid-1920s, Hungary was a bourgeois state living in relative peace, with a functioning parliament. The Communist Party was illegal. The Social Democratic Party, in order to be able to function in the cities and among the workers, renounced, in a pact, agitation among the majority agrarian population. The nation's structure contained numerous obsolete accessories and irritating features; these were distributing factors, but they did not obstruct some modernization in the spirit of conservatism and liberalism. Public education and public health improved and there were many technical courses offered in the villages; an extensive network of marketing cooperatives developed under the name of *Hangya* (Ant).

DEATH BEND

Quo vadis? Whither, man? However strange it may seem, the Horthy régime moved left from 1920 to the end of the decade. Of course, it did so not from principle or the heart but from necessity. It had started out so far to the right that it could not do anything else, and the consolidation to replace the terror quickly became its vital concern. Moreover, ever present among the Horthyites was the inferiority complex stemming from the fact that they were not the ones who brought down the Soviet Republic. They were not conquering heroes; at best they were avengers and beneficiaries. The Entente had not staked out their path from one point to the next, and yet, it was this latitude that cleared the way for them. At the same time, it did impose bounds on them for a long time.

Then the world economic crisis, which also shook the most developed countries very severely, ruined banks, ravaged money markets, and made hundreds of millions the prey of unemployment and poverty, while locomotives were being fired with wheat and coffee—and not far from us, helped Hitler come to power—that crisis reached less-developed Hungary after a brief delay. But then it immediately muddled the prosperity that was barely a few years old and just beginning to emerge at the end of the reconstruction period: it set back the regeneration of a Hungarian industry that had switched from a war to a peace economy and manufactured mostly consumer goods—and thus was very sensitive to the development of the buyers' market—and, not for the first or last time, it choked the agrarian economy into a cycle of overproduction.

The economic crisis was not yet over, but receding, when a right-wing army officer, Gyula Gömbös, pushed Bethlen aside. With Gömbös an unmistakable fascism gained ground. This was signaled by corporate endeavors, the social demagogy appropriating some of the arguments and objectives of the leftists, racism, brutal violence, and unbridled friendship with Italy and Germany, the fawning over Benito and Adolf. After a forced and modest turn to the left dictated by consolidation, the pendulum swung to the right. And when the economic crisis ended in our area, hopes for war kept the new prosperity going. In Győr, situated in the center of a strip of land along the Danube and intended to become, with no slight misstatement of dimensions, the "Hungarian Ruhr region," the new Prime Minister, Kálmán Darányi, announced the Győr Program. This conception put heavy industry in the gravitational center of industrial activity which served the rearmament long prohibited by the Entente. However, because of the shortage of time and money, it was only partially realized (which was to be clearly demonstrated by the very deficient equipment with which the Hungarian army fought in World War II). An unlimited outlet for Hungarian agricultural products quickly opened—in the Nazi Third Reich.

Smaller steps were also taken: cautious and limited land reform, social programs. The impoverished in the villages could obtain land and inexpensive homes in some places. White-collar workers and certain levels of laborers could enjoy the benefits of social insurance. Grand concepts for the development of the economy or society taking into account the nation's domain as a permanent reality were not initiated. Trianon remained the general basis of reference, the diabolical cause of every Hungarian difficulty, its rectification was held out as a promise whose possible fulfillment would solve all problems as if by magic. In case some difficulty should, by chance, still remain, that could be remedied if we, it was said, would protect Hungarians from the assimilated, from the advance of the "foreign" element that had been admitted, chiefly the Jews. With the eyes of the Hungarians closed to what Hitler openly professed in the pages of *Mein Kampf*, which was obtainable in local bookstores in Hungary, and to the shameless promises and the unhindered way in which the brown-shirted Volksbund was drawing closer to the German minority in Hungary, the illusion persisted that the future of Hungary could unfold in the shadow of Germany.

Nor was the nation brought to its senses by the *Anschluss* that liquidated the state existence of our former partner, Austria, or by the first Nazi blitzkrieg in the fall of 1939 that forced many tens of thousands to flee from Poland across the Carpathians in part to Hungary, in part across our country to other places. The expression of solidarity, kept alive by the historical Polish—Hungarian friendship, was not based on an ephemeral enthusiasm. In spite of German protests, the fate of Poles compelled to remain with us was in good hands; many of them achieved their liberation here, and those who headed across the Balkans to the south, to the Free Polish Armies siding with the British, received assistance in their journey. But this small Polish interlude and the manner in which French soldiers fleeing later to Hungary from German imprisonment found asylum with us amid the hell of war represented not even a momentary halt in our country's calamitous course.

By this time the First Vienna Award had, after all, come into being. In the fall of 1938, Ribbentrop and Ciano, the German and Italian foreign ministers respectively, functioning as a "court of arbitration," granted to Hungary considerable territories in Slovakia containing a significant number of Hungarian inhabitants. This decision was based chiefly on ethnic considerations. For this reason, the boundary line twisted and turned in such a way that for the next few years, every train heading for Kassa (Košice) had to pass through Czechoslovakian territory before reaching its destination. On the other hand, the population of the areas "returned home" was nearly 90 percent Hungarian and less than 10 percent Slovakian. (If these data did not reflect the ethnic proportions accurately, it may have been because, for example, Jews living in the areas overwhelmingly considered and declared themselves to be

Hungarians. Later, this did not much improve their fate, however.) It is worth noting that, after the First Vienna Award, many Hungarians who "returned home" bitterly observed that though they were subject to harmful discrimination as members of a national minority "over there," the bourgeois Republic of Czechoslovakia did enforce civil rights and human equality to a much greater extent, while the most minor officeholder in a still half-feudal Hungary was arrogant, its gendarmes abusive—its whole atmosphere shabby.

The Second Vienna Award was put together in the summer of 1940. In this agreement—again Ribbentrop and Ciano—gave back to Hungary a part of Transylvania in such a way that the ethnic ratio of the transferred

Miklós Horthy as Hitler's guest. *Between August 1936 and March 1944, Horthy visited Nazi Germany on eight occasions. He did so three times in 1938, though he was only Göring's hunting guest on one of the occasions. In reality, the nationalist Horthy should have fled from Hitler, who was a threat to all non-Germanic peoples living in the vicinity of Germany; but contrary to this logic, Horthy's orientation was determined by a common desire for revenge and the pursuit of advantages that could temporarily—only temporarily!—be gained through German expansion. After the bloodless "territorial acquisitions" achieved through the two Vienna Awards, in 1941, the treacherous act committed against Yugoslavia created a still not final but morally a completely unforgivable alignment between the Nazi Reich and Hungary. In this photograph, Horthy and Hitler are flanked by German naval officers; the Führer underlined his esteem for the regent's naval past during the visit in this way.*

99

population was more unfavorable because of the more complex location of the settlements: Hungarians comprised not quite 52 percent, while the Rumanians reached 42 percent.

Meanwhile, what was happening between the Soviet Union and Hungary? At the beginning of 1939, when Hungary joined Japan, Germany, and Italy in the Anti-Comintern Pact, the Soviet Union broke off the rather formal diplomatic relations which existed since 1934. But when Stalin decided on a non-aggression pact between the Soviet Union and Germany, the Soviets were apprehensive and made additional conciliatory gestures so as to guarantee their border in the area of the Carpathians too. At the Soviets' suggestion, diplomatic relations

between the Soviet Union and Hungary were restored in the autumn of 1939. A year later, the two countries signed a trade agreement. Then Hungary released and handed over two Communist leaders sentenced to life imprisonment, Mátyás Rákosi and Zoltán Vas.
As a counterbalance, at the beginning of 1941, a special train with a guard of honor transported fifty-six flags of the 1848–49 Hungarian Army from Moscow to Budapest. The czar's forces had captured them at the time of the suppression of the War of Independence. Barely a few days later, Count Pál Teleki died. Why?

The partial territorial revision with regard to Czechoslovakia and Rumania was carried out by extortionate means but without any bloodshed—data on alleged carnages in Transylvania by the Hungarian forces marching in and made public later were fabrications, ridiculous exaggerations of a few minor incidents. Sub-Carpathia (today the so-called "Trans-Carpathian" territory of the Ukraine) was similary transferred in the third stage, at the time of Czechoslovakia's complete dismemberment. The fourth stage in rectifying the Trianon decision was the last gamble in the game of chance. There was no turning back any longer. When Hitler overran the internally weak Yugoslavia in the spring of 1941 Hungary not only permitted the transit of Nazi forces against the country with which it had shortly before signed an "eternal" treaty of friendship. It also wanted to do its share or at least lend a hand in the treacherous attack.

By this time, Teleki had been Prime Minister for two years. Earlier, I mentioned that he was a noted geographer. I did not mention that he was the "chief boy scout" of the country. He was a schizoid character. A vacillating moralist. He supported serious fact-uncovering sociological investigations that produced revolting data from the depths of society. He arrived at agreements with the extremists of aggressive racism, perhaps in order to take the wind out of their sails in the spirit of his own more moderate national ideals and to form a counterweight to German racism.

Now Teleki found himself in an impossible situation. And so he threw his life away. His gesture was dramatic but futile in the long run. It is impossible not to quote the confused letter he wrote minutes before his death, his cry of distress to Admiral Horthy: "Honorable Sir! We have become perfidious—out of cowardice—with regard to the treaty of everlasting peace based on the Mohács speech. The nation senses it, and abandoned its honor. We sided with the scoundrels—because not a single word about the trumped-up atrocities is true! Not against the Hungarians and not against the Germans either! We will become bodysnatchers. The most beastly nation. I did not stop you. I am guilty."

The gesture was late politically and ineffective but absolutely genuine as a personal act. On hearing news of his death, Winston Churchill, the English Prime Minister, said that an empty chair would be reserved for Teleki at the future peace conference. This pronouncement belongs among Churchill's noble and better moments. But at the 1946–47 Paris Peace Conference, not a word was spoken about the empty chair that Pál Teleki's phantom was to occupy.

In the territory retaken from Yugoslavia at the cost of some fighting—because here some resistance did appear—only 36 or 37 percent of the inhabitants were Hungarians; true, the Germans among them formed 20 percent; the rest were Southern Slavs and other nationalities. One, however, has to take into account

Horthy at the celebration held on the return of Kolozsvár to Hungary— A photograph, 1941. *Gaining the laudatory epithet of "expander of territory" after the First Vienna Award, at the cost of Czehoslovakia, and the second, at the cost of Rumania, Horthy entered—again on a white horse, as he had Budapest in 1919—the part of the country newly returned to Hungary through the good offices of Hitler and Mussolini amid a tremendous celebration. However, it became quite apparent during the reannexation of territory that took place almost without a shot being fired that the proud Hungarian national army was hardly capable of action because of its defective equipment, inadequate training, and poor leadership. But this did not produce any sobering effects; instead, preparations for war were increased.*

the fact that a significant Serbian colonization had occurred after 1918. But even so, it is evident that during the course of Horthy's "enlargement of the country," the ethnic ratio gradually worsened.

In June 1941, Hungary entered the war against the Soviet Union (and, as a consequence, it ended up in a state of war against the Allied Powers lining up against the Axis Powers). This act was again extremely unusual. It is a fact that five days after the Nazi attack began, the Hungarian army was already rallying for a blitzkrieg against the Soviet Union. *Nota bene*: a considerable part of the army was relying on horse-drawn equipment and was composed of "fast-moving detachments" mounted on bicycles... Not consulting Parliament, Prime Minister László

Bárdossy had, in fact, launched Hungary in the war illegally; in answer to the bombing of Kassa (Košice) which, he claimed, was a Soviet provocation. But what reason would the Soviet Union have had to provoke Hungary? After all, even in the last minute it tried with gestures rare in the practice of diplomacy to keep Hungary from entering the war. Of course, as early as the summer of 1941, the rumor spread that the planes that dropped a few bombs offhandedly on Kassa—as well as on Munkács (Mukachevo) and Rahó (Rakhov)—belonged to a formation of the Nazi *Luftwaffe*. It contradicted the rumor that the German *political* leadership did not want Hungary to enter the war at the time because the undisturbed flow of Hungarian food products, bauxite, and crude oil was

The Soviet Union returns the flags of the 1848 Hungarian Army—Welcoming the flags in Budapest. *The return of the army's battle flags formerly removed as war trophies was not the only Soviet gesture aimed at keeping Hungary out of the new World War. On July 23, 1941, the day between the beginning of the treacherous German attack and the severance of diplomatic relations between the Soviet Union and Hungary, Soviet Foreign Minister Molotov, conversing in a tone uncommon in diplomacy, intimated to the Hungarian ambassador in Moscow and through him to Horthy and his supporters that the Soviet Union had no demands or requests—other than neutrality—to make of Hungary, and stood ready to support its claims to Transylvania.*

more important to its war effort, and Germany's war industry was not in the position either to supplement the armaments of the badly equipped Hungarian forces. At the same time, the *Wehrmacht* would have been pleased if the Hungarian army—in addition to the Slovakian and Rumanian—would have assisted German troops attacking on a very wide front. It was also rumored that Slovakian airplanes had carried out the mysterious attack in reprisal for the territorial annexations, and also that the planes were Rumanian because the Rumanians suspected that if the Hungarian forces did not wage war in the east, then they might devote their energy to the occupation of the remaining parts of Transylvania. As a matter of fact, it is astounding that from 1941 to the present day, no authoritative data, documents, or statements concerned with this event have come to light; not a single secret journal of war operations, not a single participant or witness, nothing.

In the beginning, the army ordered to the eastern front was limited in size, and the 1914 illusion that it would be sent home victoriously in a few weeks prevailed. However, in the spring of 1942 the Second Hungarian Army of 200 thousand was dispatched to the Russian front. In January 1943, the Russian army looked for and found the weakest point at the great bend of the River Don at Voronezh and executed a breakthrough on the front line of the Rumanian forces fighting on the side of the Nazis; then, widening the breakthrough, it routed powerful forces, encircled

them, took prisoners, and pursued them toward the west; at this time, the Second Hungarian Army lost 150 thousand of its 200 thousand men.

Many of those who fell in action or were taken prisoner were not carrying weapons. They were members of forced labor units, and they performed the hardest and most dangerous work behind the front. Members of the opposition, Jews, and national minorities under suspicion were conscripted into these units, which labored under armed guards on the eastern front and in Hungary. At first, members of the Arrow-Cross Party—the Hungarian National Socialists—were included in the opposition, but later only Social Democrats and Communists. The horrible mathematics of the war, of murder, bears witness to the fact that though it was not an exaggeration to call a part of the forced labor units, mainly those ordered to the east, a portable slaughterhouse because some commanders aimed not at working the conscripts but at exterminating them, a greater proportion of the conscripted Jewish males survived than those who were later hauled off with their families to the death camps.

After the annihilation of the Second Hungarian Army, Hungarian politics—again under a new Prime Minister, Miklós Kállay—more or less comprehended the fiasco of the path followed and began a double game. The Nazis pressed for intensification of the war effort; the Hungarians tried, instead, to diminish it and to call the Allies' attention, namely that of the Western Powers, to this effort. Feelers, apparently cautious and secretive but closely followed by the Germans, were begun to arrange the pull-out from the war—to the West. But however heterogeneous and casual the anti-Hitler coalition under Soviet and American, British and French leadership was, it did not permit a separate deal of this kind.

By the time Horthy recognized this, by the time he really came to believe that the Hungarian army fighting on the eastern front could turn to the Soviets, the "ancient enemy," only for armistice terms, it was again too late. Italy pulled out of the war somehow or other. In March 1944,

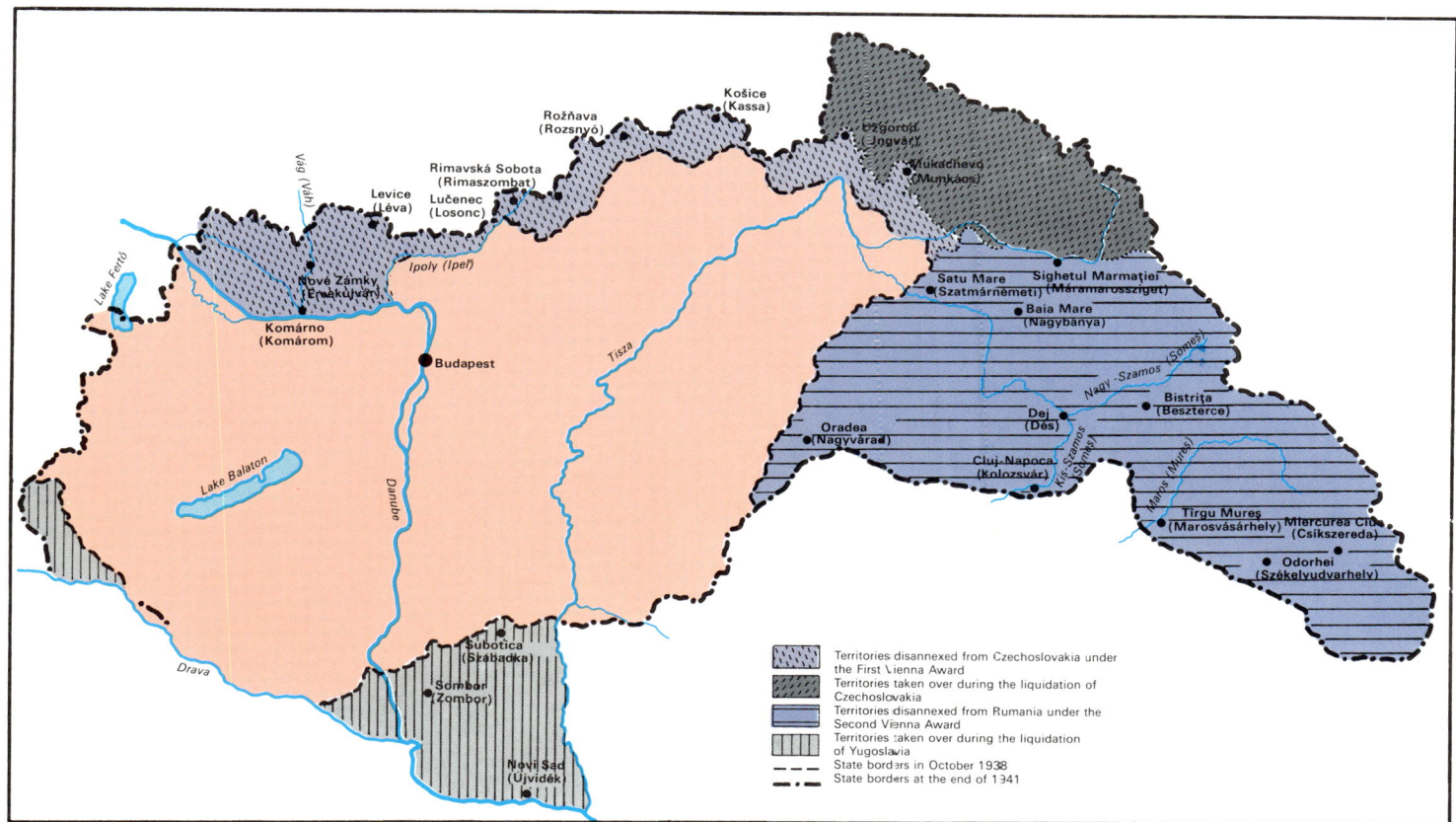

Territorial changes during World War II

while Horthy was conferring at Hitler's general headquarters, a small German army occupied Hungary. Horthy did not even have the strength to resist at least personally; no, he simply settled for a preservation of appearances, a tremendously limited sovereignty.

And now the most monstrous sowing also ripened. From the beginning, the Horthy era, which entered the stage with its White Terror, had leanings toward anti-Semitism and restrained it only temporarily. The régime produced its first Jewish law in 1938, its second in 1939, and its third in 1941, limiting ever more tightly the possibilities of activity and means of livelihood for Jewish citizens. However, their confinement to ghettos and shipment to German death camps began only after the German occupation, under Adolf Eichmann's administration but with the widespread cooperation of Hungarians. Though those in the Budapest ghetto ultimately escaped through the intense pressure of international protests, laymen and clergy rescued many Jews at great personal risk; and the cooperation of the Swedish, Swiss, and other embassies, as well as the Red Cross, was significant in the saving of lives. This is the balance sheet (approximately so, since accurate data are not ascertainable): the number of Jewish victims in Hungary during World War II was 400 thousand; 90 percent of the Hungarian Jews in the provinces were lost and nearly half of those living in Budapest.

The aim of Hungary in World War II—its first, second, and third aims – would have been the restoration of its borders to their pre-Trianon status, namely, territorial revision. This was shattered. It became clear that the First and Second Vienna Awards and then the acquisitions wrested by force of arms would have meant nothing after a war ending in defeat. More specifically, the fate of Transylvania was still in balance in the summer of 1944. According to indications, everything depended on who

would liberate the contested territories from the Germans. In addition to the constantly growing military, civilian, and economic losses, it was this factor that motivated Horthy's and his cohorts' continuing attempts to pull out of the war even after the Germans occupied Hungary. But in August 1944, Royal Rumania succeeded in pulling out. The Soviet and Rumanian armies, which had by now combined forces, immediately began their joint attack, and the weak Hungarian army, setting out from the borders drawn up in 1940, was unable to contain them. In the north, the range of the Carpathians could be stoutly defended, but in the southeast, Soviet units in September 1944 reached the border established by Trianon. Soon they were at Szeged, from where Horthy had started out with his detachments in 1919.

At the beginning of October, a gigantic tank battle commenced around Debrecen. On October 15, Horthy, in a radio address, declared a ceasefire for which he had prepared only diplomatically but not politically or militarily. The pull-out collapsed within hours. The Nazis were lying in wait. For example, the very same SS tough, Otto Skorzeny, who had freed Mussolini from captivity with his parachute commandos after the Italian pull-out, this time took young Miklós Horthy hostage in Budapest. The grief-stricken Regent handed power officially to the leader of the Hungarian National Socialists, the Arrow-Cross, Ferenc Szálasi, while he and his family were interned in Germany. (Although the Hungarian people's tribunal later condemned several ministers and generals who carried out Horthy's policies for their war crimes—most of whom were captured by the Americans who handed them over to the authorities of the new Hungary—Horthy avoided this fate; he died in exile in Portugal in 1957.)

Szálasi, this former officer of the general staff who was more muddle-headed than Hitler, created an idiotic reign of terror in the limited territory under his rule. The siege of Budapest began at the end of 1944. Actually, the German army was desperately defending here the Vienna Basin and the only oil field still at its disposal,

the one in Zala County. But the war in the country did not end even after the siege of the Hungarian capital and its capitulation.

Meanwhile, efforts were made to have regular Hungarian troops take part in the final crushing of the Nazi Third Reich... A group of soldiers who wound up as prisoners of the Soviet army initiated the establishment of a Hungarian legion, but they were not given the opportunity to carry out their plan. And the new democratic Hungarian army recruited in the liberated part of the country by the Provisional Government formed in Debrecen did not become battle-ready in time. Only the military cooperation of a single, spontaneously rallied outfit, the Buda Voluntary Regiment, could be observed in the battles for Budapest.

The last important battle of the war initiated by the Germans was the large winter breakthrough in the Ardennes in December 1944. When that faltered, the few still combat-worthy élite guards of the German army, with the still effective Sixth SS Panzer Army, were hastily transferred to Hungary, to Transdanubia, where, deployed in the Lake Balaton area, they were to hold on to the Zala oil fields. When the Soviet forces eventually liberated the last Hungarian town early in April 1945, barely a month was left of World War II in Europe.

The plaque of immunity of the Swedish Red Cross from the house at Úri utca 19. *In addition to the efforts of diplomats from Switzerland and other neutral countries, members of the Red Cross, and private individuals, Raoul Wallenberg's heroic deeds, often rich with motifs of adventure novels, stood out in his rescue of at least a part of those persons who were threatened with that deportation which led to death at the time of the Hungarian Holocaust. Swedish "protected houses" and safe conduct passes—documenting Sweden's willingness to provide shelter—extended escape from certain death to thousands, indeed tens of thousands. Wallenberg himself, who needed to be in communication with the Western Powers struggling in an alliance with the Soviet Union, disappeared at the beginning of 1945. As became obvious later, he was arrested as a "suspected spy" and thrown into a Soviet prison; to the present, his fate, his death is full of details unclarified as yet.*

The arrow-cross takeover on October 16, 1944—Szálasi's supporters enter Buda Castle. *Horthy's attempt to pull out of the war on October 15 came too late, though even then it was unprepared for. And it was not the least frustrated by the officer corps: a considerable number of them were secret members or sympathizers of the Arrow-Cross Party. They did not turn against the Germans; on the contrary, they joined the fascist "putsch," leaving the "Supreme Commander" in the lurch. Ferenc Szálasi was the leader of the Hungarian National Socialists and as "Hungarian Führer" he is shown surrounded by Hungarian officers who joined up, in the foreground, with German Storm Troopers observing the scene in the background.*

Soviet soldiers in battle in Budapest on January 14, 1945. *This photograph was taken four days before the liberation of Pest was completed. The complete defeat of German forces in the capital—including the Hungarians still supporting them—who had entrenched themselves in Buda and finally in Buda Castle took until February 13. During the fifty-day siege of Budapest, one-fourth of the buildings were destroyed and three-fourths of them damaged; not a single bridge remained over the Danube. As at Stalingrad, Hitler did not permit any negotiation by his already completely conquered armies leading to some deal. The last attempt by German forces in the Buda hills and the Pilis forests occurred through a contravention of the Führer's orders; by then it was futile to do so, however. Hitler's attempt to retain the possession of the Vienna Basin and the oil fields in Zala County in Hungary by holding out in the Budapest area and thus to gain time also failed eventually.*

FOUR AND A HALF DECADES,
OR ONE PLUS
THREE AND A HALF

Each day we all add a few bricks to the edifice of History. But those who build any one of its parts lack the perspective to survey the whole construction. Still, let us try to sketch out these past forty-five or so years, as though from a greater distance in time.

As the front rolled westwards through Hungary, behind it enormous changes were taking place as early as the end of 1944. To call them revolutionary does not seem unjustified in some respects. However Hungarian society did not achieve these by its own efforts: they were brought about with the help of foreign troops. This, however, did not mean the rapid and violent introduction of the Soviet system—at least not for the time being. In a paradoxical way, initially contradictory developments occurred. When the atrocity-laden inferno had passed, the Soviet military administration behind the lines sometimes was more inclined to entrust routine tasks to the old public administration officials (those who had not fled westwards), than to the new, often radical, organizations which were brought to life with considerable popular support. There were places where Communist veterans of 1919 wished to reintroduce immediately the earlier dictatorship of the proletariat. Such individuals were discouraged because in this part of Europe—on the surface at least—it was real democracy, and not "people's democracy," that was on the agenda. This feeling was soon reinforced by the arrival of delegates from the wartime allies; British, American, and French officers belonging to the Allied Control Commission were present to oversee the domestic situation in Hungary.

Although the fighting sometimes left large areas untouched, destruction was nationwide. According to rough calculations, the economic losses suffered during the war amounted to five times the national income of 1938, the last year of peace, or 40 percent of the total national wealth. In the fighting itself 120 to 140 thousand persons lost their lives; about a quarter of a million never returned from captivity in the Soviet Union and, to a much lesser extent, from the POW camps of the British, French, and American forces. They either died there or sought a new home elsewhere. At least half a million Hungarians were kept in these camps for longer terms; most were released after two or three years, but tens of thousands were set free only in the 1950s.

The fate of Hungarian prisoners of war in the Soviet Union cannot be dismissed so lightly. Only some of those thus held were genuine war prisoners—that is, soldiers who were captured in uniform either during the fighting or after the capitulation. Two additional facts need to be taken into account. One follows from the special history of the siege of Budapest. After the large-scale tank battle on the Great Plain (the so-called Battle of Debrecen), Marshal Malinovsky wanted to regroup his forces. On orders from Stalin, however, he was obliged to attack Budapest while still on the move. Therefore, instead of lasting a matter of days and weeks, the battle for the Hungarian capital dragged on

for months. The marshal, who was rightly fearful of Stalin, excused himself by claiming that there were many more Hungarian defenders than was really the case. Because the number of Hungarian POWs taken served to contradict this story, the Red Army rounded up additional men, among them many who had never been soldiers at all. In addition, many thousand of people—among them a large number of women—were taken to the Soviet Union for so called "reparations" work. These were mainly taken from German-inhabited "Swabian" villages and the northeastern area of the country—from both sides of the newly-restored Trianon border which in this area was now the Hungarian–Ukrainian border.

It is difficult to determine the number of civilians who died as a result of the war. (Here we must repeat that at least 400,000 Jews died as a result of the Holocaust in Hungary.)

Budapest and several hundred other settlements lay in ruins; not a single bridge across the Danube remained intact. The gold reserves of the National Bank, most of the railway rolling-stock, machinery and other equipment, farm animals, museum treasures, and a great deal of property in private hands had been taken off to the West before the fighting reached Hungary. After the battles, however, long eastward-bound trains took entire plants, large and small, to the Soviet Union. What remained of the food and livestock (there were still some reserves) naturally passed into the possession of the Red Army, which used them to supply the forces occupying Hungary and the troops carrying the fight westwards.

Even so, if they survived, Hungarians were apparently living better not long after the front passed over them—at least they were consuming more calories—than people in many other parts of Europe.

Reconstruction proceeded quickly. Land reform benefited 650,000 landless or dwarfholder peasants. Although workers wages fell to a fraction of what they had been earlier, industrial recovery was very rapid. As well as catering for the domestic market, trade began with Soviet, Czechoslovak, and Rumanian partners.

Under moderate military supervision, in the countryside local self-government bodies proved to be effective. Arbitrary revenge for past social and political slights did occur, but was rare; those who had offended were dealt with according to the law.

New possibilities for further education opened up for the children of workers and peasants. The spirit of the period found expression in the marching song chosen by an institution which served them, the National Federation of People's Colleges *(NÉKOSZ),* and much sung for a number of years:

Hey, bright breezes blow
Our flying banner;
Hey, this is writ upon it:
Long live Liberty!

Béla Bartók (1881–1945). A portrait by Nicholas Muray, 1928. (The coloring is the work of Antal Kotnyek.) *It is possible that posterity will judge Béla Bartók to be the greatest Hungarian of the twentieth century. His character is universally respected. But there was more to Bartók than his compositions, his teaching activities, and his scholarly research into folk music. Bartók's world outlook, which found expression not only in his pronouncements, but also in his music, reflected the interaction of the spirituality of peoples, and their loathing of their lot, as well as his own unbending morality. Bartók was unable to bear the fanning of anti-Semitism, and left Hungary in 1940 to settle in the United States. He was already ill at the time and died in 1945, shortly after the end of the war. His remains were brought back to Hungary in 1988, to nationwide homage. Similar posthumous tributes had been paid only to Imre Thököly, Ferenc Rákóczi II, Lajos Kossuth, and Mihály Károlyi.*

> Hey, breezes, bright breezes
> Keep blowing, blowing—
> By the morrow we'll turn
> The entire world over.

This, then, was the age of "bright breezes," whose pathos was enchanting even though the "turning over" did not entirely achieve its fine objectives.

The revival of intellectual life was also swift. The seriously-ill Bartók did not return home from his exile in the United States, but Zoltán Kodály became the distinguished and respected organizer of the new, popular culture. Albert Szent-Györgyi, the biochemist and discoverer of Vitamin C (and the only Hungarian to win the Nobel Prize while actually resident in Hungary) led the revival of domestic scholarship. (Headstrong and active, Kodály remained in the country, while Szent-Györgyi, disenchanted, moved abroad.)

The Paris Peace Treaty of 1947 did not, from the point of view of Hungary, correct the Treaty of Trianon. On the contrary: three more villages near Pozsony (Bratislava, the capital city of Slovakia) were taken away from Hungary and given to Czechoslovakia. Hungary's obligations for war reparations were extensive.

Eventually, beyond direct losses due for its undeniable part and responsibility in the war—while German wartime debts were never recovered and therefore increased the burden—Hungary had to meet the additional obligations imposed in Paris, obligations which were difficult to assess in material terms since terms of trade, prices, and accounting methods had lost touch with the actual expenditure both during and after the conflict. They were not based on proper valuations and were unconfirmed by the judgement of the market.

The wildest inflation in history raged in Hungary from spring 1945 to summer 1946. The last pengő banknote issued bore the denomination 100 quadrillion, one unit of the new currency was equal to 400 thousand quadrillion pengő. A significant part of city rubbish at the time consisted of paper money that had been thrown away. In August 1946, the stabilization, which occurred without foreign loans and essentially through the provision of goods, and the creation of the forint were masterpieces of finance. One drawback, however, was the fact that fiscal reform also meant price reform: it distorted price ratios, reducing agricultural prices and increasing those of industrial goods. Although it was not without reason that, for example, rents and services were made cheap after the war, later on this interference with market forces was to have profound effects.

The restoration of the Trianon borders caused huge migrations. Many resettled of their own accord in the motherland (some as a result of population exchanges); many were expelled to Hungary (largely from Slovakia). At the same time the Potsdam resolutions of the "Big Four" ordered the mass deportation of ethnic Germans from Hungary. Since returning Hungarians had a desperate need for land and houses, this process was taken too far in some areas. Through these means Hungary became relatively homogeneous ethnically: apart from the almost 500,000 (or 4–5 percent) Gypsy population, Hungary today has fewer than half a million German, Slovakian, Ruthenian, Rumanian, and Southern Slav inhabitants. On the basis of the suffering caused to those resettled and those who were deported (together with worsening relations with Tito's Yugoslavia in 1948), one could not, in the first decade after 1945, yet speak of reconciliation between Hungarians and the nationality groups within our borders. Moreover, discrimination also asserted itself, mainly against the Southern Slavs and Germans who remained in Hungary.

However, while the various migrations involved a quarter of a million people at most, the Hungarian borders drawn in 1920 and reaffirmed in 1947 became an enduring historical reality. At the same time this also meant that several million Hungarians, clinging to the centuries-old dwelling places of their ancestors, were also obliged to live as citizens of neighbouring countries. We cite round figures rather than exact data, as the statistical error is large for both historical and psychological reasons. In Rumania, there are colonies of ethnic Hungarians amounting to at least 2.5 million people; in Serbia and Croatia and in Slovakia, more than one million altogether; in the Ukraine, 200,000; and in Austria, 10,000 to 20,000. The often tragic post-1945 history of these people remains unwritten

The congress of Young Communists—A poster by István Czeglédi (b. 1913) and Tibor Bánhegyi (b. 1923), 1950. *At the beginning of the 1950s, every poster displayed a pure smile or healthy muscles. Portraits of Mátyás Rákosi, the "people's wise leader," filled the streets. Meanwhile, because of unrealistically ambitious plan targets, the rapid pace of industrialization (and armaments production), and of compulsory collectivization of the land, the impressive economic performance of the Coalition years could not be sustained. In the new atmosphere of fear and reprisals living standards first stagnated and then fell. Inflation began, and the shops were virtually empty (food rationing was temporarily reintroduced).*

and—for the moment at least—cannot be written. If we include the large numbers of those who dispersed throughout the world in waves of emigration who still maintain some kind of connection with us, then we must mention the one million Hungarians scattered across North America and the tens, or hundreds, of thousands living in Western Europe and South America. Nearly a quarter of a million Hungarians have settled in Israel. According to a final total, if the number of Hungarians at home in Hungary is today ten and a half million (or, subtracting the other ethnic groups, close on ten million), then more than a third of all Hungarians live outside Hungary's borders. Hungarians constitute the largest national minority in Europe.

Between 1945 and 1949 Hungary's political system altered radically and violently. The dozen or so political parties revived or established in 1945—which in the autumn of 1945 contested fair and free elections—were quickly reduced to four. Of the two peasant parties and two workers' parties remaining, the last two, the Social Democrats and the Communist Party, merged in 1948 to form the Hungarian Working People's Party. As in the rest of Eastern Europe, a "people's democracy" was established which essentially promised to follow the peaceful path dotted with compromises of socialist revolution. The leading force in this process was a single workers' party. In some countries other parties survived either in name only or in alliance with these workers' parties. In Hungary, however, political activity outside the Hungarian Working People's Party could only continue within the framework of a mass organization, the People's Front.

Among the leaders of the Hungarian Communists, who had been extraordinarily active ever since 1944–45, those who returned home from Moscow, and especially Mátyás Rákosi played a decisive role from the beginning. But in the first years the views of those who had engaged in illegal activities at home before and during the war still enjoyed some weight. After 1948, "the year of the turning-point," Rákosi and his narrow circle forced out one after the other—partly in show trials sentenced to death or long terms of imprisonment—their rivals, real or imaginary, mainly former Social Democrats or Communists who had stayed in Hungary during the war. Especially suspicious were the veterans of 1919, volunteers who had fought in the Spanish Civil War, and all those who were inclined to think and to act independently. László Rajk was executed and János Kádár was imprisoned. The latter had been one of the leaders of the party in Hungary during the difficult years of the war. Both were former interior ministers, and in the early postwar years were loyal associates of the Communists who had returned home from Moscow.

The radical dogmatic social utopianism and Machiavellian scheming used by Rákosi and his associates to win absolute power took on a Stalinist character, but had typically local traits as well. Around the "year of the turning-point" these politicians enjoyed some support among workers, intellectuals, and agricultural labourers. But their prestige was destroyed in a couple of years by the forced collectivization of agriculture, which had already begun to organize spontaneously into cooperatives; by the forced development of heavy industry (actually the revival of the wartime Győr Program); the "dilution" that "weakened" the working class by adding to it those peasants who fled the land; by the deterioration of the workers' situation at all levels; by compulsory nationalization; by centralized economic policies; by the fetishization of the paternalistic state; by the intimidation of small-scale producers and the middle layers of society, along with increasing appropriation of their often-meagre property; by the collection of material for secret personal dossiers; by discrimination against children in education on the basis of social class; by emphasizing production at the expense of consumption (with directed labor and food rationing); by illegal acts in addition to the show trials—the list could go on and on.

Although the process was more complex and the mixture of good and evil involuted, we can say, if we want to indicate phases, that most of what the period 1945–49 built up (which was not little), the period 1949–53 destroyed. After Stalin's death and the momentous Twentieth Congress of the Soviet Party, Imre Nagy, himself a former exile in Moscow, returned from the periphery of the party to the center of events. In 1944–45 he distributed land in his capacity as minister of agriculture in the Debrecen provisional government; in 1953 he was prime minister, while Rákosi remained first secretary. The next three years failed to produce the necessary

Streetscene from the 1956 revolution—*When deciding what really happened in Hungary in 1956, the basic question is whether the events were planned in advance or whether they were spontaneous. So far historical investigations have failed to prove that the siege of the Hungarian Radio building, which began in the early evening of October 23, was decided in advance and may have been a part of a larger plan. Then and afterwards, it was a rather complete randomness and blind rampage that characterized the violent events which took place in the streets—a fury and volcanic outbursts of popular rage. (An example was the toppling of the huge Stalin statue as early as 9.30 p.m. on the evening of 23th.) Only with the passage of time and as a result of the furious attempts of the old order to reassert itself did the popular movement—to which hardly any counterrevolutionary elements adhered—become ever more conscious and revolutionary. (Instances of this were, firstly, the setting up of the National Guard and then—mainly—the emergence of the workers' councils.)*
In a paradoxical way, the 1956 Hungarian October really became revolutionary and organized only after the (second) intervention of the Soviet troops on November 4, after the seizure of power by Kádár's "Revolutionary Workers' and Peasants' Government." It was then that the workers' councils were outlawed. Their complete dismantlement and a widening retribution represented the real counterrevolution.

The 1956 revolution did not break out when the country and society reached the nadir, but rather when a certain improvement had begun—weak, uncertain and easily reversible though it was. It was at the same time accidental and legitimate as the October 23 mass demonstration wished to show solidarity with the earlier movements in Poland, but the events—in the wake of the incompetence and disintegration of the party, the state, and the armed forces—became uncontrollable. Fighting broke out, strong emotions and ambitions surfaced. The intervening Soviet army restored the rule of the Communists. Admittedly, a small group of previously-compromised leaders were dropped and Reform Communists who had shown solidarity with the revolution—among them Imre Nagy—were removed.

The leading post fell to János Kádár, although the precise circumstances, motives, and pressures that led to his appointment cannot be known even today. In the name of the Hungarian Socialist Workers' Party (which had replaced the disintegrated Hungarian Working People's Party), Kádár at first announced a radical break with the past. At the same time the new government moved forcefully against those who continued political and armed resistance—in a few places not shrinking from mass terror and massacres. Accordingly, some 200 thousand people fled to the West across a border which remained open for weeks. (During the days of the 1956 revolution

political corrections that had been promised; instead the time was squandered in internal party strife, in battles between factions. Although the economy was now on a sounder basis and the rehabilitation of those sentenced unjustly had started (posthumously for some), Rákosi and his clique launched one counterattack after another.

123

some three thousand people died in the street fighting and in the armed retribution that followed. This figure includes fighters from both sides, demonstrators and chance victims; the exact number of Soviet troops who fell is unknown.)

The Kádár period, which can be dated from the end of 1956 and beginning of 1957 was, by its very nature, seriously contradictory and two sided. Retribution for 1956 lasted for years; the number of those executed for essentially political offences was around 500. The number of those imprisoned ran to many thousands. At the same time the old-new party granted concessions. First of all, in order urgently to lay the foundations for good spring work and the 1957 harvest, agricultural policy was changed. Afterwards Hungarian agriculture—although again handicapped by low prices on the world market, overproduction, western protectionism, deteriorating terms of trade, and heavy taxation—was for a long time an example and successful practising ground in "socialism as it was," for the encouragement of individual interestedness, and for the fostering of entrepreneurial spirit. Despite the fact that force was repeatedly used in the organization of the cooperatives, later on the large units differed a great deal from their Soviet kolkhoz–sovkhoz prototypes. They endeavored to become integrated with the production (crops and animal husbandry) of the remaining private (family) small farms, mainly with the small household plots and private allotments of peasants employed in cooperatives. But these agricultural cooperatives also involved themselves in different types of industrial work, thus supporting state industry and producing consumer items which had previously been in short supply.

By the summer of 1957 economic consolidation had been achieved. The process was almost too rapid. The ensuing stability, together with a counterattack by retrograde, dogmatic forces, meant that the transformation of industrial policy urged by reform economists was neglected. This came onto the agenda more than a decade later, in 1968, when the harsh atmosphere generated by the "Prague Spring" was unfavorable for cautious Hungarian renewal.

In the years after 1956 and 1968, Hungarian economic policy entered a reform period of thirty and twenty years respectively (characterized by interruptions and backsliding) which was intended to revive an economy destroyed in a few years after 1949 and bring it from a state of weak development to the level of moderate development. A few signs of the latter appeared long ago, although as a whole the Hungarian economy had remained backward. Hungary's experiments and solutions, often lumped together by the foreign press under the name of the "Hungarian model," were, in the meantime, sometimes avant-garde in character—in comparison with those in the neighboring countries. But they remained far behind the real demands of society and the economy, and, in addition, the financing of the modest results was for the most part from foreign funds given carelessly by the West and afterwards inefficiently used. This has created an enormous burden for the future.

During these decades the key social-political phrase was "national consensus." This endeavor, which however was very limited in scope, was promoted by the idea that "He who is not against us is with us." (This formula—the very opposite of the well-known biblical citation used by Stalin and Rákosi alike—was proclaimed by Kádár at the end of 1961.) This meant that politics did not wish to always force itself on the population, but that it recognized the domains of private life to be wider than hitherto; that within the country's borders choice of place of residence and workplace became free and after a while in practice anyone would be able to leave the country; that the principle of the monopoly of Marxism (which was illusory anyway) would be replaced by the principle of the hegemony of Marxism and a cautious dialogue between different world views; that state supervision and police persecution of the Churches would decrease a little and that the practice of religion, which was already finding acceptance, would show itself again (there was a certain renaissance here: religious activity among young people, building of new churches, and reviving social work by the clergy); and that more effort would be made to strengthen complete harmony and final reconciliation with Hungary's nationalities, thus supporting their endeavors to strengthen their relations with their own ethnic communities and their mother countries, while stressing the necessity of mutuality in this respect albeit without much success. Moreover, Hungarians in general could, in the course of their travels, gradually form a picture of East and West alike, and those who had spent long years abroad in exile would become free to return home.

According to sociological studies, towards the end of the 1980s there emerged two sections in Hungarian society, forming 0.5 and 10 percent, which were, respectively, very wealthy and comfortably off. These two groupings were very heterogeneous. One could find among them owners of private workshops, lawyers, professional sportsmen, some doctors, and small-scale village producers. (Members of the political and power élite only rarely featured among them, and then not in the upper 0.5 percent.) It was frequent that registerable property and/or high incomes were rooted in the more distant past. For those who had belonged to the better off, or those who received such a start from home, it was easier to ascend in the social scale, although there were also many recent self-made men. These two layers expanded from year to year.

At the other end of the spectrum, some two million people (20 percent of the population) were found to be living below the poverty line. Among them are many members of the traditional *Lumpenproletariat*—and very many alcoholics. In these groups even under the conditions of socialism poverty continues from generation to generation: only rarely are the children able to break out. Simultaneously significant is the new poverty among these people, poverty which springs from the economic and social anomalies of the recent past. Many pensions are so low that they would be inadequate even if they had succeeded in maintaining their real value; moderate pensions have been eroded by accelerating inflation which is never adequately offset. Frequent divorces, the break-up of families, and the need to create a new home again and again have impoverished many. It is paradoxical that the acquisition of property makes one poor. In certain peripheral and economically underdeveloped parts of the country, chiefly near the frontiers drawn at Trianon, whole areas live in destitution. Many from these regions undertake work in the population centers, traveling there and back, "commuting" as domestic guest workers. Their living standard may be termed poor even when their income is adequate. In such circumstances it is family members staying at home who suffer both materially and psychologically.

The reburial of the 1956 martyrs, June 16, 1989. *Although himself a former Communist exile in Moscow, back in Hungary Imre Nagy found himself outside the party's leading group. Again and again he came into conflict with Rákosi and his clique on ideological and agricultural issues. When, in 1956, popularity gained in the intervening years brought him to the fore he was drifted along by revolutionary events which he did not control. Nevertheless, for some days he was again prime minister. Later on, after the collapse and having taken refuge at a foreign embassy he was not prepared to legitimize the Kádár regime by tendering his resignation. Nagy's life now took on overtones of a Greek tragedy: he was made a scapegoat, sentenced to death, in a secret trial, and hanged on June 16, 1958. The 1989 exhumation, identification and reburial of Nagy and those executed with him—among them Pál Maléter, minister of defence in 1956—in Plot No. 301 in the Budapest Public Cemetery was a turning-point in the accelerating changes and national renewal during the decisive year 1989–90. The honoring of Nagy and his colleagues in this way confirmed the revolutionary (as opposed to "counterrevolutionary") nature of the 1956 events better than any mere legal rehabilitation could have done.*

On the other hand, in the middle, the society of this period became strongly homogenized. This came as a surprise even to those who predicted that socialist development would erode earlier class and sectional anomalies and differences. By the end of the 1980s there were fewer and fewer purely worker, peasant (i.e. agricultural worker), intelligentsia, or other families: the majority of families are of mixed composition. If not within the nuclear family (parents plus children) then in the wider family there were workers in the different sectors of the economy who, on the basis of statistical classification, could be placed in the various groups and layers of society. This was a real development, because differences accruing from life and work in industry and agriculture, in the countryside and in Budapest, in village and town, and in main occupations and supplementary occupations, were more or less evened out in such families.

This relatively static picture of Hungarian society as it had developed by the end of the 1980s needs to be sketched, even if it is now beginning to lose its validity. It came into existence during a period of almost fifty years; in comparison with a more than thousand-year history this period is not insignificant in the life of the country and nation.

What will come now is already beyond the scope of this book. Here the history of tomorrow is still the story of today—continuous happenings cannot be regarded as history.

János Kádár died in the summer of 1989, having survived his political death (that is, his complete removal from power) by only a few weeks. A few months earlier, it was openly being said that the Kádár period had come to an end. What had come into existence under his aegis was in ruins economically. And politically? His party declared its acquiescence in the restoration of the multi-party system. It did this in the knowledge that this step was equivalent to the party's decline into insignificance parallel with sharing the bitter fate of the opposition.

Thus ended the period covering almost a third of a century, the beginning of which was overcast by the shadow of the post-1956 retributions. Later, it gave Hungary its relaxed atmosphere, leading ironists to dub the country "the happiest barrack in the camp." Close to the end of the 1980s, its attempts at reform won perhaps excessive and flattering judgements in the West (these made it more suspect within the Eastern bloc). Also, the end of the third decade was overshadowed by the previously whispered, but later admitted, information that Hungary had accumulated a foreign debt of twenty billion dollars—most of it in a couple of years of recklessness. This was where the contradictory, limited, national consensus had led; this was what the divergence of production and consumption, the maintenance of a tolerable living standard, and the erroneous use of the loans received had amounted to. The heavy interest burden on these debts alone will have its effects felt for decades, and will cripple all renewal.

In the midst of the preparations for a peaceful transition of power and democratic elections Kádár's successors surprised the world at large. Eschewing the gendarme role still expected of it in the Eastern camp, Hungary allowed several hundred East German citizens to escape westwards across the Austrian border. (This move had been preceded by the taking in of Rumanian citizens, for the most part of Hungarian nationality, who had escaped across the "green border," and the recognition of their refugee status.) Later the barbed-wire fence along Hungary's western border was taken down. Like an avalanche, these steps directly led to the visible collapse of the Berlin wall and, with it, the dissolution of the East German state and the unexpected union of the two Germanys—developments unimaginable even a few weeks earlier.

Naturally, all this can, or should, be seen in connection with the rise of Mikhail Gorbachev in the Soviet Union, even if in history questions of cause and effect are not entirely settled. However the question of what went before and what happened afterwards is constantly debated in history. Hungary, desperate and euphoric at the same time, turning away from the road followed for almost a half century and hardly able to see the path of the future, and finally saying goodbye to the Soviet troops stationed on its territory since 1944–45, took state, national, and political risks with some of its decisions in 1989 in a context of a rather uncertain international situation which was not moving towards stability. This was how we arrived at the 1990s.

And this can hardly be spent with anything else but with the relearning of the almost totally forgotten rules of democracy, and also with surviving the economic depression and creating a new economic order. While difficulties will not make provision for efficient tactics,

The proclamation of the Hungarian Republic, October 23, 1989.
On April 14, 1849, at a critical stage of the Revolution, the Hungarian Parliament then sitting in Debrecen defiantly announced the dethroning of the House of Habsburg, but did not proclaim a res publica. (Lajos Kossuth now became "governor-president.") On November 16, 1918 in the wake of the bourgeois revolution that had broken out, a "people's republic" was formed, and later, on March 21, 1919, a "republic of councils." After the fall of the short-lived "Hungarian Soviet state", at the end of 1920 a newly-elected Parliament restored the kingdom, albeit without restoring a king. (Miklós Horthy served as regent.) The latter state form did not change even during the Arrow-Cross (i.e. Hungarian National Socialist) terror of 1944–45. When on December 21, 1944 the Provisional National Assembly convened (again in Debrecen), the state form was still not altered. This happened only on February 1, 1946, when Hungary became a republic: the newly-elected Parliament moved from Budapest to Debrecen for one day. From August 20, 1949 Hungary was once again a "people's republic." And finally, on October 23, 1989 the Hungarian Republic was proclaimed. In actual fact, this is Hungary's second republic after the one that existed between 1946 and 1949. May it prove to be lasting and firmly rooted.

a whole range of strategic issues should be decided on. And while the full vulnerability of the economy is only now being fully revealed for us, the necessary decrease of consumption has to be forced on society amidst expectations to the contrary.

The past—the time before 1945 and, at the other extreme, the Kádár period—is now seen nostalgically; new and old-new ideas surface. On the political scene, in the parliamentary and extra-parliamentary spheres a faltering democracy and struggles of bitter and frequently depressing content and form are developing.

In the meantime, both Eastern and Western visitors to Hungary at the beginning of the 1990s may find the country more affluent and resourceful than do its own citizens, who see it forced into worrying straits. The Eastern visitor is influenced by his own, often more miserable, position. Westerners, on the other hand, find things better than their old expectations of life behind the Iron Curtain would have suggested. This is the new Hungarian paradox: almost every outside observer values the dynamism of the country highly, but the inhabitants, who bear the burden

of most of the changes, are cautious and pessimistic. Who is, and will be, more correct?

Western capital, although in the long run it hopes for strong revival from the Hungarian economy, is procrastinating over possible investment. Rampant inflation and unemployment threaten. In a financially polarizing society, with the rich getting richer and the poor getting poorer, Hungarian citizens are already gloomy when they look around themselves. If they contemplate, beyond our borders, a crisis-ridden Eastern Europe beset by national and nationality problems and compelled to starve before the much-promised economic upturn, they are more gloomy yet.

Looking at the recent changes—perhaps ungratefully— this is how we stand in East Central Europe, in the middle of the Carpathian Basin, as we celebrate the 1100th anniversary of the Hungarian Conquest, which, in five years will be followed by the opening of the third millennium, which for us means the first millennium of the foundation of the Hungarian state reckoned from the coronation of St. Stephen.

Landscape after a battle. *The Danube Bend at Visegrád. What picture should we select, at the beginning of the 1990s, to conclude this illustrated history of Hungary? Let's choose a bird's-eye view of the Danube Bend, where the river, hemmed in by the Börzsöny and the Pilis mountains, meanders beneath the castle at Visegrád. Passing over the rich prehistoric monuments of the area, let us begin by saying that among the Roman defence walls of the Sibrik Hill important new buildings were erected as early as the time of the Árpád dynasty. After the foundation of the state, Visegrád was one of Hungary's first ecclesiastical centers, as well as being a royal estate and a county seat. After the Mongol invasion, a hill castle was built for the wife of Béla IV which, together with the riverside ramparts, constituted one of the country's most defensible fortifications. Under its protection, at the time of the Anjou kings and later King Matthias Corvinus a most magnificent palace grew up. Archaeologists are discovering more and more evidence of its greatness and pomp. On important occasions the king's cellar-master released wine into the waterpipe system of the palace; waterpipes so far discovered lend credibility to the legend that red and white wine flowed from the marble fountains of the court of honour and the palace's outer wall. After the Turkish conquest, however, the Hungarian Versailles was laid low: it was almost completely raised to the ground, and weeds grew over it. Only in this century did Visegrád begin to arise from the dust—as a resort-place and through its discovered and restored historical monuments.*

In the 1980s the Visegrád area was again brought to the forefront of public attention. Czechoslovakia and Hungary long ago planned

the building of a water-step, of which the main Slovak installation would be at Bős and the main Hungarian installation at Nagymaros, north of Visegrád. The latter would have been in close proximity to the royal castle and palace. But in East Central Europe during the 1980s growing political dissatisfaction and civic opposition found an object of focus in this gigantic project at Bős–Nagymaros. In this, ecological and political motives played a part, and these had national and international ramifications. The Hungarian domestic opposition—one half of which came to power in 1990, while the other half went into opposition—for many years had two main areas of activity: samizdat publications (their production and distribution) and the struggle against the Danube water-step. The Slovaks have stuck to the building of their own installation at Bős, although in the absence of its Hungarian counterpart it will be of limited use. The Hungarians, on the other hand, have stopped all construction work and have started to restore the area to its original natural state. No clumsy reinforced concrete seal has defiled the Danube and this historic landscape...

In conclusion, as has been written earlier in this book, in 1335 King Charles Robert of Anjou organized a trilateral summit meeting at Visegrád attended by the king of Bohemia and the king of Poland. In 1991 Hungary, Czechoslovakia and Poland, all of which find themselves in a serious economic position, concluded an important agreement, mainly concerning mutual trade, also at Visegrád. The principal theme of this was regional cooperation and mutual trade. Accordingly, Visegrád is a suitable lookout point from where to take a final look at Hungarian history.

LIST OF RULERS

House of Árpád

Árpád, Prince	c. 886–907
Zolta, Prince	907–946
Falicsi (Fajsz), Prince	948–c. 955
Taksony, Prince	955–c. 972
Géza, Prince	972–997
(Saint) Stephen I, Prince	997–1000
King	1000–1038
Peter	1038–1041
Samuel Aba	1041–1044
Peter	1044–1046
Andrew I	1046–1060
Béla I	1060–1063
Salomon	1063–1074
Géza I	1074–1077
(Saint) Ladislas I	1077–1095
Koloman	1095–1116
Stephen II	1116–1131
Béla (Blind) II	1131–1141
Géza II	1141–1162
Stephen III	1162–1172
Ladislas II	1162–1163
Stephen IV	1163–1165
Béla III	1172–1196
Emeric	1196–1204
Ladislas III	1204–1205
Andrew II	1205–1235
Béla IV	1235–1270
Stephen V	1270–1272
Ladislas (the Cuman) IV	1272–1290
Andrew III	1290–1301

Kings of different houses

Wenceslas of Bohemia	1301–1305
Charles Robert of Anjou	1301–1342
Otto of Bavaria	1305–1307
Louis I the Great of Anjou	1342–1382
Maria of Anjou	1382–1395
Charles (Small) II of Durazzo	1385–1386
Sigismund of Luxemburg	1387–1437
Albert Habsburg	1437–1439
Wladislas I Jagiello	1440–1444
Ladislas V (Posthumous) Habsburg	1440–1457
Matthias I Corvinus	1458–1490
Wladislas II Jagiello	1490–1516
Louis II Jagiello	1516–1526
John Szapolyai (Zápolya)	1526–1540

House of Habsburg

Ferdinand I	1526–1564
Maximilian	1564–1576
Rudolf	1576–1608
Matthias II	1608–1619
Ferdinand II	1618–1637
Ferdinand III	1625–1657
Ferdinand IV	1647–1654
Leopold I	1655–1705
Joseph I	1678–1711
Charles III	1711–1740
Maria Theresa	1740–1780
Joseph II	1780–1790
Leopold II	1790–1792
Francis I	1792–1835
Ferdinand V	1835–1848
Francis Joseph I	1848–1916
Charles IV	1916–1918

Heads of State since 1919

Count Mihály Károlyi	1919
Sándor Garbai	1919
Miklós Horthy	1920–1944
Ferenc Szálasi	1944–1945
Zoltán Tildy	1946–1948
Árpád Szakasits	1948–1950
Sándor Rónai	1950–1952
István Dobi	1952–1967
Pál Losonczi	1967–1987
Károly Németh	1987–1988
Brúnó F. Straub	1988–1989
Mátyás Szűrös (provisional)	1989–1990
Árpád Göncz	1990–

Heads of Government since 1945

Zoltán Tildy	1945–1946
Ferenc Nagy	1946–1947
Lajos Dinnyés	1947–1948
István Dobi	1948–1952
Mátyás Rákosi	1952–1953
Imre Nagy	1953–1955
András Hegedűs	1955–1956
Imre Nagy	1956
János Kádár	1956–1958
Ferenc Münnich	1958–1961
János Kádár	1961–1965
Gyula Kállai	1965–1967
Jenő Fock	1967–1975
György Lázár	1975–1987
Károly Grósz	1987–1988
Miklós Németh	1988–1990
József Antall	1990–1993
Péter Boross	1993–1994
Gyula Horn	1994–

CONCORDANCE OF GEOGRAPHICAL NAMES

Bécsújhely *Hung.* = *Ger.* Wiener Neustadt
Bős *Hung.* = *Slovak.* Gabčikovo
Brünn *Ger.* = *Chech* Brno
Byzantium (Constantinople) = *Turk.* Istambul
Cattaro *Ital.* = *Serb.–Croat.* Kotor
Eperjes *Hung.* = *Slovak.* Prešov
Eszék *Hung.* = *Serb.–Croat.* Ošijek (the ancient Mursia)
Kassa *Hung.* = *Slovak.* Košice
Késmárk *Hung.* = *Slovak.* Kežmarok
Kismarton *Hung.* = *Ger.* Eisenstadt
Kolozsvár *Hung.* = *Rom.* Cluj-Napoca
Komárom *Hung.* = *Slovak.* Komárno
Körmöcbánya *Hung.* = *Slovak.* Kremnica
Munkács *Hung.* = *Ukrain.* Mukachevo
Nagybánya *Hung.* = *Rum.* Baia Mare
Nagyszeben *Hung.* = *Rum.* Sibiu
Nagyszombat *Hung.* = *Slovak.* Trnava
Nagyvárad *Hung.* = *Rum.* Oradea
Nándorfehérvár *Hung.* = *Serb.–Croat.* Beograd (Belgrade)
Nyitraivánka *Hung.* = *Slovak.* Ivanka pri Nitre

Óbuda *Hung.* = *Ger.* Altofen
Olomouc *Czech* = *Ger.* Olmütz
Pozsony *Hung.* = *Slovak.* Bratislava
Ragusa *Ital.* = *Serb.–Croat.* Dubrovnik
Rahó *Hung.* = *Russ.* Rakhov
Rodosto *Hung.* = *Turk.* Tekirdağ
Segesvár *Hung.* = *Rum.* Sighişoara
Selmecbánya *Hung.* = *Slovak.* Banská Štiavnica
Sopron *Hung.* = *Ger.* Ödenburg
Spalato *Ital.* = *Serb.–Croat.* Split
Szatmár *Hung.* = *Rum.* Satu Mare
Székelyderzs *Hung.* = *Rum.* Dîrjiu
Szombathely *Hung.* = the ancient Sabaria
Trau *Ger., Hung.* = *Serb.–Croat.* Trogir
Úrvölgy *Hung.* = *Slovak.* Špana Dolina
Vajdahunyad *Hung.* = *Rum.* Hunedoara
Világos *Hung.* = *Rum.* Şiria
Zara *Hung.* = *Serb.–Croat.* Zadar
Zimony *Hung.* = *Serb.–Croat.* Zemun

LIST OF REFERENCES

Hungarian Collections

Historical Museum of Budapest 52, 73
Institute and Museum of Military History, Budapest 1, 68, 79
Jókai Memorial Home, Balatonfüred 86
Jósa András Museum, Nyíregyháza 10
Déri Museum, Debrecen 60
Christian Museum, Esztergom 25
Recent History Museum, Budapest 94, 95, 96, 97, 99, 101, 102, 103, 106
Hungarian National Gallery, Budapest 7, 11, 12, 17, 20, 52, 57, 58, 64, 71, 92, 93
Hungarian National Museum, Budapest 5, 10, 13, 16, 29, 35, 37, 41/a and 41/b, 53, 54, 65, 72, 80
Historical Picture Gallery (Hungarian National Museum) 61, 63, 66, 69, 72, 74, 77, 78, 80, 82, 84, 85, 87, 90, 92
Hungarian News Agency MTI 34, 107, 108, 109/a and 109/b
Hungarian National Archives 33/a and 33/b
Matthias Church, Budapest, 30, 50
National Széchényi Library, Budapest 19, 23, 36, 49
Petőfi Literary Museum, Budapest 75
St. Stephen's Basilica, Budapest 18
Cathedral, Esztergom 51
Cathedral, Győr 28
Museum of Fine Arts, Budapest 70

Private Collections

Buzinkay, Géza 98/a and 98/b, 104
Kotnyek, Antal 105
Undi, Flóra 9

Foreign Collections

Cathedral, Aachen 39
Heiligen-Geist-Hospital, Lübeck 32
Historisches Museum der Stadt Wien 48
Kunsthistorisches Museum, Wien 44
Mary Chapel of the Cathedral, Kraków 55
Sammlung der Gesellschaft der Musikfreunde, Wien 87
Schatzkammer, Wien 56
Cathedral Treasure House, Zagreb 24
Reformed (Calvinist) Church, Székelyderzs 26

Books

Csánki, Dezső (ed.), *Árpád és az Árpádok* (Árpád and the Árpáds) 38
Erdődi, Mihály (ed.), *A felszabadult Erdély* (The Liberated Transylvania), Budapest, 1941 100
Hauszmann, Alajos, *A magyar királyi vár* (The Hungarian Royal Castle), Budapest, 1912 88
Hellebronth, Kálmán (ed.), *A magyar testőrség könyve* (The Book of the Hungarian Guardsmen), Budapest, n.d. 67
Kordos, László, *Emberelődök* (The Ancestors of Man), Móra, Budapest, 1982 3
László, Gyula, *Hunor és Magyar nyomában* (In the Tracks of Hunor and Magyar), Gondolat, Budapest, 1967 2, 14
The Thuróczi Chronicle, Brünn edition 46

The photographs were taken by:

Antall, Péter 26
Bakos, Ágnes 73
Balogh, P. László 108
Bókay, László 75
Buzinkay, Géza 81
Dabasi, András 5, 6, 10, 13, 16, 29, 35, 41/a and 41/b, 53, 54, 63, 65, 66, 69, 72, 74, 77, 78, 80, 82, 84, 85, 87, 90, 92, 110
Dékány, Ágoston (graphics) 2
Farkas, Árpád 99, 102, 103
Hasznos, Zoltán 17
Hász, András 9, 14/a and 14/b, 21, 30, 33, 38, 40, 45, 50, 59, 67, 86, 94, 95, 96, 97, 98/a and 98/b, 99, 100, 101, 104, 106
Kolozsvári, Grandpierre Miklós (graphics) 3
Kotnyek, Antal (color technique) 105
Manek, Attila 109/a and 109/b
Makky, György 33/a and 33/b
Michła, Stanisław 55
Mihalik, Tamás 31, 62
Mudrák, Attila 25
Muray, Nicholas 105
Németh, Ferenc 1, 68, 79
Rafael, Csaba 51
Róka, Lajos 86
Schiller, Alfréd 58, 61, 84, 93
Szacsvay, Imre 47
Szelényi, Károly 18, 21, 27, 28, 37, 60, 70
Szepsi Szűcs, Levente 7, 11, 12, 20, 52, 57, 64, 71, 92
Szerencsés, János 76
Tihanyi, Bence 4, 43
Tóth, Béla 6, 22, 40, 42, 83, 89